11-99

MORALITY:
MES FLESH

CHRISTIAN MORALITY: THE WORD BECOMES FLESH

Josef Fuchs, S.J.

Translated by Brian McNeil

Gill and Macmillan, Dublin
Georgetown University Press, Washington, D.C.

Published in Ireland by
Gill and Macmillan Ltd
Goldenbridge
Dublin 8
with associated companies in
Auckland, Dallas, Delhi, Hong Kong,
Johannesburg, Lagos, London, Manzini,
Melbourne, Nairobi, New York, Singapore,
Tokyo, Washington

ISBN: 0 7171 1564 X

British Library Cataloguing in Publication Data
Fuchs, Josef
Christian Morality: The Word Becomes Flesh.
1. Christian Ethics
1. Title
241   BJ1251
ISBN 0-7171-1564-X

Published in the United States of America by
Georgetown University Press
Washington, D.C. 20057
ISBN 0-87840-451-1
ISBN 0-87840-452-A (pbk.)

Library of Congress Cataloging-in-Publication Data
Fuchs, Josef, 1912–
Christian Morality.

1. Christian ethics – Catholic authors. I. Title.
BJ1249.F753   1987   241'.042   87-9138
ISBN 0-87840-451-1
ISBN 0-87840-452-A (pbk.)

Print origination in Ireland by
Design and Art Facilities, Dublin
Printed in Great Britain by
The Camelot Press, Southampton

Table of Contents

Introduction

Christian moral theology — in keeping with Jesus Christ — has a divine-human character. In what sense is it "divine", and in what sense is it "human"? There is no answer as yet to this question that would put an end to the discussion; for the human possibility of indicating a path for human life worthy of human beings ("natural law") is a created, and in this sense human, participation in the wisdom of God ("eternal law"). The mission on which Jesus Christ sends the Christian on a path through the world in his Spirit is a divine-human mission. In both cases, a divine and a human element are distinct but still united. In both cases, the word becomes flesh — the word in which all was created, and which has appeared to us in Jesus of Nazareth. This did not happen exclusively on one occasion: the incarnation of the word continually takes place in the search for right morality.

The essays collected in this book, dated from the last few years, deal with this question in various ways. The first part addresses the question and the scholarly discussion systematically and theoretically. The second part reflects on the status of the moral person who acts — bearing in mind the question that has been posed fundamentally and theoretically. The third part seeks to clarify the question that has been posed by means of some concrete examples.

Rome, September 1987   Josef Fuchs

PART 1

Christian Morality

Christian Morality: Biblical Orientation and
Human Evaluation

Vatican II: Salvation, Personal Morality,
Right Behavior

Our Image of God and the Morality of
Innerworldly Behavior

God's Incarnation in a Human Morality

Christian Faith and the Disposing of Human
Life

Early Christianity in Search of a Christian
Morality: 1 Cor 7

I. Christian Morality: Biblical Orientation and Human Evaluation

The title of this essay points to a problem that continues to be relevant. It concerns one Christian morality into which two elements clearly enter that may be distinguished but not divided. If the two elements are to be distinguished, one must ask what precise contribution each of them makes to Christian morality. Here lies the problem.

1. Introduction to the Problem

Bernhard Fraling once formulated the question as follows: the exegetes tell us that the Bible does not have much to offer us by way of material ethical norms, while the theologians ask how a nonbiblical morality based on natural law can give expression to what is properly Christian.[1] His reply to the question is similar to that, for example of Raymond F. Collins: Christian morality has a theological context, but the kingdom of God has no distinctive material *a priori* norms. The theological context makes Christian morality Christian: its normative content is secular.[2] Other moral theologians would formulate the reply differently. Paul Hoffmann and Volker Eid, for example, see it thus: Christian communities stand ethically under the influence of the relevance of Jesus, but their ethical norms are pluralistic and therefore cannot be definitive – as long as they do not betray the clear intentions of Jesus. Jesus opens perspectives, and the community responds, but not without making its own particular self-understanding a part of its response.[3] Some Polish moral theologians also point to the fact that Christian morality, which as such naturally brings in Christian faith, cannot do this unless the autonomous(!) moral experience, which requires the free affirmation of value, is (logically) antecedent to faith;

thus, faith as such cannot (logically) be the original starting-point of morality.[4] These few remarks may suffice as a short introduction to the problematic which we shall treat; they ought to be complemented, however, by a short historical retrospective.

The Second Vatican Council emphasized the need to provide a more solid biblical foundation for traditional moral theology; but this directive was not the first of its kind.[5] Rather, the Council's mandate presupposed earlier theological reflections and discussions. These had their precursors in the first half of the last century (Sailer, Hirscher), but began anew in the thirties of this century. The first — rather "biblicist" — attempt by Fritz Tillmann[6] was followed by various others, including that of Bernard Häring.[7] The opponents of such tendencies feared the elimination of the traditional natural-law elements of moral theology; they drew attention above all to the fact that, as even Tillmann's studies showed, the Bible gives no answer to the manifold ethical questions confronting Christians in the modern world.

As has been said, the Second Vatican Council, despite the hesitations of some moral theologians, accepted positively the case for a stronger biblical approach to morality. It was not afraid that the traditional natural law element might disappear in the process; this confidence is evident in the wording of *Gaudium et Spes* (the Pastoral Constitution on the Church in the Modern World), no. 16.

The directive of the Council was universally accepted within the church, but occasionally with one-sided enthusiasm. This means that, of the two elements of Christian morality conjoined in the title of this essay, that of human evaluation received insufficient consideration in discussions concerning normative morality; in other words, natural law thinking was often excluded practically (or also theoretically) from normative moral theology. This process was reinforced by the fact that the defenders of the natural law approach, which stresses human evaluation, demonstrated only insufficiently how biblical thought in fact was operative enough in their reasoning to justify the specification of their conclusions as "Christian." In short, it became obvious that in the discussions of the preceding decades there had been an inadequate awareness of the complexity of providing a biblical foundation to moral theology.[8] A balanced view of the problematic, as suggested in the title of this essay, requires thorough reflection and prolonged discussion of an exegetical, theological and philosophico-ethical character. By way of simplification it can be said that so far a double tendency has resulted: that of a biblico-theological ethics of faith (also briefly called faith-ethics) and that of a heightened emphasis on human evaluation carried out in a Christian context (for short, ethical autonomy in a Christian context). The study by Vincent McNamara of the relevant problems in the last decade, which appeared last year,[9] narrows the problematic to the two tendencies of "faith-ethics" and "ethical autonomy in a Christian context." The distinction formulated in this way obviously integrates nuances of various kinds, but less clearly indicates tendencies and questions which do not enter fully into the dual alternative (e.g. Klaus Demmer and Hans Rotter).

2. Moral Norms of Behavior and Judgment in the Bible

The discussion in recent decades has chiefly concentrated on the problematic of moral norms and moral judgment with regard to behavior in our human world. Whether there are fundamental religious and moral attitudes, that is, whether a rich and specifically Christian *ethos* exists,[10] is in fact nowhere being challenged or at least not fundamentally. The reduction of moral-theological reflection to the determination of a normative morality of behavior is, therefore, broadly accepted, although occasional warnings are voiced about the one-sidedness of this state of affairs.

In recent years the question of the *proprium* of Christian norms of behavior on the basis of biblical statements has been examined very critically. In view of their genesis, are these norms independent, in that they arise from Christianity as such? Do they comprise a *distinctivum*, that is, a set of moral judgments that are possible only in Christianity? Do they belong to the *specificum* of what is Christian, that is, do they appertain absolutely (if not also exclusively) to Christian morality? Does the Bible itself regard them as universal norms not bound by time, or rather as answers to questions which were posed by a specific culture? Finally, do they intend to be understood at all — at least generally — as a moral *doctrine*, indeed as revealed moral truths, or rather as *paranetic* warnings in which the norm as such is presupposed but not explicitly taught? Such questions, of course, make the problematic of the *validity* of such norms inescapable, and specifically that of their validity for Christians of subsequent generations.

Above all, it has been correctly stated that one-sided recourse to the Bible so as to establish norms of moral behavior not only comes close to a fundamentalistic understanding of the sacred writings, but also is rendered, by the relatively few statements of the Bible itself, a hopeless project for one who must make decisions about the immense field of innerworldly behaviour. In particular, this way of proceeding contra-dicts the whole tendency of the Bible, above all of the New Testament, not to offer itself primarily as a help for the right ordering of the human world, but as a help for salvation, and therefore, for conversion and for personal goodness, now that the kingdom of God has broken into the world. This proper view of biblical norms is evident both in the tendency of the Sermon on the Mount and in the paranesis of the Apostle Paul. Obviously, the conversion to personal goodness will have consequences in the domain of behavior; but Christians must determine what these consequences are to be.

It has been pointed out that even the Decalogue should not be regarded as a direct revelation of moral behavior by God, but rather as a brief synthesis of religious prescriptions imposed on the people of Israel (first to third commandments) and of fundamental modes of societal action in Israel — parallel to those of the neighboring peoples (fourth to tenth commandments). It is indeed true that the observance of these precepts will be Israel's expression of fidelity to the covenant that God has offered to his people, and thus indicates a deep religious sense that goes beyond its apparent moral import.[11] Nevertheless, the observance of the precepts does not directly flow, as far as their content is concerned, from the essence of the covenant and of the covenant God. Moreover, as studies have begun to show,[12] the Sermon on the Mount embodies the best moral wisdom of the Jewish tradition and leads Christians back, by means of the correctives added by Jesus, to behavior that is truly *humanum*. Such behavior is opposed chiefly to that of sinners, and of those who yield in the face of perverted hardheartedness. Thus, Jesus is presented as calling people to what is human and not to a superhuman, "distinctively Christian" behavior in the world. In those who follow the moral stance which Jesus demands, however, the world is given a sign of the religious transformation of those converted to the kingdom of God which he proclaimed. In his paranesis, St. Paul also adopted the best moral norms of behavior proposed by then contemporary thinkers, whenever he believed there was no incompatibility between them and Jesus' understanding of God and the world (that is, of human beings). This compatibility, of course, was a guiding criterion, because in and through morality, religious union with Christ had to be able to express itself in a vital way. As was already the case in the Old Testament, so it is clear also in Paul and in Jesus that they wished to give the appropriate answer for precisely the questions posed by the people of their time and their culture. This fact obviously can relativize the lasting significance of their answers to particular questions for other times, cultures and worldviews.

Fundamental considerations expressed in many publications of the last decades show that the reflections being made here are *per se* necessary. This is the case not only because Christian faith (and the normative morality that corresponds to it) presupposes (logically) the fundamental moral experience of the human person. More important is the fact that the rational structure of the world and of human beings, and thus also of their morality, does not allow for a structure of moral norms that is fundamentalistic or mysterious. A moral claim that is fundamentally inscrutable for human beings cannot be a factor in the process of moral self-realization that is their task — even if it does present itself as a general norm or as a concrete requirement. Many moral theologians wish to characterize precisely this rational process as moral autonomy: that is, that humanity itself — because of its share in being the image of God — is to seek and discover the morally binding way of acting in the world. Such responsible autonomy is "theonomous," "relational," the gift and task bestowed on humanity by the Creator and demanded of it by Jesus; morover, this responsible autonomy can be experienced even when the explicit recognition of its *raison d'être* is not present. In the end, such reflections inevitably lead to the realization that the competence of the church's magisterium in questions of normative morality for innerworldly behavior is not simply and indistinguishably the same as its competence in questions of faith.

It is interesting that not only many moralists but also dogmaticians and exegetes are concerned about the ongoing debate in the field of moral theology, and some indeed not without serious misgivings. Because of this concern and in the wake of previously held discussions of the Pontifical International Theological Commission, a small book, *Principles of Christian Moral Theology*, edited by Joseph Ratzinger, appeared in 1975. Even today it remains typical of a particular way of trying to arrive at a truly Christian moral theology. The book contains three essays, two by dogmaticians (Hans Urs von Balthasar and Joseph Ratzinger) and one by an exegete (Heinz Schürmann).[13] It is instructive to know what concerns and suggestions the non-moral theologians have to offer with regard to the research presently being undertaken in moral theology. For this small book was conceived as a dogmatic-exegetical protest against a tendency in moral theology to defend the human-rational, and thus the autonomous, element of decision-making so as to offset a one-sided emphasis on a Christian *proprium* of Christian morality.

The "Nine Propositions about Christian Ethics" of von Balthasar, which have been reprinted in various languages, generally correspond to his *Theology of History*, which appeared many years earlier. The author defends a markedly biblical christocentrism, basing his argument to a large extent on Col 1: 15–18: *everything* has its existence in Christ. Consequently, Christ is simply *the* moral imperative of all human morality; the preceding Old Testament is taken up into the New Testament norm, "Christ"; the instances of "extrabiblical" authority — conscience and natural moral law — arrive at their true meaning only in Christ, at least insofar as their fullness is concerned. Even if the author seems to have a rather reductionist understanding of the "extrabiblical" elements (especially of the natural moral law), what he says of Jesus as the "concrete universal" norm (containing in himself all moral norm-making) is theologically first-rate; but it does not provide much help for the discussion taking place in moral theology concerning the relationship between biblical and concrete "human" morality which the above-mentioned publication was basically meant to aid. An exception to this is the fact that the "extrabiblical" elements, conscience and natural law, seem to be embedded and fully actualized in the morality which has Christ as its only imperative.[14]

Like von Balthasar, the dogmatician Ratzinger, in his essay "Magisterium of the Church, Faith and Moral Theology," addresses in a substantial way the discussion being carried on by moral theologians about the *proprium* of Christian morality. He does admit that, while the Bible does teach some ethical principles, the *proprium* of biblical morality does not consist of a list of exclusive norms; but on the other hand, elements that have their origin elsewhere (traditions, rational insights) can become a *specificum* of biblical morality. However, the criterion for selecting the norms that come from elsewhere is biblical faith itself. This statement is explained in the following terms: "Christian originality consists . . . in the new shape of the whole, into which the seeking and struggling of humanity has been melted down by the orientating midpoint which is faith in the God of Abraham, in the God of Jesus Christ".[15] Thus, Ratzinger considers that the norms of the Decalogue reflect the specific holiness of Yahweh, and therefore cannot be separated from him. But surely this must not mean that Yahweh's holiness itself grants the norms of the Decalogue their truth and validity — is it not rather the case that it contradicts the holiness of Yahweh to do what is considered to be morally unacceptable? The name "Christians" accounts for the second "new shape of the whole," attention being paid to the occasional interchange of *christos* and *chrestos* (good); since they belong to Christ, Christians must be fundamentally good. This truth obviously has little to offer to the search for concrete normative morality. The apostolic paranesis is described as the third "new shape of the whole," that is, the demand to live according to the teaching of Jesus and the recognition of the correct concept of God. According to Ratzinger, this principle provides not only a formal intention but also a material ethical content. Modern exegesis would scarcely agree with this view; and even Paul could not make his choice of moral norms simply by following the criterion of this "new shape of the whole." However, it is indeed true that normative morality is concerned with the faith, and that formal non observance of this morality stands in contradiction to Jesus and Yahweh; but it is hardly true to say that the entirety of Christian normative morality is, with regard to *its contents*, inherent in the faith and determined by the faith. This conclusion should be of no small importance for the specific competence of the magisterium regarding such questions of morality, a matter in which Ratzinger shows himself especially interested.[16]

Heinz Schürmann, an exegete, examines the moral statements of the Bible in the light of the problematic confronting moral theologians in search of a concrete and normative morality of Christian action: what does the Bible offer in terms of concrete norms for the daily decisions of Christians living in the world today? Schürmann's intention is to affirm: very much; yet his findings affirm: very little that is concrete. Even he seems to be rather disappointed with the results. Schürmann's attempt represents an impressive endeavor to relate the behavioral morality of today's Christians with that of the Bible. A difficulty inherent in this enterprise is the translation of the categories of the Bible into those of the moral-theological problematic of today.

According to Schürmann, the New Testament understands Jesus' style of life as obligatory for Christians: this is true also of his words — although not in a "legal" sense.[17] In the same way, the imperative character of the apostolic instructions — in some fashion given in the name of Jesus and in the Holy Spirit — is acknowledged. Most obligatory are the general spiritual, Christian-theological-eschatological attitudes (for example, love). The same also applies, moreover, to particular moral instructions about conduct, even if these were in part conditioned by their own time, or arose from an insufficient understanding of the given realities. The obligatory character of these instructions does not therefore exclude the fact that for today's Christians, to use Schürmann's formulation, they are often imperative and can be put into action only in an approximate, analogous, related or even merely intentional manner. This is indeed also true of some particular "spiritual" instructions.[18] As a result, according to Schürmann, the instructions of Jesus and of the apostles must be read hermeneutically; however, this implies the human-rational-autonomous activity of evaluating and judging — even if the latter is always done in the light of faith (Vatican II: "in the light of the Gospel"). The exposition of Schürmann (as an exegete) fails to bring forth more abundant results than those of von Balthasar and Ratzinger (as dogmaticians).

3. The Problem of "Reason and Faith"

In the essay already cited, Ratzinger has pointed out, as have many others, the importance of the problem of "reason and faith" in determining the properly Christian character of Christian morality: "The problem which arises here is how we are to understand the inter-relationship of faith with reason, or with thought patterns which are human in the general sense; and finally the question arises concerning the possibilities and the boundaries of reason vis-à-vis faith."[19]

Several representatives of the approach to morality that is called "faith-ethics" for short (e.g. Bernhard Stöckle),[20] have a rather skeptical view of the ability of human reason to determine what is proper human action. They maintain that reason is powerless in this regard, unless it is energized by Christian faith. This is indeed a devastating message for humanity, which is to a great extent non-Christian or de-Christianized! The first question these moral theologians raise is that concerning the *origo* and *finis*, the source and goal of human existence. Although it is admitted that the human person may well be in a position to discover meaningful patterns of behavior, this capacity is viewed as greatly limited because of their conviction that some ethical questions — e.g., suicide, extramarital sexuality, love of neighbor, pardon of enemies, acknowledgment of the worth of every human being, etc. — can be properly solved only on the basis of a *fides quae christiana*. It is, however, more important for such moralists that the absolutely binding character of such behavioral norms cannot be made evident; without Christian faith, therefore, every type of activity is seen as fundamentally permissible. Today's ethical pluralism and behavioral inconsistency (both of which can be established to exist) could well make such considerations seem plausible; but contrary considerations are likewise plausible, if one were to recognize the ethical sincerity and behavioral consistency to be found in those committed to other forms of faith, and even in agnostics and atheists.

Other moral theologians, each in a particular way, resist such skepticism about human morality (e.g. Bruno Schüller, Franz Böckle, Alfons Auer, Dietmar Mieth, Richard McCormick). First of all, some "faith-ethicians" seem to attribute to their "opponents" a one-sidedly rationalistic concept of *ratio*, as if these less skeptical moralists did not understand that it is not the *ratio* which thinks, but the human beings making use of it, with the result that they always stand — even in their thinking — under influences of various kinds (inclinations, experiences, options, "faith", etc.). The faith-ethicians themselves seem scarcely to admit the fact that there are many kinds of experiences and insights which cannot be formulated conceptually but which persons freely accept in the course of determining their lives and making their decisions. It has already been observed that many adherents of a Polish school of ethics understand human moral experience, that is, the experience of conscience, to be necessarily — therefore logically — presupposed by faith and by every other moral insight. This stance does not exclude the possibility that the implicit experience of grace, or even of revelation (not consciously reflected upon), may be active in such moral decisions; but, even if this is true, it is the human person as such, capable of experiencing and *understanding* (hence as *ratio*), who actually understands and experiences. Furthermore, human persons often arrive at insights, which they can in principle understand, only through the *removens-prohibens* of many impulses, which do not

spring from their own ego, but which set them free to be truly themselves, or to come to a deeper self-understanding; some of these
impulses are: the words of the Bible, the anthropological implications
of the act of faith, the church, etc. Nevertheless, it is always the *ratio*
itself by which we evaluate, understand and judge — even if it is true
that what is meant is not "pure" *ratio*, but *ratio* set free in the manner
just described. The observation of the Polish moral theologians means
that human recognition of behavioral norms, which is accepted even by
many "faith-ethicians", is certainly experienced as moral (i.e.,
absolute). Therefore, one should not be dismayed by the lack of
evidence which characterizes the content of practical moral judgments,
for there are contingent realities and experiences implied in such
recognitions, which do not permit a metaphysically, but "only" a
morally, certain knowledge. Even faith itself does not in all circumstances prevent a moral pluralism, as the Second Vatican Council
expressly states. [21] Furthermore, the understanding of faith, which provides support for the recognition of moral norms, is a *human*
understanding of faith (Schüller) empowered by that *ratio* — with all its
weaknesses — in which one finds it hard to have confidence; even faith
does not simply exempt one from the *conditio humana*. Finally, "faith-
ethics" which puts its trust in understanding based on belief has until
now not demonstrated how it actually arrives at a normative behavioral
ethics without a healthy confidence in the *ratio* (Auer).

On the other hand, those who emphasize the fundamental
rationality — *ratio* (!) — of all moral norms of behavior have never
wanted to say, and have never said, that Christians could ignore the
Bible in the process of determining norms of behavior. The only
question is: which function should one attribute to the Bible and which
to human reason? For it is absolutely necessary to distinguish in this
matter. Demmer has been pointing out for years that the attempt to
formulate moral norms and judgments always takes place within a process which entails an interaction of both faith and reason. It is in this
new process, and not in the search for new behavioral norms, that the
proprium of biblical morality is to be found. Therefore, Demmer does
not begin his moral reflections by posing the question concerning
normative morality which was treated above, because it does not seem
to be very significant. He writes in a recent study: "The history of the
efficacy of revelation ... creates in the believer a new self-
understanding, which as it develops arrives at moral consequences . . .
The moral reason of the believer operates so as to come to moral
norms, and thus functions as insight working under altered, transcendental conditions . . . The believer approaches moral obligations with a
different pre-understanding than does the non-believer, and this pre-
understanding does not remain external to moral reason." [22] In this

sense, Demmer can speak elsewhere of a *ratio nova* – parallel to St. Paul's concept of the *homo novus*.[23] Despite this *real* interaction of faith and reason within one process, one must maintain the *distinction* between the two elements and between the particular functions of each within the moral process. There is no doubt that the function of reason, and its exclusive function, is to be concerned about the moral correctness of the behavior.

What then is the contribution of biblical faith (both as *fides qua* and as *fides quae*) to the process of formulating moral norms and judgments? As *fides qua*, it helps Christians accept themselves as those believing, loving and whole persons in whom the self-communication of the God revealing himself in Jesus Christ has taken hold. As *fides quae*, biblical faith means the acceptance (the taking into oneself) both of the vision of God and of the world which is contained in this self-communication and of an ethos that corresponds to it. Thus, a development of human self-awareness takes place in the believer; one could speak, in a way parallel to formulations proposed above, of a "new" self-consciousness and of a correspondingly "new" conscience; the "novelty" is essentially proper to the self-consciousness and to the conscience of Christians. In using their *ratio* to evaluate norms and judgments, Christians who search for truth cannot abstract from this novelty, even when it does not present itself in an explicit and reflective manner.

Is it possible to say something more about the "novelty" of the consciousness and the conscience of Christians? Obviously, one can attempt this in various ways. Above all, one could perhaps point to the holistic character of the fundamental attitude of Christians toward life. Christ shows us his and our *God*, and the relationship that now exists between the God of love and the human being who is taken up into this love and is called to a hope and thus to a deeply meaningful life. Paul shows us *Jesus* as the Christ, his self-sacrificing relationship to us and the loving and self-giving relationship of Christians to their Lord. The *Spirit* of God and of Jesus Christ is revealed as present and operative. Human beings may now know that they are accepted despite their weaknesses and sinfulness, and as a result they can comprehend their profound dignity; they can also recognize the dignity of every other human being, and understand that it must be taken seriously. However, it should be noted that this line of reasoning does not represent the primary basis for asserting the dignity of the human person; rather, this human trait is understood here in its deepest sense.

Other important aspects of the novelty of Christian self-understanding are the biblical figure and the teaching of Christ, as well as the content of the apostolic paranesis. Even when it is evident that influences on the latter are determined by a particular time and culture, it nevertheless remains true that both Christ and his disciples and apostles believed that they could regard the forms of conduct which they approved as compatible with the ethos and fundamental attitude of the disciple in the kingdom of God, or that they could understand these forms of conduct as possible ways of expressing the fundamental Christian attitude toward the world. One is thus required to undertake a serious hermeneutical reading of the appropriate biblical texts – a task that is to be carried out by the *ratio*.

Finally, attention should be given to the functional thrust of the Sermon on the Mount. It has been correctly emphasized that its proper characteristic is the radicality that will be lived by the true disciple of Jesus, the human person who has been converted to the kingdom of God and acts in the power of such a calling. Yet, such radicality should not be interpreted to imply a superhuman morality, that is, one in which something "more" is said to be operative in Christian moral acts vis-à-vis genuine human morality. The radicality of the Sermon on the Mount has a double meaning: first, a radically serious living of humanity (= morality) as opposed to confining oneself to what even the sinners do ("even the sinners do that"); second, an equally serious living of humanity (= morality) as opposed to adopting an egoistic moral stance, e.g. the limitation of full fidelity in marriage to the matrimonial legislation of Moses ("But I say to you"). This affirmation of Jesus also suggests that the "novelty" of Christian consciousness consists in bestowing new power so that it is possible to opt for good and correct conduct.

All these considerations indicate that believers possess a new "Christian" meaning, a new intentionality, a new and deepened insight into Christian anthropology and ethics, a new motivation for action, and a new readiness to live seriously: in short, a specifically Christian orientation both for the moral life itself and for the discovery of moral norms and judgments with a view to correct behavior in the human world. It is indeed true that this orientation does not explicitly contain teaching concerning moral norms; moreover, moral norms and judgments cannot be grounded in such a way that, without this orientation, they would have to remain necessarily closed to human insight. The biblical orientation will therefore be concretized by Christians themselves; they must decide which innerworldly behavior is or can be an expression of the biblical orientation. Christians must choose, however, within the concretely given reality with all its historical particularities and on the basis of the moral understanding which they have thus far attained. Such Christian decision-making must be undertaken with the aid of human reason which evaluates all human and worldly reality and pronounces moral judgment on it – although always in the light of the ever-present biblical orientation in its reflective or non-reflective form. Therefore, the biblical orientation does not determine any moral norms of behavior which are not accessible to human insight. This point of view corresponds to a centuries-old Christian tradition: Thomas Aquinas taught that, like the action-oriented morality of the Old Testament,[24] that of the New Testament also is rational-human morality;[25] as was already the case in the Old Testament, natural reason is to inspire Christians to works of virtue.

4. Moral Rightness

Morality in the proper sense can be predicated only of persons and of their free attitudes and decisions; morality is also called moral *goodness*; its opposite would be personal immorality (= badness). Moral goodness necessarily expresses itself through behavior in the world of human beings, and hence in the further activation and shaping of this world. Moral goodness is therefore inherently directed to the responsible and thus right shaping of the world. Yet the right shaping of the world is not the only aim of morality; it is also concerned in an essential way with the task of incarnating moral goodness in the world — precisely through right behavior. In this sense, one can also speak of *moral* rightness (the opposite: moral wrongness) of behavior in the world.

The problem of moral behavioral norms is concerned with this rightness. The corresponding normative moral theology seeks to investigate which modes of human behavior serve to enhance the world of human persons — of the individual, of interpersonal relationships, of human society, of the subpersonal world — and thus to realize the true good of the human person (of humanity).[26] This enhancement of the human world is, first of all, a purely material human question, and for this reason morally neutral. But since rightness of conduct in the world is sought, found and actualized by the human person, this process of seeking, finding and actualizing is always moral in the narrower sense; this means that it is supported by moral goodness and, in a corresponding fashion for Christians, by their fundamental biblical orientation (at any particular moment perhaps scarcely reflected upon); one could speak analogously of non-Christians and of their fundamental stance rooted in a world view or a religious tradition.

Guided by their search for moral goodness and by their biblical orientation, Christians attempt responsibly to understand and to evaluate the human person, humanity and the world — the latter not only as a whole and as particular realities but also in terms of the relationship of the particulars to the whole. Therefore, it is possible to understand and judge the different kinds of projects aimed at shaping reality — projects of things to be done and things to be left undone — by inquiring about their convenience and rightness with regard to the actualization of the individual person and of the formation of a human world. Such understanding and judging are proper tasks of human reason. As far as it can, reason probes the whole of reality; only by use of reason is it possible to discover moral rightness. Rational reflection allows itself to be led from the reality of the ego toward the reality of the whole world, into which the ego expands itself; rational reflection is guided by the whole of reality, and evaluates and judges in what way and through what behavior it can be further activated and developed in a manner that is meaningful and human. It is therefore human reality itself that poses questions to reason (which is illumined by Christianity) as it carries out an evaluation and judgment of it, and fosters its development so that it always remains a personal reality.

The biblical-Christian orientation, therefore, cannot overlook the fact that moral rightness can be discovered by reason only when the latter knows and understands the "reality" and the "realities" of the human person. Today, if one wishes to make a moral judgment concerning atomic armaments, one must understand much about social psychology, about chemistry and physics, about law and politics; for only if this is done can one be confident in making a sound evaluation and judgment from the moral point of view. If one wishes to speak about sexual or family morality, it is not sufficient to have a medieval knowledge of the respective areas of life to be considered; current knowledge of these matters helps one form a morally correct judgment and not just *any* judgment. The biblical orientation cannot take the place of human factual knowledge and human-rational evaluation and judgment; on the contrary, the Christian biblical orientation requires these, since it seeks after the very same rightness of human behavior that is demanded by human reality itself — and no other form of rightness whatsoever.

The steadily groping attempts of reason never take place outside history, never, as it were, in an air-free space or from a neutral standpoint. There have always been norms of moral rightness, although often they were based on another level of knowledge, on a partially different picture of the world, on other experiences, other patterns of interpreting human persons and their world, or perhaps even on a different kind of availability (than that of today). The hermeneutical reading of such circumstances with the aid of rational reflection also has a contribution to make to the human search for conduct that is correct today, that is, here and now. It is not a matter of finding an abstract rightness as such.

Even inherited norms, or those that we have accepted or indeed worked out ourselves — this "we" is always to be understood within a cultural context — are abstract and therefore in need of a hermeneutical reading, so that we may arrive with their help at a reasonable judgment concerning concrete behavior here and now. For an abstractly formulated norm does not state what it in fact intends to pronounce about the concrete, and hence more complex, reality. The decree which reason makes about historically concrete conduct is therefore never the pure application of an abstract norm, but the extensive interpretation of it.

Norms and judgments of morally right behavior require an evalua-' tion and a comparison of the good/ills or values/nonvalues implied by particular conduct in the human world; for responsible behavior must strive to augment human goods and values. The observance of the relative character of such goods and values is possible and necessary because they do not constitute an *absolutum*, that is, they do not represent realities which are unconditionally required by the human person. One should interpret this position neither as simple utilitarianism nor as calculating consequentialism; for in such an endeavor to explain right behavior it is not the case that either means alone or consequences alone are considered in isolation; rather, the entire reality of a moral act is taken into account — its own meaningfulness as seen within the context of the meaningfulness which the entire act and its result represent and signify. Proportionalism, a term customary today chiefly in America, is therefore a better name for this process of comparative evaluation. Occasionally, the accusation of a certain impracticability is brought against this explanation of right behavior, but the accusation is more theoretical than real: the practice of such evaluation is well established both in theory (e.g., with reference to action involving the principle of double effect, or to the ordering of the works of fraternal love, etc.) and in the area of practical life. Many opponents of proportionalism fear above all that it considers individual acts (e.g., masturbation, contraceptive behavior) simply as physical realities rather than as human acts which are therefore to be judged morally. This is obviously a distorted description of proportionalism, and should not be employed in criticizing it. For the proponents of proportionalism state something quite different, namely, that although such acts are always subject to moral evaluation, final judgment about them cannot be made in the abstract, that is, without simultaneously taking into account the circumstances and intentions of such acts; only in this way can the moral judgment about them be objective.[27]

Both Kant and a certain Catholic tradition would like to escape this conclusion, and they would do so in two different ways. First, they appeal to the natural goals of human faculties, for example, sexuality or language, and they interpret these as natural and hence God-given instructions. This is the typical naturalistic fallacy. For what is given in nature can communicate to us only what it is and how it functions —

that is, the reality which the Creator intended it to be. But it cannot provide us with moral instruction about how we are to use it; its meaningful use by human beings — in the entire context of human reality — is discovered by reason, which must interpret, evaluate and judge, so as to decide what the moral will of God is concerning its use. Next, appeal is made to God's ordinances and rights — for example, with regard to the disposing of human life. Thereby the transcendent reality of God is placed alongside (not "above" or "in") the categorical realities of creation: this presupposes a false image of God and therefore represents an attempt to judge natural gifts in an ethically impossible manner.[28] As has been stated above, the evaluating reason, in the face of these questions, must concretize the biblical orientation in a human way.[29]

Correct human behavior in this human world is to be discovered by the partner created by the Creator, and with the aid of the human reason of the creature which reflects the wisdom of the Creator. Biblical faith necessitates this process and gives its own orientation as a help toward fulfilling it, without however substituting itself for human reason. Enlightened human reason itself must seek the moral rightness of inner-worldly behavior (and truly evaluate it), thus concretizing the biblical orientation in a manner which is independent of it.

NOTES

1 B. Fraling, "Glaube und Ethos. Normfindung in der Gemeinschaft der Gläubigen", *Theol. u. Glaube* 63 (1973), 81–105, see 82.

2 R. Collins, "Scripture and Christian Ethics", in: *The Cathol. Theol. Soc. of America, Proceedings of the 31st Annual Conv.* 29 (1974), 215–240.

3 P. Hoffmann and V. Eid, *Jesus von Nazaret und eine christliche Moral. Sittliche Perspektiven der Verkündigung Jesu*, Freiburg i. Br. 1975, 19–24.

4 H. Juros and T. Styczén, "Methodologische Ansätze ethischen Denkens und ihre Folgen für die theologische Ethik", in: J. Pfammater and F. Furger (eds.), *Theologische Berichte* IV, Einsiedeln 1974, 89–181; see 105.

5 *Optatam totius*, 16.

6 F. Tillmann, *Die Idee der Nachfolge Christi*, Düsseldorf 1933 (3rd edn., Düsseldorf 1949).

7 B. Häring, *The Law of Christ*, 3 vols, Westminster, Md., 1961–66.

8 V. MacNamara points this out in his most recent work: *Faith and Ethics. Recent Roman Catholicism*, Dublin and Washington 1985.

9 See note 8 above.

10 F. Böckle, "Unfehlbare Normen?", in: H. Küng (ed.), *Fehlbar?*, Zürich 1973, 280–304.

11 On the problem of the decalogue, cf. the synthesis in H. Schüngel-Straumann, *Der Dekalog — Gottes Gebot?* Stuttgart 1973. Most recently: F.L. Hossfeld, *Der Dekalog. Seine späteren Fassungen, die originale Komposition und seine Vorstufen*, Göttingen 1982.

12 Cf. e.g. R. Neudecker, "The Sermon on the Mount as a Witness to 'Inculturation'. The first two Antithetical Cases (Mt 5:21–32)", in: *Bible and Inculturation* (ed. A. Roest Crollius). From a Jewish point of view: P.E. Lapide, *Die Bergpredigt, Utopie oder Programm?*, Mainz 1982 (2nd end.).

13 J. Ratzinger (ed.), *Prinzipien christlicher Moral*, 1975 (2nd edn.).

14 It is interesting that an exegete, J.P. Meier, offered, although in a different perspective, but at the same time as the systematic theologian H. Urs von Balthasar the following formulation: "For the Christian disciple, Jesus is the Norm of Morality". The author means that the disciples of Jesus follow a requirement, not because of its contents, but because it is the requirement of Jesus. – Nonetheless, like Jesus himself, the disciples too must always be guided by what could be regarded as correct – as we see later in Paul. But this, according to the author, is then not what Jesus commanded and commanded to be handed on to the future. See J.P. Meier, *Law and History in Matthew's Gospel. A Redactional Study of Matthew 5:17–48*, Rome 1976, 169.

15 J. Ratzinger (ed.), *Prinzipien christlicher Moral* (cf. n. 13), 48f.

16 The idea of the "shape of the whole" is found again, when J. Ratzinger (1984, now Archbishop, Cardinal and Prefect of the Congregation for the Doctrine of the Faith) required a few years ago at the Congress in Dallas that the American bishops as teachers of Christian morality quite simply "attest" the moral "wisdom" of the church across the centuries. This can doubtless mean an ethos that is based in Jesus, but scarcely the concrete normative behavioral moral theology that is varied in itself, experiences alteration in various elements, and is not to be shown as coming from Yahweh and Jesus. This cannot be "attested", but must be established through *human-rational* observation, evaluation and moral judgment (*in faith*) of the particular empirical reality and experience. (Cf. Cardinal J. Ratzinger's lecture in: *Moral Theology Today: Certitudes and Doubts*, St Louis, The Pope John Center, 1984).

By way of parenthesis: whenever the Prefect of a Pontifical Congregation speaks, there arises the question who exactly is speaking: a Congregation, a Cardinal or Archbishop, or a theologian? The question goes parallel to that put forward in the carefully prepared essay of *La Civiltà Cattolica* on infallibilism as opposed to the doctrine of infallibility ("Il ministero del Papa dopo i due Concili del Vaticano", *La Civiltà Cattolica* 136, 1985 IV, 209–221). The danger is real that every utterance of a representative of the Vatican may be taken as the official position of the Vatican itself. This would be naïve integralism.

17 Schürmann refers to 1 Cor 7, 12–16.

18 Schürmann refers to 1 Cor 7, 7–14.

19 Ratzinger, *Prinzipien christlicher Moral* (cf. note 13 above), 47.

20 B. Stöckle, *Grenzen der autonomen Moral*, München 1974.

21 *Gaudium et Spes* no. 43.

22 K. Demmer, *Deuten und Handeln*, Freiburg i. Br./Freiburg i. Uc. 1985, 82.

23 E.g. Rom 6,4.

24 Cf. *S.T.* I–II 100,1; 102,2 ad 1.

25 Cf. *S.T.* I–II 108, 2 ad 1.

26 Cf. Thomas Aquinas, *S.C.G.* 3, 122; introduction.

27 This mistaken interpretation of proportionalism is found also in Cardinal Ratzinger's address in Dallas on the question of proportionalism; cf. *Moral Theology Today* (cf. note 16 above), 343.

28 Cf. J. Fuchs, Our Image of God and the Morality of Innerwordly Behavior, see below, 28–49.

29 On the question of universal norms, cf. the excellent lecture (with discussion) by J.S. Cahill, "Contemporary Challenges to Exceptionless Moral Norms", in: *Moral Theology Today* (cf. note 16 above), 121–35 and 193–202.

II. Vatican II: Salvation, Personal Morality, Right Behavior

The theme "salvation, moral goodness, moral rightness" was not treated explicitly by the Second Vatican Council — as is true in general of the basic questions of Christian fundamental moral theology. In *Gaudium et Specs* (GS), the Pastoral Constitution on the Church in the Modern World, although significant things are said about responsible *behavior in the world* in general, and above all about particular questions in a special way, a theory of behavior is not developed. Nevertheless, one quickly realizes that in the background there is another deeper moral problem, namely, that of the inner *morality of the personal human being* as such, who intervenes in the human world with behavior that is ultimately grounded in his personal morality. Personal morality in its turn presupposes, according to the Council's statements, that "healing" and "sanctifying" transformation of the human person, who, left to himself, is a sinner; this transformation is the salvation given by God as a gift that calls the human person and makes him "good" — before God. The three themes named — salvation, personal morality, right behavior — are neither systematically distinguished nor treated separately by the Council. But one would misunderstand the Council's Christian moral teaching if one failed to see that the fundamental theme in the Council's statements about the human person is salvation, to which is joined the question of personal morality; both become incarnate in right behaviour in the world.

1. God's Salvation

One can grasp how much the central anthropological idea of the Council is the salvation of the human person by and through God when one sees its endeavor not to exclude from the possibility of salvation, as a sharing in the earthly and eternal paschal mystery, those many people who, through no fault of their own, live without any knowledge of God and Christ, but in fidelity to their conscience

(*Lumen Gentium* (LG) 16, GS 22, *Ad Gentes* (AG) 7; cf. LG 14). Because of their special thematic, the two documents which deal more than any other with the central significance of the salvation that God gives are the Dogmatic Constitution on Divine Revelation, *Dei Verbum* (DV) and the Dogmatic Constitution on the Church, *Lumen Gentium*.

According to *Dei Verbum*, the reason for God's self-revelation to men and for its being handed on is that it is a message of salvation (DV 1). On the basis of this fact, the Council wishes to determine how the revelation that has been handed on to us is to be understood as a whole and in detail. The Council speaks of a history of the revelation of God which we accept in faith, hope and love (DV 1,5). The gospel is seen as a handing on and therefore as the "source of every truth of salvation" (DV 7). Everything that the Bible says "for the sake of our salvation" is truth (DV 11). This is true both of the "history of salvation" in the Old Testament (DV 14) and of what Jesus "truly did and taught for our salvation" in the New Testament (DV 19). The word "moral teaching" is joined only once to the word "truth of salvation" – though without reference to an interior union; the text speaks here about the gospel (DV 7).

The Constitution on the Church, *Lumen Gentium*, understands the mystery of the church most deeply as the mystery of salvation. The church is seen fundamentally as "sign and instrument of the most intimate joining to God" and of the unity of mankind as "full unity in Christ" (LG 1). If creation already is aimed at "participation in the divine life," and "aids to salvation in Christ" have been given to us after sin (LG 2), then in the continuation of Christ's mission through the church the salvific work of God has already grown mightily (LG 3); the Spirit who works in mankind is power that aims at eternal life (LG 4). In the church, the already present "kingdom of God" has become a visible reality (LG 5). The teaching of *Lumen Gentium* about the church as "people of God" points in the same direction: God reveals his "counsel of salvation," sanctifies his "people" for himself, changes its interior (its "heart," according to Jer 31:31–34) and concludes a covenant with it in the blood of Christ and in the Holy Spirit (LG 9). Here, we see more clearly than before that the one who is in "salvation" is personally "holy" in personal moral "goodness."

The primacy of the reality of salvation is also found in other Council documents. When the decree *Optatam Totius* (OT) speaks of the theological education of future priests, it insists upon a first course of introduction "to the mystery of salvation" (OT 14), while all the theological disciplines for their part should be taught "in contact with the mystery of Christ and salvation history." The relationship between salvation and morality is suggested in the exhortation that moral theology should not proclaim first of all human morality, but the salvific action of God (OT 16). A remark in the Decree on the Lay Apostolate *Apostolicam Actuositatem* (AA) is also interesting, where it is said unambiguously: "The aim of the redemptive work of Christ *per se* is the salvation of man"; in the same decree, however, the observation is added, though without any explanation, that the work of salvation also includes the "temporal order of this world" (AA 5). Whoever neglects his (earthly) duties, we read in *Gaudium et Spes*, "imperils his eternal salvation" (GS 43). In the text about the primacy of divine salvation, then, there is also, even if only occasionally, a pointer to the relationship of salvation not only to personal morality, but also to the right ordering of the world.

The Pastoral Constitution *Gaudium et Spes*, as already noted, has its starting-point, in accord with its particular aim, in the problematic of the ordering of the world of the human person as God's creation (GS 1), but also sees our attempts to further shape the created world (GS 34, 57) as a (moral and religious) perfecting of the active human person himself (GS 37–39, 57) and as a requirement of the "kingdom of Christ" (GS 39), for the ordering of this world takes place in the "expectation of the new earth" (GS 39).

2. Personal Morality

Salvation is not a "something," but a call that comes from God and the inner reshaping of the personal man; according to the Council, salvation is in man's free acceptance, which is itself a gift of God — in faith, hope and love. The personal decision for the God of salvation therefore does not directly concern the innerworldly behavior of man, but man himself as person. He lets himself be reshaped, and reshapes himself in inner freedom; thus he is not a sinner, but redeemed — whether this be in categorial knowledge of God's salvific action (GS 11–13) or without such knowledge (cf. GS 22).

It is important, in reflecting on the statements of the Council, that salvation be viewed in direct relation, not to acting in the world, but to the person in his freedom. Morality in the genuine sense of the word can be predicated only of the free person, not of actions as such. Indeed, in all free behavior in the world, the principal matter is at the same time and most deeply the self-shaping of the person (GS 52, 37–39) and the person's inner disposition (GS 26, 71). Personal morality means the opposite of egotism that is closed in upon itself, i.e., personal morality means the openness of the person as such — for God, for men, for all that is good and right; it is thus a "sacrificial gift acceptable to God" (GS 38). Personal morality is also, therefore, inner openness and readiness to work for the good of others (GS 39), to care for the right shaping of the world of man (GS 39); it is a tendency toward the correct "act and truth of life" (GS 42), a readiness to become involved for the sake of the world (GS 43), a motivation in the correct shaping of the world (GS 4). Righteousness, generosity, fidelity, chastity are like openness and readiness for right behavior, and so they are just as much moral goodness as openness and readiness for right behavior in civil, economic, international affairs, etc.

Instead of speaking about personal openness as the opposite of closed egotism, the Council repeatedly speaks of *love* as the fundamental attitude of personal morality. Love is termed "the fundamental law of human perfection" (GS 38). Love becomes effective in bearing fruit for the life of the world (GS 16), love is the readiness to see that the brothers receive help and justice (GS 72) and to work together to change the world (GS 38). In accordance with Scripture and tradition, the commandment of love is called the "new commandment" of love (e.g., GS 38, LG 2). Naturally, this does not mean that, without Christianity, love would not still be the fundamental attitude of personal morality. The Council's Decree on the Lay Apostolate, thinking principally about the history of its influence, calls love of neighbor a command that is especially "characteristic" of "Christian" morality, that receives a new and richer meaning in the entirety of the Christian context (AA 8).

It is charactistic of the concept of personal morality — goodness — in the texts of the Council that frequent appeal is made to the *conscience* (judgment of conscience) rather than to laws, commandments and norms as the reference-point of moral decision and hence of personal morality. Fundamentally, a phrase in *Gaudium et Spes* speaks of the "right to behave in accordance with the right norm of conscience" (GS 26); the addition of the word "right" certainly intends to deny to a conscience that is culpably insufficiently formed the function of "norm." For the Council, the reason for the appeal to the conscience in our moral decisions, which are always interior, is that norms and commandments, and hence also the "will of God," are known and acknowledged in the conscience and thereby become our "interior"; fidelity to the "interior" of the conscience is therefore the morality of the "interior" of the person (cf. *Dignitatis Humanae* (DH) 3). In other words, the only possible reference-point for the inner moral decision is interior knowledge of right behavior, i.e., the conscience. Therefore the conscience retains its dignity in the realm of personal morality even when it inculpably considers a false opinion about human conduct to be correct (GS 16). Atheism and nonmembership in the church are personal faults that exclude from salvation only if the conscience signals the possibility and necessity of belief in God and of belonging to the church (GS 14, 16, 19). The Council holds that the church respects conscience (GS 41) and requires that the state do likewise, above all with regard to religious freedom (DH 2).

3. Right Behavior in the World

One never experiences moral goodness and salvation in a pure state, but always in the simultaneous realization of our human world in time and space. The realization of the world itself, as such, is first of all itself only the shaping and developing of the world. Moral goodness requires that the realization of the world actually takes place, and that it not happen arbitrarily, but "rightly," for the Council understands the shaping of the world as a task that comes from creation, with the aim of developing and perfecting this world (e.g. GS 34, 57), as the reshaping in human culture of what is given in creation (GS 43). Therefore faith and love and eschatological hope motivate the Christian to this act of shaping the world.

The Council understands the world as the world of the human being: the personal individual in his dignity (also seen religiously and morally), the various inter-personal relationships, the many institutions, human society, scientific acquisitions of knowledge and technical possibilities, etc. In accordance with their particular theme, it is above all the Constitution on the Church in the Modern World and the Decree on the Lay Apostolate that address this question. They see the necessity to do so primarily because of the enormous questions concerning mankind that are raised with regard to human society, its institutions and individuals, and on account of the immense possibilities of a humanity that lives "in dynamic evolution" (GS 5). While the Council addresses above all the "great questions of humanity," it must not be overlooked that questions like marriage also belong to the shaping of the world and to the cultural creative activity of mankind (e.g., GS 53–62), along with questions of sexuality, of more "private" interpersonal relationships, and cultural creation in general (cf., e.g., GS 53–62), etc.; this means that they are not per se questions of personal morality.

Both documents named begin with the obvious fact that the reality of today's world is to an unimagined extent a new reality that presupposes much technical knowledge for the right realization of the world, and sets an extremely difficult task. The fact of this task is no problem for these two documents; but how to find a solution for it is problematical. It is interesting that both documents explicitly say that the "rightness" of the solutions is important (GS 21, AA 7). It is clear, therefore, that the problematic of the right human realization of the world is distinct from the question of personal moral goodness. One should note the typical statement that, confronted with the problems of today's human society, a good intention (i.e., personal morality) does not suffice; rather, an alteration of society itself — as the material right realization of the world — is also required (GS 26). The term "human behavior" therefore, covers reflection on the criteria for the rightness of such behavior in this world in all spheres.

From this point of view, the subtitle of the third chapter of *Gaudium et Spes* is eloquent: "Human creativity in the world." Two things are meant by this: "As the creative activity of man proceeds from man, so is it also directed to man" (GS 35). It is astonishing to see how frequently this orientation, and hence the *humanum* as the concrete criterion of rightness of conduct in today's world, is emphasized in the Council's texts — perhaps more frequently than the reference to given norms. Obviously, the norms of right behavior have their criterion in the *humanum*. Finally, it is in this way — and only in this way, that the Council can explain (GS 2) its addressing not only Christians but all mankind.

The Council sees a new kind of humanism at work in the contemporary attempt to resolve the great questions of mankind (GS 55). It intends to speak of a humanism which seeks to arrive at "the true and full realization of the human being" through a true "culture, i.e., the development and nurturing of the goods and values of nature" (GS 53); at the development "of the full human personality" (GS 56); at a continuous alteration of the human person "above himself" (GS 35); and correspondingly, at the shaping of a "human" life (GS 38), of a "more human" society (GS 53); and at the "building up of a more human world" (GS 57). Therefore all form-giving activity in this world must "be in accord with the genuine good of humanity" (GS 35), taking into account everything "that belongs to a life that is human in every aspect" (GS 74). In short, according to the humanism proposed by the Council, the "human person" is the criterion for "right" behavior in humanity's world. In this sense, it accepts, together with the other religions, "the voice of God . . . through the voice of creatures" (GS 36). This is the well-understood teaching of the Council on natural law; it does not exclude, but rather includes the possibility of different cultures and therefore of different lifestyles and "moralities," even if in today's world lifestyles and ethical behavior tend rather to become ever more unified (GS 53f., cf. 43).

In many individual questions too, the Council insists upon the *humanum* of behavior: the family should be "a school of humanity that develops itself" (GS 52); the marital act should be "human" (GS 47); procreation should take place "in a human fashion," and should be "truly human procreation" (GS 51); and one must think of conscientious objectors "in a human way" (GS 79).

It is not always easy, however, to discover what can be human *in concreto* and a human (and thus "right") solution to humanity's problems. The Council affirms this, and consequently urges the cooperation of all who are competent in particular areas, including the cooperation both of believing Christians and of non believers, since it is a question of "human" and not of distinctively "Christian" problems (GS 21, 43, 57, AA 7). The Council fathers also explicitly emphasize that even truly believing and conscientious Christians can arrive "legitimately" at different or opposed solutions in many concrete questions (GS 43), and that the church as such (GS 33) and its pastors (GS 43) do not always have a ready solution for concrete questions, for this does not belong to their mission (GS 43). This does not exclude the possibility that precisely the religious proclamation of the "Church" (GS 11, 42), the light of faith or of the "gospel" (GS 11, 43), true "holiness" (LG 40) and the knowledge of "divine wisdom" (GS 15) and of the "divine law" — although none of these can itself offer a solution — can nevertheless be very helpful in discovering human solutions (the word "human" is used in each of the statements noted), or indeed can tend forcefully toward such solutions.

The factor common to these remarks of the Council is that the questions of today's humanity, although belonging neither to those questions which *Dei Verbum* states have been revealed "for our salvation" nor to the formal substance of personal morality, are nevertheless human questions, and remain human questions, within the one reality of redemption. It is above all the Council's Decree of the Lay Apostolate that emphasizes that the work of redemption also includes "the building up of the whole temporal order" (AA 5), and that one must speak of a "Christian orientation of the temporal order" (AA 31).

Similarly, *Gravissimum Educationis* (GE) sees "all natural values" as taken up into the panorama of the human person redeemed by Christ (GE 2). This must be linked to the rather vague statement of *Lumen Gentium* that the message of faith is to be applied to moral life (LG 25); the only question is, what concretely could be meant by this? One could suppose a possible answer to lie in the observation of *Gaudium et Spes* that the "luminous principles that come from Christ are clarified" on the part of the church through the answers given to concrete individual questions (GS 46). This clarification, however, is possible only through a "human" evaluation of the concrete human reality of life. One may see a further answer in the observation of the same constitution that our values that are valid today "proceed indeed from the God-given character of the human person" and are thus "good," but in fact lack their "necessary final orientation because of the perversion of the human heart, so that they need to be purified" (GS 11); that is, they need to be brought to their true and full humanity. The attempt in the Decree on the Lay Apostolate (AA 16) is more problematical, for it says that Christians must "seek to find higher principles of activity in the light of the gospel" for their conduct in the world. This seems to require more than a mere deepened understanding of "human" norms; it could refer also to purification, and thus to more genuine humanization of such principles. It would not be readily comprehensible if the observation meant what it seems to say on a first reading — that one should seek "higher" principles in the sense of "superhuman" principles.

One should not overlook the fact that when the Council speaks of human conduct in the world, it does not deal formally with morality in the truest sense, but with the problem of the rightness of the active shaping of man's world by man. The Council is aware, however, that man is bound by his personal morality to accept responsibility for mankind's world, and must therefore undertake the search for right action in the world, in order to act in accordance with the solution he finds. For this reason, it is customary today, and rightly so, to describe the problematic dealt with under the title "human activity in the world" (whether dealing with Christians or with non-believers) as the problematic of *"moral* rightness." It is, therefore, not without a relationship to moral goodness, i.e., to morality in the most genuine sense of the word; indeed, it is required by it and signifies the incarnation of personal goodness in humanity's world. Yet moral goodness and moral rightness are to be distinguished; in its remarks on moral goodness, the Council therefore repeatedly drew attention to fidelity to the inner word of conscience, not to the moral rightness or wrongness of actions as such.

4. A Complementary Reflection

The Council did not achieve a systematic account of the various statements about salvation, personal morality and rightness of behavior. Certainly, such a systematic account would have been significant, because the failure to distinguish, or the confusion of the person and the rightness of behavior had often led to regrettable consequences both in discussions of moral theologians and in interventions of the church's magisterium. But the contemporary status quo of the discussion among moral theologians did not enable the Council fathers to make such a reflection.

No one expected that the Council would positively reflect upon the questions which would later be addressed by the post-conciliar moral theologians. Moral theology on its own initiative, then, entered a discussion that leads to significant consequences. First, there is an effect on the discussion which develops with its own impetus, of a differentiated competence of the church's magisterium in questions of the moral goodness of the person and of the moral rightness of behavior. Next, there is a contribution to the further clarification of the question of how one can come by argument to judgments on the moral rightness of behavior. Here, many theologians and others emphasize the necessity of a judgment that makes a "teleological" evaluation of morally relevant values that are not in themselves already moral (and thus absolute) earthly goods/values.

But not all moral theologians are able to follow this development, especially because the distinction between "morally good" and "morally right", though rooted in tradition, is either ignored, misunderstood or rejected. Apart from this, they overlook the fact that the teleological manner of reasoning is restricted solely to questions of moral rightness, not to those of moral goodness, because statements about moral goodness are exclusively justified "deontologically." Universality and *intrinsice malum* belong therefore to their essence, which is not the case in questions of moral rightness, although even in those questions they are not absolutely excluded. Correspondingly, such moral theologians do not accept in principle the further, and necessary, pinpoint of the *res (fidei et) morum* as the sphere of the competence of the church's magisterium, although recent studies on the two Vatican Councils show that the Councils themselves did not attempt such a clarification.[1]

The manner of speaking in the postconciliar period about the church's magisterium on questions of fundamental moral theology is somewhat similar to that of the Council fathers. Some will regret this. Where individual members of the college of bishops become aware of the new reflections in moral theology, their inner continuity with tradition is often not seen; statements (such as those about what, primarily in the United States, is called "proportionalism") are fundamentally misunderstood where there is dependence upon certain theologians, and the consequence is a negative and occasionally polemical attitude.

NOTES

1 Cf. W. Levada, 'Infallible Church Magisterium and the Natural Law', excerpts from dissertation, Pontifical Gregorian University (Rome, 1971); A. Riedl, *Die kirchliche Lehrautorität nach den Aussagen des Ersten Vatikanischen Konzils* (Freiburg i. Br., 1975); F.A. Sullivan, *Magisterium. Teaching Authority in the Catholic Church* (Dublin, 1983); J. Schuster, *Ethos und kirchliches Lehramt* (Frankf. St. 31) (Frankfurt, 1984).

III. Our Image of God and the Morality of Innerworldly Behavior
translated by James Keenan, S.J.

This chapter deals with problems concerning the right realization of the world. Naturally, this problematic involves God, insofar as we understand the human world as gift and task coming from God. The right realization of the human world is without doubt the will of its Creator and Savior. The question is: *how* does the willing, fostering, and acting God intervene through humanity in the realization of the world? Obviously, much depends here on our image of God.

Theologically understood, the realization of the world is the task given to human beings through the gift of their environment. For this reason, one must hold as theologically suspect any position in which God appears somehow to be *alongside* the human (therefore, to be categorial) whenever a question arises concerning the right realization of the world, that is, the right behavior of human beings in their world. Some instances of this suspect approach are the imposition of commandments, the requirement of particular rights, and disjointed interventions in the historical process and emerging order of the world. Certainly, God fosters — in divine transcendence — the *right* realization of the world in every case; this is God's will. But this will and the possibility of its execution are embedded in human beings and in their world. Behind many attempts to propose a categorial extension of God's hand into the realization of the world, is there not an extremely anthropomorphic image of God?

Indeed, all human talk about God is necessarily anthropomorphic to some extent. However, if one wants by such talk to come to theological or ethical principles or conclusions concerning human behavior in this world, one must take care to see to it that no specifically human element of talk about God is also projected inadvertently onto God. Otherwise, one can imply a competition between the rights and interests of human beings who experience themselves as commissioned by God to realize the world and those rights and interests of the same God who is categorially active in the world. This could place demands on human persons pursuing the realization of the world, demands which do not result from the reality itself which is to be realized and which therefore even Christians are not able to understand, in spite of their generous willingness to order reality responsibly before their Creator and Savior. And it is all too evident that non-Christians and nonbelievers would then view their Christian collaborators in the realization of the world as facing problems which are unintelligible to them and which encumber their cooperation with Christians.

Such problems stemming from an overly anthropomorphic image of God are undoubtedly to be found in Catholic moral theology. Although the development of theology calls for a clear withdrawal from the tendencies indicated above, nonetheless we should not be surprised that traces of such tendencies were found and are still to be found today in views advocated by the official church. We must reckon with this possibility: it cannot and should not be allowed to disturb us and hinder our further efforts to illumine the issues we are addressing. In the following pages, this effort will be made with regard to several concrete contemporary problems.

It should be noted explicitly that the whole problematic, as was stated in the beginning, concerns only questions of the real (and, therefore, morally obliging) *rightness* of the human realization of the world — through culture, education, technology, the state, marriage, sexuality, etc. — and not the question of the personal *goodness* of human beings — fidelity to conscience, loving faith, desire for genuine self-realization, readiness to order the world rightly, dedication to God and God's will, etc. It is clearly certain that even morally good human persons do not always know the really *right* act to practice in this world, whereas "wicked" human beings are often able to contribute much to the right realization of the world.

The following pages examine two extremely anthropomorphic images of God and their influence on ethical considerations and principles: the image of the commanding God and that of the ruling God. The third part of the chapter will reflect briefly but thoroughly on the problematic of the "image of God and the image of the human person" with regard to moral theological considerations about human behavior in the world.

A. A COMMANDING GOD?

The expression "commanding God" means that God is understood as Lord, that from beyond the world God simultaneously sends commands into the categorial world and binds humanity to order and develop reality in exact accordance with commands which have been issued: human persons accept the commands and carry them out in conscientious, loving obedience. There are different types and corresponding consequences of this understanding of God.

1. Fundamental Option and Categorial Behavior in the World

At the 1983 Bishops' Synod in Rome, the concept "fundamental option" naturally emerged in the treatment of the themes "sin" and "confession." This was inevitable insofar as, on the one hand, this concept has been used for many years in theology (dogmatics, fundamentals, morals), and on the other hand, the Vatican Congregation for the Doctrine of the Faith commented on the theme "fundamental option and sin" for the first time (even if rather reluctantly and apologetically) in number 10 of the "Declaration on Certain Questions concerning Sexual Ethics" (*Persona humana*, 1975). Thus, it seems fitting to reflect further on our thematic by considering the Vatican's Declaration, rather than by treating theological publications. It is worth noting in passing that it was evident at the Synod that the problem of "fundamental option and sin" was not familiar to many of its participants.

Many theologians who deal with the concept "fundamental option" understand it to mean the *self*-disposition of human persons as such (that is, as a whole), fully realized in their innermost core (and for this reason, conceptually not fully subject to reflection, and ultimately athematic); this disposition of self occurs before an Absolute (we say: God, Christ) experienced in the person's very depths.[1] Naturally, at this point we cannot enter into a more specific discussion of this concept. Those theologians who collaborated in formulating the Declaration for the Congregation for the Doctrine of the Faith argue erroneously that the fundamental option is to be understood as the "direct and formal" acceptance or rejection of the love of God (and of neighbor). However, it is expressly admitted: "In reality it is precisely the fundamental option which in the last resort determines a person's moral disposition." It is also correctly emphasized that personal (mortal) sin — the problem treated in number 10 of the Declaration — is to be understood as the retreat of human beings into themselves, the enclosure of self in self. This is a refusal of love, while its opposite is a loving openness.

But, as has been noted, the Declaration's theologians do not really grasp the true depth of the person which is intended in the teaching on the fundamental option. Nevertheless, it is explicitly and correctly emphasized that in the concrete act the refusal of love does not necessarily have to occur in an explicit manner (whereas for a while some pastors were, in fact, under the impression that only the "direct and formal" refusal of love could render a morally incorrect act a mortal sin). The Declaration's formulation is clearly concerned with defending a particular opinion found in many manuals of the not so distant past, concerning the inherent relationship between the concretely incorrect *act* and the refusal of the openness of love, which constitutes sinful *wickedness.*

Here the issue which concerns our problem emerges. The Roman Declaration defensively and apologetically stresses that a mortal sin is caused not only by "the formal and direct rejection of the command-ment of love" but also by the refusal of love *implicit* in every violation of the moral order with regard to serious matter. Here the Declaration refers to the words of Jesus to the young man, "Keep the command-ments" (of the Decalogue), and it adds that not even the compassion of a pastor is allowed "to undermine *the commandments of God*" or to "diminish in any way the saving *teaching* of Christ." But the Declaration does not ask *in which sense* actually the (only ten) "Commandments of God" in the Decalogue pertain to us (here the exegetes must be consulted) and similarly *to what extent* the "teaching of Christ" contains concrete commandments for the right realization of the world, as for example, in the area of sexuality, the theme of the Vatican Declaration. (The latter considers these questions in a very minimal way and without any reference to the issues arising from them).

In brief, translating "moral order" by the terms "commandments of God" or "commandments of Christ" must awaken the impression that individual mistakes in realizing the human world run contrary to the God-given commandments and precisely for this reason, at least impli-citly, these mistakes constitute a refusal to love God. The widely acknowledged qualification "insofar as the commandments refer to serious matter" rather confirms this impression; yet this same qualifi-cation implies that acting contrary to God's commandments is not necessarily understood as denial of God's love, even though such action is against God's commandments; God seems to differentiate between one commandment and another, although they are all *God's* commandments.

It is to be feared that behind these formulations there is the idea of a commanding God who hands commandments down to us "from above" (thus, from outside the world) and whose numerous commandments (concerning the entire realization of our world) demand obedience; and that precisely for this reason, every single instance of not obeying the commandments (with regard to a serious matter) is aimed *directly against God* and hence proves to be a refusal to love the God of these commandments. This accounts for the skepticism which the Declaration manifests toward the theological teaching of the fundamental option. Thus, the Declaration recommends that it is better to reflect on individual personal actions which conflict with God's commandments.

However, if the human world were viewed as gift and task for humanity and not so much as the human world "under God's commandments," another understanding would result. The human person would then be someone who has conscientiously (certainly, with the aid of Christian grace and "in the light of the Gospel"[2]) to discover how the human world of God should be realized so as to better humanity and to correspond to the task bestowed on human persons through creation itself. The self-opening person, that is, the loving human person, would seek and carry out what best corresponds to the realization and development of the world. Whenever persons refuse this task in weighty matters, they will be able to discover in the depths of their own self that their behavior stems from a deeply shattered relationship with the Absolute (God, Christ), that is, from a negative fundamental option. In this case, God is obviously refused love. We recall the words of Thomas Aquinas, that God is only offended through behavior by which persons go against their own well-being.[3] How very different this approach is from the formulation of the refusal to love due to the failure to obey a God-given commandment.

It should not be denied that with a bit of effort one could somehow reconcile the two views outlined above. Nonetheless, it cannot be overlooked that a somewhat different image of God forms the basis of each of the two views.

It is noted that the language of the first part of the Vatican's Declaration of 1975 (not necessarily prepared by the same theologians as no. 10) rings somewhat differently. There is less talk of God's commandments as a "law" which the human discovers within his conscience, and which he has "not given to himself." Rather God has written it (Rom. 2) "into the person's heart"; the human must obey it. That is, the "law" is grounded in "the eternal, objective, and universal divine law." And the human can recognize this. As far as its content is concerned, this law corresponds to the essential order of human nature; the law can be here recognized precisely from its correlation to this order. Many principles of this order are viewed as universal and unchangeable and hence independent of historical and cultural factors. The Roman Declaration views such principles as determinative not only of general statements, e.g., that the human should be conscientious, true, just, chaste, etc., but also of concrete norms of action, e.g., those treated in the Declaration (extra-marital intercourse, homosexual behavior, masturbation). It is therefore talk of a law coming from God and thus absolutely valid, which expresses itself in the conscience and in the nature of the human person. The idea of a commanding God, even regarding the very concrete (e.g., sexual-ethical) norms, is not wrong, but this is to be linked to the idea of a Creator God, in whose creation (conscience and human nature) moral principles and norms can be discovered: yet, it does not arrive at a balanced formulation (cf. nos. 3–5). The added expression: "With the Holy Spirit's assistance, she [the Church] ceaselessly preserves and transmits without error the truths of the moral order" seems from the purely historical point of view, not only to be uncritical and triumphalistic but also to imply the character of the "givenness" of moral "law." It is suggested that even every "authentic interpretation" of the moral law must be understood, whereby this interpretation includes both the "revealed positive law" as well as "the principles of the moral order which have their origin in human nature itself and which concern man's full development (sic! thus, e.g., the questions of sexual morality treated in the Declaration) and sanctification." (no. 4).

2. The Law of Graduality and the Graduality of the Law

More clearly than in considerations of the fundamental option and of God's commandment, the above-outlined understanding of "commandment of God" appears, since the Bishops' Synod in 1980 (on marriage and the family), in a recurring view which opposes a "graduality of the law." This view was briefly formulated in the Pope's address at the close of the Synod and was repeated both in the Apostolic Letter *Familiaris Consortio* (22 November 1981, no. 34) and also in the Pope's address at a seminar on marriage on 17 September 1983.[4] Dionigi Tettamanzi is the author of a precise exposition and defense of the refusal to accept any notion of "graduality of the law." His contribution[5] is the basis of the following considerations.

The occasion for the discussion at the Synod was the problematic of an obviously existing and clearly voiced discrepancy between an official ecclesiastical teaching (the encyclical, *Humanae Vitae*) and the actual practice of many Christian couples. The problematic of the law of graduality was therefore applied to a particular case, although in itself it is of greater importance. Some Synod members recalled this law as one method, known especially in the missions, for pastorally and prudently guiding a Christian toward the fullness of Christian behavior. They believed that a genuine acknowledgment and consideration of such "graduality" would make understandable to some extent the de facto presently widespread situation within the church and would avoid assessing the situation as a catastrophe. Even Tettamanzi affirms the law of graduality in his contribution: human persons as historical beings are day by day "on the way" and know the progressive steps toward the good. Certainly, this presupposes that they affirm and strive for the goal of their search and that they observe the conditions for a successful arrival at the goal. However, the author adds to this affirmation a warning that the law of graduality does not mean the graduality of the law. This view will now be examined without restricting the problematic to the Synod's particular concern, marriage.

By "graduality" of the law is meant the view that one must accept in the "divine law" varying degrees and forms of a commandment for different people and life situations. Here Tettamanzi objects that in such a view the "divine law" actually is measured not by a divine but by a human standard. This stance is at variance with the fact that the "divine law" expresses the need of the human person for the truth. Consequently all concrete difficulties which emerge in the realization of human reality must find their solution in the law of God, simply because the difficulties ought to accept the truth, and only the truth, as valid. Whoever thinks otherwise either sees the divine law only as an utter ideal instead of a genuine commandment (which Christ challenges us to obey) or tries to replace it with a human order different from the "divine law."

Tettamanzi's presentation is to a certain extent convincing. Insofar as it is really a question of a divine law, the truth about humanity from a moral point of view is defined in it. Because it is law it can be a question not simply of a pure ideal, necessarily unreal and unrealizable, but rather of a genuine demand. Because it is a demand originating from God, neither various degrees of fulfillment nor various ways of execution are open to question. Because it is a definition of the truth of humanity, the realization of human reality must correspond to it without any qualifications.

And yet a rather difficult problem appears to lie behind the author's explanation, namely, a distinctly inadequate and suspicious concept of God. The real question is: what really is the "divine law" which is so self-evidently brought into the discussion and where may it be found?

Therefore, how is the "law of God," so often cited by the author, actually understood? It is hardly (or better still, only in rather rare cases) to be understood as a positively given and revealed commandment of God; for there are no such commandments which correspond to the unlimited variety of problems regarding the realization of human reality. Thus, in the light of this fact, the concept of a commanding God is eliminated. Therefore, "divine law" can mean only that moral order which God has written "as law" into the human heart and into human nature, and which is also called the moral natural law. Now Tettamanzi repeatedly takes it for granted that we know without a doubt the contents of this moral order in its unlimited variety and that we "have" them formulated, in the same way we "have" a positively given law. Is there not in this a secretly positivistic understanding of the natural moral law as "God's law," whereby a corresponding commanding God is tacitly assumed? Or is an "ecclesial possession" or an ecclesial "positivization" of the orders of the natural law simply pre-supposed, though neither idea is explicitly discussed anywhere? (First, however, such a "possession" and such a "positivization" can only concern a very small number of the truths of the natural law. Second, people who make up the church and its teaching office must recognize such laws "autonomously" (through "theonomous" autonomy), without any special revelation, even if not without "the light of the gospel." Third, such moral knowledge and judgment must necessarily reckon with human and time-conditioned inaccuracies.)

But if the "laws of God" which we possess are due to human know-ledge, evaluation, and judgment, then a number of problems result. It is in fact possible, as well as very probable, that many of our "divine laws" have been formulated very unclearly by us humans, and thus they only inadequately express the real "divine laws" as the moral truth of the human person. In many such formulations, which are unilaterally derived by man (that is deontologically), one may fear that one single element of a more complex concrete human reality has been considered and absolutized. But this means that it would be forbidden to include in concrete moral judgments which are to be "objective" the diverse, concrete ways of realizing that one factor in people and situations. (It is clear what this meant for the problematic of marriage which was treated at the Bishops' Synod.) A "law of God" so understood would lack the required objectivity and, therefore, the quality of genuine "divinity."

A different method of making moral judgments (teleology), aimed at greater objectivity — that is, consideration also of the objective differences in the realization of definite human conditions — would mean that the demand for truth about the person in certain circum-stances requires a much greater number of objective "divine laws" than Tettamanzi is willing to accept. By their very nature, such more numerous and more detailed "laws of God" would not so easily give rise to the idea of the "graduality of the law." If some of the too precise — and for that very reason, too imprecise — "laws of God" leave us tacitly to presuppose a secretly (positivistic) commanding God, then this tacit presupposition can be dropped from the proposed solution to the problem. Not the often undifferentiated letter of the "law of God" but rather the more differentiated sense (spirit) of an undifferen-tiatedly formulated law conditions the real truth and radicality of the moral action.

However, if someone, along with Tettamanzi, does not agree to the considerations just proposed then there are still further consequences to be feared. First, the "divine laws," which one seeks to protect from the "graduality of the law," are perhaps basically only "pure ideals," withdrawn from the concrete circumstances of human reality and therefore unreal and unrealizable [6] and even, therefore, exposed to the danger of the "graduality of the law."

Second, where the singular "law of God" is very generally understood and the recognition of different nuances is denied, the danger exists of having to fall into the widely accepted Lutheran moral ethic concerning the solution of conflictual situations. This teaching was advocated chiefly by Helmut Thielicke in his *Theological Ethics*. Rainer Mayer summarizes it briefly in his essay "Morality and Christian Ethics":

> A conflict situation exists ... whenever the commandment of God no longer admits any unambiguous decision, insofar as the observance of one commandment leads to the violation of another, and even passivity renders one truly guilty.[7]

Now, insofar as the commandment of God (and all commandments of God) is unambiguous and consequently demands an impossible obedience, there can be no right or justified action on the part of the person in this case; only God can justify the human person (not the human person's action) from beyond. That there are ethical demands which can be formulated as "divine commandments" and which in the concrete are incompatible with one another, has been stressed repeatedly in recent decades, even among Catholics. The often held solution, which would render only one of the ("deontological") "laws" involved in the conflict absolute and the others merely relative, does not allow itself to be theoretically defended, if one observes the values grounding the "laws."

In recent moral theology attention has been drawn repeatedly to the point that the "laws" formulated by us humans (thus not by God) are often vaguely formulated and thus not at all absolute, as their wordings might suggest (e.g., Tettamanzi: "intrinsic evil"), and that therefore the *real* "law of God" is not at all so clear and "free of gradations" as it might seem at first sight. Whoever views in this way the "laws of God" recognized and formulated by us humans as well as possible, need not fall into the Lutheran attempt at a solution of so-called conflicts. One of the fundamental weaknesses of this attempt consists in the fact that some absolute "laws of God" are adopted whose derivation and absolute validity have not been grounded at all, and indeed cannot be grounded. For the commanding God which such a teaching presupposes does not exist.

In order to make clear the intended problematic of the "law of God" of a commanding God, the following question can be posed: Will the rejection of the "graduality of the law" in the way proposed by Tettamanzi result in the "law of graduality" or the "graduality of the law" in concrete considerations of sexual ethics? The German bishops noted in their pastoral letter on the question of human sexuality (1973) that premarital intercourse on the part of an engaged couple is not truly in order, but is essentially different from impersonal and uncommitted sexual intercourse; only the latter is the true form of fornication. In contrast to this differentiation and gradation, the Declaration *Persona humana* (1975) knows only the one undifferentiated law of God: Sexual relations are valid only in the context of marriage. Is there between partners on the way to marriage an introduction to marriage or is there only a universal and undifferentiated assignment of every sexual experience to marriage? Is there a sexual ethic corresponding to the different phases of sexual development or only a uniform and global sexual ethics? Does masturbation, performed at different stages of life and for different reasons, come under one single undifferentiated "law of God" (as is the case in *Persona humana*)?

3. Moral Theology and the Image of Evolving Man

Speaking about "God's commandment" and "God's law" undoubtedly makes good sense. For God continually creates and maintains human reality, its intelligibility, and thus also the ground for its right conduct in and for this world. "Acting rightly" is consequently God's will, and in this sense, "God's commandment" or "God's law". But the formulations "God's commandment" and "God's law" express not only the fact that God with eternal wisdom maintains the "eternal law," that is, both the most universal principles and the concrete moral norms (based on the realities determined by time and circumstances); they also express the fact that God acts as the ground of all true concrete moral demands. Besides, these formulations also imply that God has in some way given the "commandments" and/or the "laws." Indeed, the hearers of these formulations understand them thus and they are quite mistaken in this understanding. It is to be feared that even a number of those who use formulations and transmit them to the Christian people hardly note that the formulations implicitly depend on this understanding. If those who use such formulations were asked, they would probably deny this understanding and subscribe thoroughly to the human act of discovering and finding, with the help of grace and in "the light of the gospel," moral norms for human conduct in this world. But probably they do not notice that human insight and knowledge discover not only moral "commandments" and "laws" which are very undifferentiated and universal, but also an extremely differentiated wealth of moral norms and judgments.

A real (that is, not static) understanding of natural law already justifies these considerations. Furthermore, there are evolutionary-based tendencies, which do not exactly recommend frequent mention of "God's commandments" and "God's laws" as given to us. In the years of fruitful discussion during and after the Council and before *Humanae Vitae*, the Dutch philosopher of nature, van Melsen, along with others, constantly warned the ethicians who argued from natural law: Is there a nature "given" *in this way* by God to us, through which God wants to communicate ways for human conduct and activity, or is the actual "human nature" not largely a (partly accidental) product of evolution? Is it therefore advisable constantly to talk of "God's commandment" or "God's law"? (Van Melsen neither spoke of a spiritual hominization nor did he deny the presence of God which knows and sustains all developments.)

With regard to "an essential norm" for traditional sexual ethics, formerly judged to be universal and static, today the great diversity of materially similar sexual behavior is frequently pointed out. This diversity is above all grounded on generally observed phases of sexual development but also on ascertainable individual developments of human sexuality. The proposed question seeks to determine whether this manifold reality is adequately assessed by means of some "essential norms" or by "God's commandments" or by "God's laws."

One speaks with good reason of the morally obliging protection of human life. Now human life unfolds itself by evolving, not only as a hominization occurring in natural history but also as a becoming and passing of individual human lives. But the term "human life" must be used in a way thoroughly conscious of its analogous meaning. Even if the fertilized ovum should already contain in itself all the possibilities which will develop themselves into a future human person, it is still not yet established from this fact alone that one is dealing with not only a potential life but rather with an actual life of an individual person. One can view it as problematic to consider a fertilized ovum as an individual "human," during the period when this ovum can dissolve itself through division (into 2-4-8-16 cells) and thereafter develop itself again into an indivisible unity, that is, an individual. That this is so is a finding of contemporary biology. Even the "Declaration on Procured Abortion" (1974) of the Congregation for the Doctrine of the Faith refused to take a clear position on this question, as it so states in note 19. This consideration has a parallel in a doctrinal teaching advocated in the church for centuries, and based on particular biological and philosophical assumptions concerning the "ensoulment" of the human person.

Furthermore, concerning the end of human life, a certain analogy is largely accepted today, that is, that ascertainable brain death can be viewed as signaling the end of the individual-personal life of a human, even though certain functions (thus, "human life") may be present. The analogical use of the words "human life," which is grounded in the evolutionary nature of the human person, ought to indicate as less appropriate earlier undifferentiated use of the terms "God's commandment" and "God's law."

At a recent international symposium attended by leading biologists and physicians with Catholic philosophers and moralists, a Catholic geneticist, who is a theologian as well, voiced the opinion that theology does not yet take sufficient account of human reality as an evolution and a process reality, and that it thinks all too statically and consequently understands laws and commandments in the same way. Preference was given, hypothetically, to the formulation: which phases in the process of the development of human life demand human protection – and to what degree? This formulation may best be judged as a challenge. Whoever would like to give a response which to some extent is worthy of consideration, however it may be worded, certainly ought not simply to refer to "God's commandment" or "God's law." For it is exactly the latter terms which must be made precise.

B. A RULING GOD?

The formula "ruling God" suggests that God is often understood as the Lord, who, although transcendent, reaches into the categorial world of humanity and, through demands and interventions, reserves particular rights within our human world or else delegates these rights to us. Two ways in which belief in such a God-ruling-as-Lord is expressed are to be examined here.

1. God's Lordship and the Human Disposition of Self

One of the ways in which God reaches into our human world has been accepted by a long theological tradition and still resounds today. For example, in the pastoral letter of the German bishops on euthanasia (1975), the illicit nature of this act is grounded on the argument that the human person is not lord over life and death, but rather God alone is. The prohibition against euthanasia is described as "God's commandment" and its origin is traced, by means of a thoroughly uncritical theological understanding, to the fifth commandment of the Decalogue, "Thou shalt not kill." Similarly, the corresponding Declaration of the Vatican Congregation for the Doctrine of the Faith (1980) sees in euthanasia and voluntary death a "rejection of the supremacy of God" and a "violation of the divine law" (obviously, of the fifth commandment of the Decalogue).

Since 1973, Bruno Schüller has correctly observed[8] that formulations like those of the two documents just cited basically say only that human beings are not God and consequently, that they are not lord of their own lives in the same sense in which God is Lord of life. Surely, God is the "transcendent" Lord of human life and human existence. Now, God is Lord in this sense not only of human life but in the same way of created reality in its entirety. Whoever treats *any* area of reality arbitrarily and thus abuses the creation entrusted to humanity — by going against its integrity and hence against its well-being — acts against God and violates the "rights" of the "transcendent" Lord over creation. A person acts against God, therefore, not just through an abusive disposition of earthly *human* existence.

But this truth illustrates that specific discourse about God as the only Lord over human life — or human existence — is often understood to mean something different from God's "transcendent" lordship over all creation. This discourse implies more than an abusive disposition toward human life and toward every creature, and in this sense a contradiction of the transcendent lordship of God. Rather such discourse tends to consider God as filling the role of higher Sovereign *within* our human (categorial) world; thus, in the area of categorial activity and law, God is said to reserve certain rights — namely, the disposition of human life and human existence. Correspondingly, an advocate of such a view would say that, where the right of human beings to kill is partially accepted — for example, the death penalty, killing in a "just" (defensive) war and in self-defense, and "indirect" killing — a "delegation" of the right of God is given to human beings. In saying all this, only slight reflection is given to how and why this delegation occurs within the human world.

Obviously, what is at question here is an extremely anthropomorphic, and at the same time somehow voluntaristic, image of God. Reference to the "commandment" of God (as has already been said, in a theologically uncritical understanding of the fifth commandment of the Decalogue) ought very well to confirm the supposition of an extremely anthropomorphic concept of God as the only Lord, in this world, over life and death. And this supposition is quite different from that which stresses the all-encompassing and transcendent lordship of God over created reality.

Discourse about God as the Lord of every human existence is ambiguous. It can mean the transcendent lordship of God over all creation. It can also, but falsely, mean the transcendent God's "legal status," understood in an overly anthropomorphic manner and projected onto the sphere of the human world. These two ways of speaking of God as the Lord of human life are consequently to be differentiated properly. It is important that a clear distinction be made between correct and erroneous talk of God's lordship over human existence.

This difference must produce practical results for moral judgments concerning the human disposition of human life. Namely, if one can appeal neither to a specifically reserved "right of God" nor to a corresponding "commandment of God" given to us, then the *moral permissibility* or prohibition of the actual use of the human *possibility* of disposing human life must be sought after, and then judged by means of reflection (for Christians: "in the light of the gospel") on the dignity of human life and of the categorial right to human existence. And these decisions must be made and judged by comparing them with other competing categorial values and goods. Only in this way can society and the individual existing in it come to a judgment as to whether *under certain circumstances* self-defense through killing, the death penalty, killing in a "just" (defensive) war, terminating pregnancy, suicide on the part of bearers of state secrets, euthanasia, etc., are morally justified or not. Such a judgment occurs, insofar as we stand under the "transcendent lordship" of the Creator who is always "sustaining" us humans. An undifferentiated appeal to "God's commandment," or a specific appeal to the "exclusive lordship of God over human life," is, in contrast to what has just been said, not theologically defensible.

Talk of God's exclusive lordship over life and death, although theologically not entirely false and yet theologically so often completely misunderstood, has its consequences not only in normative morality, but also in the daily faith, lives and conversations of many Christians, priests and laity, about dying. Volker Eid has very clearly drawn attention to this state of affairs in his book about euthanasia.[9] He objects to "the naive idea, found in my opinion among people, that God acts concretely in each death: that God actually determines whether persons lose their life in youth or in advanced age, through a traffic accident or a war, whether through cancer or a heart attack, whether after a short or a long final agony. As a result of an anthropomorphically and uncritically formulated theological argument, God is here given the role of an officer of execution." The author adds that talk about the unfathomable ways of divine decisions or about being tested by God is in fact not completely theologically false but can even serve in a moment of spiritual distress as a kind of "helpful bridge." However, such discourse functions in the end as a "whitewash over the mysterious and angst-producing dimension of human existence." And whoever might remark that God employs terrestrial realities only as "secondary causes," must surely add that then in concrete cases it is after all always God who, as Lord over life and death, "uses" a meaningless traffic accident, a famine or a total war.

2. God's Transcendence and Human Self-Transcendence

A further example of an overly anthropomorphic understanding of God which has corresponding consequences for morally right conduct

in this world is found in a recent attempt to defend the main thesis of
the encyclical *Humanae Vitae*, on the prohibition of contraceptive
means. During and after the Synod of Bishops at Rome in 1980, the
bishops and the pope called on theologians to seek new and more
convincing arguments, especially of a biblical and anthropological
nature, for this thesis. Instead of a biblical argument, an attempt at a
theological one has in the meantime been developed. The pope himself
presented this argument in September 1983 before a symposium
aimed at studying the question of marriage.[10] The Italian moral
theologian, C. Caffarra, has written an article to explain the theological
value of the argumentation.[11] The reflection which follows here
is based on Caffarra's article, generally considered to be the
most detailed to date. It will be shown that it presents a typical
extremely anthropomorphic image of God as the foundation of
moral considerations.

The point of departure of the author's reflections is the idea,
commonly advocated in the church's teaching, that the personal
(spiritual) being (this is Vatican II's formulation, whereas otherwise
one used to talk of "soul") of human persons cannot be the direct
product of the human biological act of reproduction, but must be
traced directly back to God's creative activity. From this statement, the
author concludes that a new human being emerges as a person only
through the fact that in the reproductive act not only the parents, but
also the creative activity of God, work in cooperation. However, this
cooperation presupposes that the two human partners in the procreative act are biologically fertile. In this case, or so the author
interprets the data, God the Creator certainly wills to cooperate in
bringing forth new personal life. Consequently, in this case,
contraception would mean an encroachment on the rights of God. The
reason for this conclusion is seen to be that, because the parents are
as such incapable of awakening personal life, not they but God must
decide about the coming-to-be of new personal life. Whoever would
hinder God's active presence in the procreative act through contraception would evidently understand human procreation as a purely
human possibility. Such persons would hinder God "from being God,"
that is, prevent God from assuming a role as Creator-God in the sexual
consummation of the human partners and thus from exercising a
divine right and creative work. Caffarra maintains that his reflection is
fundamental, that even if it is less explicit in the church's tradition, it
was almost always present there (presumably in the teaching that only
God is the Creator of the human soul) and that it is the truth.
Therefore, he claims categorically: "Each is forced 'to put his cards on
the table': for the truth is either simply accepted or rejected: there is no
third option."

Caffarra obviously takes it for granted that his audience are believers; still, that is not of interest here. Concerning the problematic of his article, it is also unimportant whether Caffarra's argument is conclusive from his own theological presuppositions. Likewise, it need not be asked here, why the interpretation of the divine will of the Creator advocated should not also be valid for the systematic obstruction (permanently or temporarily) of the divine will with regard to marital sexual life regulated (justifiably or not) through the choice of infertile periods, even if Caffarra himself attempts explicitly to negate this parallel. Likewise, it does not interest us here, whether on the basis of the above interpretation one must not say that God is "wrongfully forced" into creative activity in actual marital relations which, for important reasons, are illegitimate: in extra- and pre-marital sexual intercourse, as well as in the (unjustified) fertilization of the human ovum outside the sexual act.

Rather, fundamental considerations with regard to Caffarra's article interest us here: which underlying image of God does it depict and to what extent does it condition these moral norms of conduct in our world? The author has rightly abandoned language, used through the centuries, describing the creation of the human spiritual soul, and prefers the formulation of the Second Vatican Council, since he speaks of the effectiveness of God in the development of a personal human life. Furthermore, he is completely correct in presuming that a personal human being can come into existence neither through a division of the spiritual principle or soul of the parents nor as a product of a human biological act. Consequently, a specific effective act of God is required. However, it would have been better to speak of God's effectiveness not in the parental act of intercourse itself, but rather, as Karl Rahner has put it, "in connection with the biological development of the human person."[12] The question, after all, is: when does the existence of the person (thus, the "ensoulment") of the fruit of the sexual act take place? The question was under discussion in the early centuries as it still is today, even if it is raised because of different issues, and it is still considered a point of discussion by the Congregation for the Doctrine of the Faith.[13] Furthermore, the question would be asked in a different way in the case of artificial fertilization outside of sexual union.

Obviously, Caffarra places himself after all in the long tradition of creationism, i.e., the teaching of the "creation of the human soul directly by God." The cooperation of the procreating parents with God's creative activity seems to be understood in the sense that God is the cause of the existence of the being of the person, while the parents are the cause of the biological substratum. Thus God's activity would be the categorial cause (that is, in this world) alongside the categorial causality of the parents. According to this understanding, however, the competition and conflict between the two categorial causes of action are not excluded, and one can speak without any difficulty of the categorial rights of God which can be impeded by the acting human being. But here the singularity of divine activity is most surely not sufficiently distinguished from creaturely causality: the whole construct preserves "a tinge of the miraculous."[14]

For some time theologians have sensed the problematic of creationism which Caffarra has not sufficiently worked out. It was perhaps above all Karl Rahner who first proposed, in connection with the theological explanation of evolution, a new interpretation which in the meantime seems to have met widespread approval. Fundamental to his position is the metaphysically compelling distinction between *creaturely causality* in this world and God's efficaciousness as the *transcendent* ground of all created reality; the latter is thus not categorial (within this world) causal activity. However, God as transcendent ground is not a deistic God, but God is a cause in this world only *through created secondary causes*, as contemporary theology generally accepts. Accordingly, if the existence of a human person can come to be only through God, then God must be the ground of this coming-to-be through creaturely causes, that is, through the parents.

It is thus established that parental action is the cause of personal existence through genuine self-transcendence and self-surpassing, i.e., a genuine increase of being or existence. The properly human-biological parental causality as such does not make this fact possible, but rather it is the empowerment to self-transcendence given by God to the parents. For God, as the lasting and always present transcendent ground of creaturely being, grants to parents (as secondary causes) the power to extend themselves beyond their own parental reality.

If "divine activity and human *development* of the world intimately condition each other, then transcendent and immanent causalities must meet where the world plainly exceeds itself by becoming that which it is in itself. This self-transcendence can be described as the creation of the soul."[15] In this way the possibility of conflictual and competitive situations arising from Caffarra's required cooperation are done away with and therefore can no longer serve as a foundation for moral-theological arguments. "God and creatureliness are not two entities, which can be divided into their own proper sphere of work. Rather God enables the creature to grow beyond itself. Whatever happens in this way is completely due to God's initiative, but it is realized in such a way that it emerges completely from the creature itself."[16]

C. IMAGE OF GOD AND IMAGE OF THE HUMAN PERSON

A definite image of God, which is expressed in the few examples of moral theological statements treated here, seems to presume that we can know very well God's laws and commandments, God's rights and interventions in the world. Is this presupposition justified?

1. God — the Transcendent Mystery

We know about the mystery which grounds and bears us, and we call this mystery God. We know far better our human worldly reality, but we know this mystery precisely as its lasting and always present ground. Indeed, this world, above all the human being, is in many ways an unknown mystery, but still it is a mystery in an entirely different sense from the transcendent mystery, which we are accustomed to call God.

Divine revelation and our faith also speak about God and the human person or about the divine-human dialogical relationship. Indeed, there is much stated and much implied about God and the divine-human relationship. But even the statements of the revelation given to us are passed on to us in human language and images — yes, even in the language and images of a particular epoch and culture of humanity, and thus not in a language transcending time.

Every discourse about God, because it is *our* discourse, is necessarily anthropomorphic and consequently symbolic. Certainly, we must talk about God and the divine-human relationship, and we can do so only in an incomplete, anthropomorphic and symbolic way. Human language of this kind can be true without, however, expressing even to some degree the entire truth, and without ever being able to have as the direct object of our knowledge God, divine action, commanding or ruling, or divine rights and interventions.

The historical background of our contemporary reflection on divine mystery is an extremely anthropomorphic and mythologizing discourse about God. In large measure, it comes from the Old Testament, in whose deep religious language God is constantly "close by" in world events, intervening, working, speaking, judging, praising, and punishing. This way of thinking and speaking has partially endured in the New Testament and through many Christian centuries.

In Christian moral teaching, the influence of natural law in past centuries has reduced to a certain extent the relevance of talk about "God's commandments/laws" and about "God's intervening presence" in world events. On the other hand, in the nineteenth century, the renaissance of the natural law theory generated a strong opposing tendency to earlier interpretations, including that of St. Thomas Aquinas. This renaissance has not only taught that the final validity of moral norms and judgments undoubtedly goes back to God as its origin, but also declared without thorough reflection that the countless concrete expressions of norms, although they stem from human insight, are "God's law/commandment." Believing Christians see themselves personally and also their work within the human world as confronted by "divine" laws, commandments, rights, and by "divine" actions and "divine" interventions. God is more or less experienced as the true transcendent standard over (or in) all beings and yet, as such, the one standing *alongside* us in this categorial world of ours. Is this not in fact the God whom Nietzsche thought he discovered in the imagination of many Christians and for that very reason had to reject as the competitor of humanity? Certainly, this is the image of God instilled even today in a multitude of ways through catechesis, sermons, devotional literature, several theologies, and even official church interventions. Nevertheless, it has to be admitted that it is not at all easy, when one must speak of God (and humanity) anthropomorphically, to avoid a false image of God.

It is more important that such an image of God and corresponding talk about God and humanity do not determine theological — moral theological — reflections and statements; otherwise statements not properly grounded would give the impression of being scientific. In his article, "Befreiende Rede von Gott in der praktizierten Moraltheologie" (1975), Volker Eid has formulated the decisive issue in the following way:

> The question is whether the image of God which at any one time dominates in practice guides humanity to pursue morally *alienating* action or whether by *liberating* humanity to go out of and beyond itself, it encourages humanity to develop a more realistic and more mature morality.[17]

In the light of this question, the image of God and the corresponding image of the human being which are found in the moral theological statements reviewed above, ought to be examined.

2. An Overly Anthropomorphic Image of God

In spite of their explicit claim to think through natural law teaching within a Christian and believing context, the above-analyzed moral theological formulations spring in the final analysis from an image of God which advocates truly rigid universal "divine laws and commandments" and does not concern itself with practical (human) distinctions and differences. This image insists on upholding God's reserved rights within the categorial world and on stressing that God alone and in every case intends to decide in a direct manner about the coming-to-be of new human life. Without doubt this God is recognized as a transcendent God. But this God is not so much seen as a God *in* whom we live and act and who, as the most intimate ground supports our lives and actions, but rather as a God who always and emphatically stands *alongside* us in our categorial world and makes demands on us. It is ultimately a matter of the image of a God who from a moral point of view basically demands only one thing: obedience; and all other moral values and possible human evaluations are relativized in comparison. Rather than responsible human cooperation with God as transcendent Creator, this image of God demands obedience. Therefore, one designates as sin every act of insufficient obedience toward that which is proclaimed as "God's law" and consequently as "the truth about humanity." Let it be repeated: Theoretically, the human discovery of moral norms ("natural law") is not denied; but the manner of presenting the contents of the natural law takes on to a great extent the character of a positivistic and voluntaristic understanding of such law. And therefore what is emphasized is neither the natural law justified by the Creator God through the act of creation nor the corresponding act of moral ordering on the part of humankind. Instead, we see ourselves confronted rather with the image of a God who has created in humanity something more than an earthly partner and collaborator — indeed has created God's own image.

3. An Image of the Human Person "Not in the Image of God"

We have already indicated in the preceding pages a decisive element related to the image of the human person in which are found the above-examined moral theological interpretations. In accordance with the image of God which has been sketched, the human person does not appear in these interpretations to resemble the human being described in the first book of the Old Testament, that is, a dialoging and cooperating partner whose existence is distinct from the rest of the created world. The human being does not seem to be the effective categorial lord in the world but rather "the remote-controlled agent of a 'divine law' formulated in an abstract way which is alienated from life."[18] But in fact, human beings are constituted by the Creator as "lords of themselves and remain such all throughout their existence, because the lordship of God is a transcendent one; God does not act by constantly intervening in the course of human history. Rather God has set human beings free for the whole duration of history."[19] To this a quotation from Thomas Aquinas should be added: "God is offended by the action of human beings only when they act against their own welfare."[20] This statement is incompatible with the view that the human is to be seen only as a manager (e.g., regarding the goods of human life), in contrast to the divine sovereign who is the actual proprietor. And this statement is also incompatible with mysterious talk of divine "authorization" or "delegation," wherever the human disposition of human life is approved (whereas in human interventions to overcome sterility or to maintain or prolong life, no such authorization or delegation is spoken of).

If the human person is constituted by the Creator as dialogical and cooperative partner and thus as lord in the world, then neither such talk nor the recurring reference to God's law and right has an adequately justifiable ground. Human authority does not become true authority because of the fact that God adds a genuinely binding character to human "authoritative" decrees; rather, in itself true categorial authority is a created participation in God's transcendent authority.[21] Similarly, the human search and discovery of morally right conduct and action in this world have the character of moral norms because of the fact that God has established the earthly lordship of human persons, certainly not only with regard to some universal laws, but also through their *insights* which go into detail and hence are very differentiated. This will be more easily grasped if it is understood that *in the concrete* it can be right to speak of an "original identity of norm and conscience." In this sense, therefore, talk about the application of "divine law" to individual human situations loses meaning.[22]

NOTES

1 In his writings, Karl Rahner wrote again and again of the fundamental option as the "self-disposition of the person as a disposition of the entire self."

2 Vatican II, *Gaudium et Spes*, nos. 46 and 43.

3 Thomas Aquinas, *Summa contra Gentiles*, 3, 122.

4 *L'Osservatore Romano*, 18 September 1983.

5 D. Tettamanzi, "Verità ed Ethos", in: *L'Osservatore Romano*, 28 September 1983. Tettamanzi is professor of moral theology at the diocesan seminary in Milan.

6 Cf. A. Molinaro in the first volume of T. Goffi and G. Piana's *Corso di Teologia Morale* (Brescia, 1983), 461.

7 R. Mayer, *Moral und christliche Ethik* (Stuttgart, 1976) 58.

8 B. Schüller, *Die Begründung sittlicher Urteile. Typen ethischer Argumentation in der katolischen Moraltheologie* (Düsseldorf, 1973), 182–98. This work has since been expanded in the 2nd edition, 1980.

9 *Euthanasie oder Soll man auf Verlangen töten?*, edited by V. Eid (Mainz, 1975), 82ff.

10 *L'Osservatore Romano*, 18 September 1983.

11 C. Caffarra, "Diritti di Dio e bene dell'uomo," in: *L'Osservatore Romano*, October 1, 1983. The author is director of the Institute for Questions on Marriage and the Family (Lateran University), founded by John Paul II. A briefer form of his thesis appeared in an article which he wrote in 1982 and can be found in: *Demographic Policies from a Christian Point of View*, edited by F. Biffi (Rome, 1984), 41ff.

12 K. Rahner, in: P. Overhage–K. Rahner, *Das Problem der Hominisation* (Freiburg, 1961), 80.

13 As in note 19 of the Vatican's "Declaration on Procured Abortion" (1974).

14 K. Rahner, loc. cit., 81.

15 E. Klinger, "Seele," in: *Herder's Theol. Wörterbuch* 6 (Freiburg, 1973), 397.

16 H. Vorgrimler, *Wir werden auferstehen* (Freiburg, 1981) 30ff.

17 V. Eid, "Befreiende Rede von Gott in der praktizierten Moraltheologie", in: *Th. Qu.* 155 (1975), 117–31, here 117.

18 D. Seeber, "Personalismus: Der Papst und 'Humanae vitae'", in *Herder-Korresp.* 37 (1983), 492–94, here 494.

19 A. Auer, "Die Unverfügbarkeit des Lebens und das Recht auf einen naturlichen Tod," in: A. Auer, H. Menzel, A. Eser, *Zwischen Heilauftrag und Sterbehilfe. Zum*

Behandlungsabbruch aus ethischer, medizinischer und rechtlicher Sicht (Cologne, 1977), 1–51, here 32.

20 Thomas Aquinas, *Summa contra Gentiles*, 3, 122.

21 Cf. J. Fuchs, "Human Authority – between the Sacral and the Secular," *Christian Ethics in a Secular Arena* (Washington, D.C.: Georgetown University Press, 1984), 100–13.

22 Cf. A. Molinaro, loc. cit., 453.

IV. God's Incarnation in a Human Morality

When I read the New Testament, I hear about God and his Spirit who transforms us, "breaking into" our world in Jesus Christ. Something new, something that we ourselves simply are not, something that is not human, joins us and penetrates us and our freedom. It is this that leads the human person, morally alienated from himself and hence from his God, back to his true self, to genuine humanity: conversion. The moral attitude of the disciple of Jesus, about which the Lord speaks, for example, in the Sermon on the Mount, is characterized not as "superhuman," but as the "genuinely" human attitude which has been lost by the sinner. The moral attitude of those who follow Jesus and belong to the kingdom of God is not set by the Lord in opposition to a genuinely human attitude, but to the attitude of the sinner, i.e. of the non-human human being, to the good conduct that is merely self-interest — "even sinners do that," says the Lord.

With the incarnation of God, the morality of the non-sinner, of the human human being, and thus truly human humanity, is given to humanity through Jesus Christ. Through sharing in his Spirit, according to Paul, "carnal" (i.e. sinful) human persons become "spiritual" (i.e., filled by the Spirit of Jesus); from being sinful, they become non-sinful, i.e. truly "human" human persons.

Thus God's incarnation in Jesus Christ leads to the only morality that is in accord with the human person on the basis of his creaturely being. God, the creative and continuing origin and fundamental active source, has come forth from himself and has entered into the other whom he willed: a first incarnation of God. Thereby, "having become man," he has also entered into the morality which alone can allow the human person to become truly human: because the creator Spirit of God is in it. In order that men may live for him — i.e. in a human manner, not sinfully — he became man in Jesus Christ and imparted a share in his Spirit.

I know that I could have used a different language here and say, perhaps, that God "became man" in the creation of one who was different from himself, with a view to the incarnation of God in Jesus Christ and to man's sharing in his Spirit. The truly human morality is the creator Spirit of God; it is in this morality that the disciple of Jesus expresses his participation in the Spirit of his Lord.

I shall speak, therefore, of this morality, which is based first on the order to be found in creation and finally on God, who became man in Jesus Christ. In the first section I shall speak of the Second Vatican Council: the "divine law" and human morality; in the second section, I shall speak of God's "innerworldly" rights and human morality.

1. The Second Vatican Council: The "Divine Law" and Human Morality

It is natural that the Second Vatican Council should have dealt with the problematic of the morality of the human person, just as it is natural that the Council puts it in relationship to the God in whom this morality somehow has its foundation. But there is no systematic development of this problematic in the Council; rather, it falls back on some formulas well known in tradition, and thus comes on occasion to use formulations that are scarcely compatible with each other, which then need to be interpreted if we are to be able to reflect upon them.

At the beginning of the Decree on Religious Liberty, it is said that the "divine law" is the highest norm of human conduct (no. 3). It is clear from the context that it is not a positively "given" divine law that is being spoken about here, but simply our human morality. The formulation "divine law" could give the impression (and in fact, does give the impression to many believers) that our morality is in reality a divine decree. It may be that even some Council fathers — like some present-day statements, incidentally — understood it so without explicit reflection. Such an understanding, which is indubitably mistaken, can profoundly condition the religious and ethical life of the faithful.

The formulation "divine law" certainly intends to be identical to the formulation that was dear to St. Augustine and to St. Thomas Aquinas after him: the "eternal law." This formulation wishes to affirm that every ordering of created reality, including the moral order of the human person, is present in the eternal reality of the all-wise God, in whom all that is created has its existence: since his reality is eternal, it is permanently near to us. This is true both of the most general moral insights and of the moral norms which concretize these; it is true of moral divergences which are culturally and historically determined and of the concrete ethical judgments which are made in individual situations. In short, what is meant is the entire fullness of right moral insights, which can never be wholly defined. Since the "eternal law" and the "divine law," thus understood, are God himself and his eternal wisdom, they are not directly accessible to us in any way; we do not "possess" this "law" and therefore we cannot draw any direct consequences for the morality of humanity from it.

Access to the "eternal" and "divine" law lies elsewhere. The God who is himself this moral "law" reveals himself to us through his creature "man." In the text of the Decree on Religious Liberty, already quoted, the Council says that God makes us sharers in his "law" by means of the conscience. It is clear that conscience is not understood here in the narrower sense as the concrete ethical judgment of a situation here and now (or the empowering of such a judgment), but as the possibility inherent in the human person of understanding himself as a moral being and of attempting to bring the manifold ethical problems and questions to a valid solution.

This means, however, that the "divine" or "eternal" law is nothing other than the natural ethical law (often also called natural law) which the Council itself repeatedly cites. Alfons Auer once observed correctly that "eternal law" and "divine law" are nothing other than an interpretation of the so-called ethical natural law. The God who gives us through creation a share in his own reality — a created participation — makes us thereby share also in the reality of "divine law" or "eternal law" which is identical with himself. The divine-eternal law is not handed over to man in any old fashion, but is given to him in the same way as humanity itself. In the human being and his morality, God has translated himself into the reality of the human being in the mode of participation: an "incarnation" into human morality.

It follows that our human morality, also called the ethical natural law, is the divine-eternal law itself, though only by participation. Thus we may also say that human morality is identical with what it is to be human, just as what is divine is identical with what it is to be God.

In the Decree on the Church in the Modern World, the Council shows that in many religions it is held that the "voice of God" can be heard in the "language of the creatures" (no. 50). Ultimately, however, "the creatures" are personal man himself together with the personal and subpersonal world that "belongs to him" (as the extension of himself). It is thanks to his participation in God's wisdom through rational insight as a human person in the image of God, that he can hear the reality of creatures and ultimately his own reality as a "voice," and that he can understand himself and thus also the right manner of his active self-realization in his human world, by means of his reason in its perceptions and projects. From this point of view, Thomas Aquinas also terms the natural moral law simply the *ratio recta*, the right insight of reason that interprets man's personal being with a view to dynamic self-realization. The Council, therefore, can call the self-interpretation in its perception and project "the voice of God" because it understands personal man, together with his reason, as a created participation in the reality of God and of his wisdom, and accordingly also in the "divine" or "eternal" law.

Seen thus, human morality cannot be other than "genuinely human," or as we also say, "humane": human because it is fundamentally identical with the human person; humane in the best sense of this word because it is "divine" — even if only by participation — divine wisdom which has become human. The church's tradition has therefore continually called the natural ethical law also "divine law." Inasmuch as God himself is present in it — in a human fashion — it cannot be an inhumane or nonhuman order; it cannot contain anything that is nonhuman or inhumane. True morality of the human person must therefore insist on genuine humanity, humaneness, and human self-realization; as God cannot be other than divine, so must the human person be nothing less than human. One could set a question-mark only in cases where, according to responsible human evaluation, certain requirements or the concrete solution to a problem would have to be judged as being too much to ask of the human person; the question would then be whether such requirements genuinely belong to the moral order and correspond to the divine wisdom which seeks to express itself in that order.

This question is possible because our morality is not handed on to us in a positive manner through a divine document (and even the few points of the Old Testament Decalogue are fundamentally human instructions that are accessible to the human person himself), nor does it present itself directly as a divine understanding, but rather as a simple human understanding. It belongs, in fact, to the human character of human morality — as only a participation — that it is not given to us directly as divine wisdom, but by means of human reason which only participates in divine wisdom; it is therefore often given to us as the insufficient and also fundamentally fallible perception of the human person (of humanity), a perception determined by a long historical development and experience. Even the light of the gospel, the power of the Holy Spirit who gives us life, and the teaching wisdom of the church — for this too, despite the support of the Holy Spirit, is fundamentally human — cannot fully remove these possibilities of human failure in humanity's perception of morality. That is how things stand when God's wisdom proceeds from its own reality and enters the merely shared reality created by itself, and in this sense "becomes man"!

Understood in this way, the "divine" or "eternal" law is truly "human" morality precisely because we — humanity — believe that we ourselves can understand and develop human morality; it is a morality of reason that is developed through perception and on the basis of experience by the "partner" whom God has created in his own image. Through his participation in the wisdom of God, the partner has the power — as partner — to attain a moral insight that is in accord with the humanity that is the image of God, and thus in accord with divine wisdom, with the eternal divine law. But since the partner remains only a created partner, he does not attain the fullness of divine wisdom and of the divine eternal law.

Since the Council did not deal thematically with the question that interests us, its documents occasionally contain somewhat incoherent formulations. First, one of these formulations is found in the Constitution on the Church in the Modern World (no. 50), where we are exhorted to orientate ourselves in our "conscience" toward the "divine law." Even from the simple point of terminology, the difficulty arises of how the conscience is to orientate itself toward the divine law if the latter is not accessible to us in itself (as has already been said), but only in the "incarnate" manner of the human "conscience." Obviously, a different way of seeing things is dominant here, presupposing a givenness, a "possession" of the divine law — presumably, a givenness and a possession in the church's fellowship and above all in the church's teaching office and its pronouncements. In fact, reference is made to the church's teaching office in this context (nos. 50 and 51; cf. also *Lumen Gentium*, no. 25).

Naturally, this other way of seeing things contains something that is absolutely right and important. Through the incarnation in Jesus Christ, the believing man receives for knowledge of morality (as the incarnate wisdom of God in creation) what the Council calls the "light of the gospel," and likewise the word of the church of God who has become man in Jesus Christ. But it would be a mistake to suppose that the "light of the gospel" was more than a light that helps us in a genuine way in the attainment of knowledge of morality; for it is only a help, not a revelation of human morality. We have already pointed out, with regard to the teaching office of the church, that it can have knowledge of morality — despite the support of the Spirit — only via the conscience of men, or by recourse to such insights. The teaching office, like the individual, has no direct access to God and to his "divine law"; from this point of view, it belongs to the realm of divine wisdom which is incarnate in creation. In the case of the concrete questions of right human conduct in the world, one cannot speak of a "possession" on the part of the church's teaching authority, but at most of a "presumptive" possession.

Second, in the text about religious freedom already quoted, the

Council speaks without conscious reflection, and therefore unsatisfactorily, about the difficulty we have mentioned, when it terms the "divine law" eternal, objective and universal. This statement is easily understood, if one thinks simply of a "divine law" in itself. But it can cause problems when we reflect that we have this divine law only in the manner, and in the measure, of human insight. In what sense can the *epitheta* of divine wisdom be valid also for moral insights into the divine wisdom which has become incarnate in human reason? It is not possible for a human reality — even the most complicated, most ignoble, and least transparent — to exist without the immanence in it of the God who sees through all things and judges them, and is eternally transcendent; every human reality is necessarily present to eternal wisdom, and this also from an ethical point of view. But the human translation of eternal wisdom must take place in human time. How difficult it is then, to bear in mind all the elements of human situations, societal problems, social injustices, and individual situations in their objective-external and subjective-internal complexity, with a view to right ethical judgment, and to analyze them thoroughly in their mutual relationships, to evaluate them and to understand them with a view to future conduct!

It is clear that the God who is permanently present to all this human reality can know in his wisdom only an objective "law" for each future human realization of the entire reality: this is true not only for sublime and utterly general principles of human morality, but also for the significance of these principles in relation to the most concrete and least transparent circumstances, both exterior and interior. Against this, there is a great danger that the human person may arbitrarily turn away from the required objectivity, not only because, as God's human partner, he has a limited capacity to evaluate and a limited insight, but also because his heart is self-interested and often egotistical. This turning away may take the all too human form of overlooking genuine and concrete moral truth, but it may likewise often take the form of anxiety about personal "security" in the face of decisions to be made, with a desire to escape societal or ecclesiastical unpleasantnesses. In such cases, the relative significance of principles or norms — relative, that is, to the entire reality of the given situation — is arbitrarily sacrificed. The Council did not deal explicitly with this question, which was, however, present in an unthematic way to the mind of the Council when it spoke — in different documents — in one place about moral principles and axioms with regard to the church's teaching authority in moral questions, and in another place about ethical solutions with regard to the concrete weight of individual spheres of life. But the Council did not reflect exhaustively upon this question.

There is no problem when the divine law, understood in its own proper character, which is not directly accessible to us, is called universal, for nothing can escape the wise creator Spirit. But much can escape the spirit of man which participates in this Spirit. There is no doubt that the requirements of personal goodness, known to us human beings, are absolutely universal: the requirement of the attitude of readiness for the good, for genuine self-realization in the individual, interpersonal, social and world spheres, as well as in the realms of economics, politics, justice, family, marriage, sexuality, etc. But only with difficulty can one establish through human wisdom what is materially, in ultimate concreteness, morally right in each case in the many spheres of human reality; and the solutions found are mostly only general, rather than universal. It is certainly possible to live on these terms! Apart from this, is it not ultimately necessary, in each decision, to establish the full concreteness of the actual situation here and now, even if this absolutely must take place in the light of the hermeneutic reading of general (or also universal) attempts at solutions which have already been worked out or already exist? This demands moral responsibility for every human decision, even if it is scarcely felt in everyday decisions.

In short, the Council uses a correct formulation when it says that the divine law is eternal, objective and universal. But when it is said that this divine law guides us, because we know it in the manner of the natural ethical law, this formulation surely tends to lead not a few believers to a mistaken and also dangerous understanding; for it does not say that the wise God and his divine law have been revealed in the mode of creation, and that they are available to us only through creaturely, human participation. The adjectives "eternal – objective – universal" do not have the same validity when applied to a merely human reading of the divine law. Were this not so, then fundamentally there would exist neither what the Council itself calls the natural "ethical law," i.e., a human ethical order which is accessible to the human person himself and yet ultimately has its basis in God's wisdom, nor the possibility of ethical knowledge, ethical insight, ethical experience, that is to say, the possibility of a human and "humane" morality.

In the case of questions of contemporary humanity, the Council itself has seen this and said it, though in places where it does not refer explicitly to the eternal law of God. Nothing else is meant by the observation in the Pastoral Constitution on the Church in the Modern World (no. 43) that even believing and responsible Christians can legitimately arrive at diverse solutions to various questions. The incarnation of God and of his wisdom through creation brings with it the possibility of a legitimate pluralism; not even the Christian faith and its proclamation through the Church can prevent this. To insist on this is genuinely human and — for human beings — humane, in the best sense of the word.

2. God's "Innerworldly" Rights and Human Morality

If this is true of the incarnation of God and of his wisdom in the creation of the human person and thereby in the foundation of a human morality, then there is an important consequence which, as far as I can see, is often given insufficient attention up to the present day: one must not directly involve the creator God further in the process of finding knowledge of the divine wisdom which has, in fact, become incarnate — i.e., in finding knowledge of the morality of the created human being. This does not mean that God is to be bracketed off, or that he does not count as the ontologically transcendent and yet present ultimate foundation of human morality, and cannot be known and acknowledged as such. But he must not appear on the scene with specific innerworldly demands and rights within this morality and alongside created human reality. Such a God would not be the transcendent God; such a humanity would not be the incarnation of God through the created participation of the human person in the divine reality; such a morality would not be incarnate divine wisdom. This formulation of mine is not, as has been said, "radical agnosticism,"[1] but rather the acknowledgment of God as God and the humble acknowledgment of human morality as merely human participation in God's wisdom — on the basis of his incarnation through creation. If God went beyond his incarnation through creation and intervened in relation to us by means of commands or prohibitions, reserving rights to himself in the sphere of human activity, then he would not take the human world with full seriousness as a gift of participation in God's reality and wisdom. In other words, he would not take seriously his own original entry into this world as its inmost ground, and into the inner moral order of the world of human persons. It is the human interpretation of human reality itself that must discover how human conduct is to be judged in the light of divine wisdom: in this way, we are to arrive at a morality that is human and "humane." But it does not always happen that way.

A *first example.* It becomes clearer every day to all of us what problems are posed today by the many extremely varied possibilities regarding the human disposal of human life. This question demands the attention of the healthy and the sick, of doctors and researchers, of churches and parliaments. An appeal to God's lordship over human life will not cut much ice among biomedical experts or parliamentary legislators. The solution must therefore be sought by considering the dignity and value of human life in the world of human persons; as with many other questions, one must reckon here with the possibility that not all who take part in the search will make their evaluation in the same way. The question remains, whether those who believe in God have another starting-point for a solution to these numerous problems, viz., the lordship over human life that belongs to God alone.

We are all familiar with the following kind of argument: God alone is the lord of all human life, and therefore no human person has the right to dispose of human life. The pastoral letter of the German Bishops on the problem of euthanasia (1975) and the document of the Roman Congregation for the Doctrine of the Faith on the problem of euthanasia and voluntary death (1980) argue precisely in this way. Thus they do not seek the solution in a human interpretation of the human reality which God and his wisdom have entered.

I believe that Bruno Schüller was correct when he stated several years ago[2] that to speak of God as the sole lord of human life fundamentally means only that the human person is not God and therefore is not lord of his own life in the same sense in which God is lord of his life. For God's lordship is transcendent, whereas any right to dispose of human life that might possibly be attributed to the human person is immanent in this world. Besides this, God's transcendent lordship is related not only to human life, but in the same manner to all created reality. One who behaves arbitrarily — i.e., against the ("incarnate") wisdom of God which has been posited in human reality — in *any* sphere of reality misuses God's creation; this is therefore not only the case when he disposes of human life in an arbitrary way, i.e., in a way that cannot be justified in innerworldly terms. Insofar as justifying reasons exist, the human person does not abuse the commission given him through creation to shape the world that has been entrusted to him.

In point of fact, human beings and the Christian churches too have considered the direct or indirect human disposal of human life — not only of other realities — to be justified, within certain limits. One may think of the accepted doctrine about conduct in a war taken to be just, about the human penal code, and of self-defense or defense of another in the case of an unjustified attack. Today, several other possibilities for justified intervention are pointed out.

Nevertheless, the difficulty of combining the justified disposing of human life and the exclusive lordship of God over life was noticed in a certain way, for it was emphasized that in these cases, God delegated to human beings the right that was his alone. No one has ever said how this delegation took place; it had to be simply presumed. This means in effect, however, that we human beings recognize the necessity of such acts of disposing of life in particular cases in our human world. If this necessity exists, it follows that the innerworldly justification of such acts of disposing of life has been posited, by the God who enters creation, in the world of man. It would in any case be impossible to understand how God could, in innerworldly terms, delegate his transcendent lordship to the human persons of this world.

A second example. Not only in the realm of the disposal of human life, but in many other realms of life too, believers in Christ are at times confronted by individual ethical norms proclaimed in the church which they believe ask too much in certain specific situations, and therefore, despite their wording, are not applicable. Appeal is made to St. Paul, who in the seventh chapter of his first letter to the Corinthians upholds the demand for marital fidelity made by Jesus himself, while he does not oppose divorce in the particular case of the difficulty of a marriage between a pagan partner and a partner who has in the meantime become a Christian.

Such reflections can contain the danger of a desire to escape true ethical requirements and the seriousness of the commission to be and to live as a human person in a genuinely human manner. But this does not mean that they cannot also have a justified sense.

Christian pastoral work has always known of a law of gradualism, both with regard to the coming into being of Christian life in mission territories and with regard to the growth of the individual toward Christian and ethical maturity: maturity takes time. In the last few years, the fear has been loudly expressed that an attempt is being made among Christian people to defend something else, viz., a certain gradualism of the law itself — i.e., of the moral order and moral norms. As has already been said, the observance of particular ethical norms becomes too much to ask of human persons in certain situations; but this is not to propose an un-Christian moral laxity.

The fear of such a tendency exists within the church. It is argued that God's law knows and expresses the truth, the whole truth and nothing but the truth: hence one may not seek to build into this commandment stages of gradual obligatoriness, for then man would no longer let God be God, making himself the standard of morality. We cannot simply contradict this consideration if we are truly speaking of the divine, i.e. the eternal law in the sense set out above. It is here, however, that the difficulty begins: in day-to-day human living, we know the divine-eternal law in general only as this knowledge is disclosed through the conscience of human beings, in whom God and his "law" cannot be approached directly, but only by means of the interpretation of our humanity, in which God has disclosed himself through creation. We should be very cautious about calling human ethical insights "divine law," although this is done very frequently. We could thereby create the false impression that the entire content of our morality is simply a divine law, and that, precisely for this reason, the idea of a gradualism of the law must be completely excluded from our morality.

If we reflect, however, that our morality has come into being through human knowledge, and that one must therefore reckon with the incompleteness and insufficiency of human knowledge and of the formulation of ethical norms — indeed, occasionally with error too — then we cannot wholly exclude the idea of the gradualism of such norms. When human beings seek to recognize and formulate ethical norms — sometimes in a very general and imprecise fashion — we must reckon with the fact that they responsibly come to see the inner boundaries of such norms when it is clear that established norms make excessively high demands. It is indeed not true to say that one introduces the concept of gradualism into moral theology in this way: one is only bringing a better insight and formulation to the insights and formulations that already exist. That would be a service to human reality, which should express as perfectly as possible the divine wisdom which has been posited in it. This second example also shows that one should be wary of mingling or confusing the eternal wisdom of the transcendent God with the participatory wisdom of the human discovery of morality — even if only by giving too quickly, too frequently or too thoughtlessly the name of "God's law" to what is due to human evaluation and insight. We do indeed hope that this human wisdom, which we wish to trust in our life, genuinely and broadly expresses the eternal wisdom which has become incarnate in us human persons through participation and has become human reality: if this is so, then its content will indeed be the "divine law."

In what has been said earlier, we have spoken of the incarnation of God and of his wisdom through the creation of the human person who is partner in God's own image. It belongs to the human character of this morality that it is not a "divine law" imposed *ab extra*, nor does it know additional requirements and rights on the part of a God who intervenes directly in his world. In this sense, human morality is the incarnate wisdom of God. God's incarnation in Jesus Christ is often understood to mean that through Jesus Christ God brings the human person, who has become sinful and without understanding, back to knowledge of the content of genuinely human — i.e., humane, morality — of the "incarnate divine law" — for example, in the Sermon on the Mount. This is proposed as the understanding of the redemption given us through Christ; but the redemption of the human person is something different from this, something significantly greater.

It is not as if the incarnation in Christ had absolutely no significance for our human knowledge of genuinely human morality; but Jesus did not bring us a new codex of human morality, for that would be a negative judgment on the part of God concerning his first incarnation in the creation of the human being together with his participation in God's wisdom. It would also be a degradation of the human person, reducing him to one who observes laws imposed on him rather than one commissioned to seek ways of actively shaping God's creation in the extremely manifold situations of human reality, which cannot at all be grasped through a positively introduced "law."

On the other hand, it is true that God's revelation about the human person and his God, and their mutual relationship — the "light of the gospel" – and the maieutic power of the figure, deeds and judgments of Jesus help us to discover norms and judgments of human morality more easily and more securely. Besides this, the true redemption of the human person, setting him free from his sinful egotism, makes him readier to strive for true knowledge of human morality. This all contributes to a stronger "humanization" (a word much loved by Vatican II) of human reality and thus also of human-humane morality.

But redemption through God's incarnation in Jesus Christ means above all something else: the liberation and redemption of the human being (alienated from himself, from his own being and thus also from God) from his state of being closed in upon himself, making him in his inmost being open to God and men, to all that is true and good, and thus to the renewed and better discovery of his own self, to peace and joy at the condescension of our God "who loves mankind" (Tit 3:4) in his incarnation in his Son.

NOTES

1 The two "examples" which follow are given in a larger context in the author's essay "Das Gottesbild und die Moral innerweltlichen Handelns," *Stimmen der Zeit* 202 (1984), 363–82. There I have shown that although all human discourse about God is necessarily anthropomorphic and thus analogous, nevertheless a "hyperanthropomorphic" language applied to God is unacceptable, if thereby it asserts categorial commanding on the part of a God who has rights and is effectively at work alongside the being and activity of the human person, in order to provide a foundation for individual ethical norms. In his answer, "Gott und die Sittlichkeit innerweltlichen Handelns" (God and the Morality of Innerworldly Behavior) *Forum kath. Theol.* 1 (1985), 27–47. J. Seifert believes he must accuse the author and K. Rahner of a "radical agnosticism." See the 1984 essay above, Chapter III.

2 *Die Bergründung sittlicher Urteile*, Düsseldorf, 1973, 182–98; second edn 1980.

V. Christian Faith and the Disposing of Human Life

The topic of this essay is not the problem of the disposing of human life — whether considered from the point of view of philosophy or of moral theology. Nor is our concern the fundamental ethical or the concrete casuistical problems which belong to that topic. Rather, in this essay I will deal with the basic question of the significance attached to the Christian faith in solving normative problems on the level of morally correct (right) behavior. But this question is not to be approached theoretically; it will be presented exclusively by means of one example: the disposing of human life.

When we speak of the disposing of human life, one thinks immediately and to a large extent of biological life. This is not wrong, but more basically it is a question of earthly human existence. As such, the various possibilities of disposing of human life in some way through biological means play their particular roles. Here I am interested above all in the question of life/death, existence/nonexistence — and precisely as this question depends on human control, or lack of control, over these alternatives.

There is no doubt that this involves causing the death of other persons. This problem not only involves reflections on the value and dignity of human life and the so-called right of God as the Lord of human life; it also merits a reflection on the person's right to life within society. The question of prenatal killing (abortion) and of the killing of the newborn would belong to this group of problems. In this area there are certainly still many points which are open to discussion. Yet in general, neither philosophy nor theology considers the prohibition against taking the life of another as admitting of absolutely no exception. In the case of taking of one's own life, the question of the right to life does not arise; rather, it raises the question of the moral justification of killing in view of the value and dignity of human life as well as that of the sovereign right of God over all human life.

In what follows, I shall limit myself (though not exclusively) to the problem of taking of one's own life, whether in suicide or in a sacrificial death or in euthanasia. The problem of "Christian faith and the disposing of human life" seems to be especially acute today in this area.

Before I enter the actual problem, it seems reasonable to reflect briefly on (1) how Christians in the past and in the present have seen the problem of the disposing of human life, and (2) human or philosophical insights into the problem.

The fact that Christians from the very beginning opted for life, thus distinguishing themselves markedly from the position of, for example, the Stoics, whom they were often glad to follow in other questions, is presumably connected with their knowledge of the fifth commandment of the Decalogue as they understood it in that period. It was a question of the right of one's neighbor. Moreover, it is clear that their reflection on Jesus' teaching about respect for one's neighbor and his teaching about nonviolence found in the Sermon on the Mount was also important. It took a relatively long time for their position regarding military service, especially when it involved killing the enemy, to develop away from the original absolute "Christian" severity. But despite the growing inclination to take a less absolute view of the prohibition against the taking of life, the position of Christians even today in regard to the life of one's neighbor is surely influenced strongly by both the word of God on Sinai and of Jesus of Nazareth. Obviously, we have to do here with a kind of attitude of faith.

In addition to and independently of this respect for the neighbor and for his life, there is also the respect for human life as such. Human life is accepted — to use a word that is familiar though often misunderstood today — as "holy"; it is God's gift and belongs in this sense to him alone. This respect for life comes to expression in early Christianity, for example, in the sharp rejection of the interruption of pregnancy. It is also expressed in the prohibition against hindering what is still only "potential" life – for example, through contraception, through homosexual conduct, and (from the sixth century on) through masturbation. To this there corresponds the traditionally sharp condemnation of suicide and, when relevant, of euthanasia. Thus the Christians' respect for human life seems, to a large extent, to be in accord with their faith and religiously qualified. The formulation, found recently in both agnostics and Christian theologians, that the rejection of suicide and euthanasia presupposes a theistic (or Christian) faith, is significant on this point.

A reflection on the disposing of human life that is less dependent on faith but is simply "human" or even "philosophical" is becoming more and more widespread. The opinion which holds that only the (Christian) faith can substantiate a prohibition against suicide and euthanasia corroborates the approach of those humanists who, without faith in God, are unable to find any reason to reject these practices vis-à-vis a neighbor who is dying. Here it may be that a right to determine one's own life is held to belong to the dignity of the human person; or it may be held that the prohibition — which has somehow been established — against the disposal of one's own life is not absolute, i.e., not without exceptions, especially in conflict situations; or it may be that one doubts the sufficient evidential value in the reasons offered for the prohibition.

The distinction between human insight and philosophical insight is not unimportant here, because it is possible that, despite deep human insights, we may not succeed in formulating convincing philosophical reasons. Apart from this, there are certainly initial insights which cannot be reduced to reasons that already exist.

. As has been said, one frequently encounters today the formulation that only a theistic (Christian) belief in God could make a prohibition of the disposing of one's own life comprehensible; the problem would therefore be more religious than ethical. This formulation parallels the saying that everything is basically allowed when belief in God is lacking. Not only Kant and a good many (agnostic) humanists, but also many Protestant and Catholic philosophers and theologians, take issue with this saying. In other words, one certainly is able to suppose an authentic human self-understanding that in principle knows something of the dignity of human existence in our time, and of a corresponding limitation on the disposing of this existence. Even where such an original insight is not admitted, plausible philosophical reasons for these intimations can be offered.

Furthermore, there is a false alternative in the formulations "Without faith everything is allowed" and "Without faith there is no good reason to prohibit the taking of one's own life." Theism and atheism do not form the human (or philosophical) basis for a solution to the problem facing us here — the disposing of one's life. Rather, the solution's foundation is human self-understanding qua human. At least in explicit reflection, however, this will always be influenced beforehand by a theistic, atheistic, or agnostic option or "faith." Yet the dignity of the human person, as an end in himself or herself and as a moral being capable of responsible self-realization, is fundamentally accessible to insightful experience. But since this dignity presupposes biological life, there may be more to be said about the question of the disposing of such life.

There is yet another question: Precisely to what level of detail are we able to find convincing or at least sufficiently plausible solutions relative to our problem? At what level will they appear reasonable to others? We may perhaps believe that we have moral, though not metaphysical, certainty in the case of particular solutions. But, as already suggested, the exceedingly various human or philosophical convictions are presumably influenced by a set of global options or beliefs in an unconscious way.

What set of comprehensive beliefs with its corresponding self-understanding conditions the formulations asserting that the disposing of one's own life, or at least a "rational" self-realization understood in terms of freedom, belongs to the essential dignity of the human person? Or that accordingly it is not necessary that every realization of life that is possible-in-itself must be realized? Or that finally, by way of comparison, death must not be considered the greatest evil for a human person?

Against this stand several prohibitory considerations that may perhaps be influenced by another set of beliefs. We are told that self-destruction is still in principle a self-affirmation and therein it contains an internal contradiction: Is this a valid argument? We are told that the taking of one's own life makes the person lord over himself and thereby confronted with an internal contradiction: Is this argument valid? We are told that taking one's own life contradicts the innermost natural tendency for self-preservation: Does this argument hold without exception? We are told that one who takes his own life escapes from the obligatory full development of himself as a person as well as from his essential role in the society to which he belongs: Is this a valid argument? We are told that it would be a contradiction to say that by hastening death freedom would deprive itself of the life that is a necessary condition of freedom's own existence: Is this a conclusive argument?

It appears that behind such arguments lies the philosophical thesis that by taking one's own life a person assumes that which rightfully belongs only to the Creator; one evades the Creator's will that we should fully develop the life he has given us; one escapes from the time of testing that the Creator has ordained. Both Thomas Aquinas[1] and Pius XII[2] understand these questions to be philosophical. But are they not really hidden theological questions? Are they not questions that have arisen out of an inspiration of faith, but are then accessible to human reflection? This is how they are understood, e.g., by Edward Schillebeeckx in his second book on Christ.[3] Similarly, Helmut Thielicke[4] holds that solutions discovered in the area of faith bearing on the human right to dispose of life must not be lost in a secularized society. Both authors imply, then, that the questions concerning the disposing of human life are fundamentally problems of human ethics and not only of faith and religion. However, this does not exclude the possibility that they are concerned with Christian faith as well.

So we see that one must not underestimate the importance that the Christian faith has in its relationship to the ethical question of the disposing of human life. The question becomes all the more pressing since today not only atheists but also Protestant and Catholic theologians speak in favor of a complete reduction of the problem to theology alone. The theologians who hold this to be necessary do so particularly because the attempts at philosophical solutions seem to them to lack insight and are indeed very uncertain. The questions that arise are these: Does the Christian faith supply essential insights and solutions to the problem of the disposing of human life, insights and solutions that cannot be understood on the basis of any other *Weltanschauung?* Or does Christian faith deepen genuine human insights, maieutically open the way for an understanding that is humanly possible? Can faith say something more precise about the absoluteness, or perhaps only a "limited absoluteness" (*sit venia verbo*), of accepted solutions? Can faith give a greater certainty if human attempts at a solution remain more or less open to discussion? Finally, should faith be a help primarily against atheistic positions or against the weakness of merely human attempts at solution?

1. Fundamental Problem: Does Christian Faith Make the Normative Decision?

(a) *Theological considerations against an excessive demand on faith.* At the beginning of my reflection on this concrete problem, I should like to proffer a general admonition by the respected Protestant theologian Gerhard Ebeling: "There is urgent need to warn against hastily bringing the subject matter of theology to bear against philosophy, rather than patiently wrestling with the reasonableness of reason."[5] Ebeling is speaking along the line of Paul Tillich's words: "one becomes bitter if one sees how theologians, who explain the concepts of the Old and the New Testament, use many expressions which have been developed by the deep reflections of the philosophers and the creative power of the speculative spirit, and then condemn with cheap objections those very expressions which have so extraordinarily enriched the language. No theologian should be taken as a serious theologian, even if he is a good Christian and a great scholar, when his work shows that he does not take philosophy seriously . . ."[6] On the other hand, especially with the topic of this essay, it is necessary to emphasize the theological necessity of investigating the possible and the actual significance of the Christian faith for the ethical problem of the disposing of human life. No one denies that faith is significant in this ethical question. The real question is *what* significance faith has for the question of a normative moral system. Does the ethical question become fundamentally a religious one? Then will faith determine the content of the solution to the ethical question either by establishing a solution that could not *de facto* be found or understood by ethics, or else by supporting ethical attempts at a solution by means of a wholly different set of criteria? Or does faith provide a model of how the Christian, as a Christian, must attempt to provide the world with a corresponding solution? Or is it the case that the Christian faith and theological love are in fact concretized in the humanly possible attempts at a solution? That is, does a human ethical solution find in faith a dimension and meaningfulness that transcends itself and thus, at the same time, offers to the Christian who is searching for a solution a further and specific motivation for the respectful treatment of human life that is ethically required, and for the conscientious observance of the answers that are sought and found?

When I reflect on the ethical question of the disposing of human life — that of others and one's own — I naturally do this as a believing Christian. Hence the reflection as a personal act is always at once religious and human. In this sense I can never arrive at solutions which would be hypostatized abstractions, either of faith or of human (indeed ahistorical) reason. The Chalcedonian doctrine of the unity of Christ does indeed permit a "communication of the properties," but not the abandonment of the distinction between divinity and historical humanity with the individual and particular function of each. The single religious reflection on the ethical question about the disposing of human life may not back away from the question of what human insight and what Christian faith contribute to the solution of the question.

The Christian faith itself, which should help us in the search for moral answers, bears in itself as a condition of its own possibility a human self-understanding and a human moral experience. We need not settle here the question of how far human and ethical self-understanding precedes faith, or whether it first becomes active *in* the encounter with the offer and the acceptance of faith. Human and moral self-understanding is nothing other than the gift of the truth about oneself, and thereby of the meaning of one's own self as this meaning forms the basis for the multiple values and norms of human realities.

Such a self-understanding is impossible without a final reference that is not further reducible and beyond which no questions can be asked. At a congress of moral theologians in 1977,[7] Schillebeeckx, together with other contemporary theologians and philosophers, called this a basic experience, a fundamental confidence, for which it is possible to adduce reasons that are perhaps philosophically good but not probative (although they can become certainty in faith for one who is able to believe). Karol Wojtyla and his Polish friends speak a similar language.

The Christian faith in creation points in the same direction. God "is really able to create" in man "a free Other over against Himself and oriented toward Himself."[8] "God can set us so free in His omnipotence that we indeed are something over against Him and oriented toward Him. Here, dependence and autonomy are realities that stand in equal proportions and not in inverse proportions to each other."[9] The human person, experiencing himself in this way as open to transcendence,[10] experiences the moral task that belongs to his most inner being. He seeks a clear understanding of the multiplicity of the values available to him, of their hierarchy, and of their capacity to make a demand on him. For this, however, the attempts of immense periods of humanity's history and continually new efforts are required. Most certainly, life — man's human existence — is among the values declared by man as good. How is he to manage this, dispose of this, and deal with the continuance of life and with death? The question is all the more acute when he realizes that life is not the highest of goods. It is only in the case of "a life that is led in free responsibility . . . that one can and must say: it is the highest of goods for the human person, an absolutely untouchable value."[11]

The openness to transcendence which the person experiences makes it possible for him to accept the freely offered gift of faith and of God's self-communication in grace. These are seen as gifts given to the human person precisely in his freedom as the "Other" created by God. It follows that all of human freedom and all ethical striving are integrated in these.[12] They can, accordingly, also give light and inspiration in the human person's difficult ethical quest. But insofar as this is only a light,[13] there must still be in principle the question of accessible moral truth that is comprehensible to human and moral self-understanding. It is a case then, of genuine humanism (not, therefore, specifically atheistic or agnostic or theistic humanism), and not of an ethics of faith that is added on to this or stretched out before this.

In treating the problem of the right to life and the right to take life, reference has been made in some way in all periods since Aristotle to the dignity of the human person, of his existence, and of his life. This dignity has been understood as a dignity that belongs to the human person who in freedom lives and historically actuates the meaning of his own self; so Kant saw man as "an end in himself." From the standpoint of creation theology, man is the "Other" who has been sent forth in freedom through God's omnipotence. The question about the disposing of human life, that of others and one's own, must respect this "truth" of the human person. It is not solved by merely accepting an "instruction" that comes from outside — from God, for instance. Because earthly existence, life, is not an absolute good, and not the highest good of man, it can be understood why the problem of the disposing of human life will never find a generally accepted solution that goes into points of detail.

Since Dietrich Bonhoeffer[14] and Karl Barth,[15] and continuing in Germany under the influence of "Barth's disciple" U. Eibach,[16] there has been for some time a very strong tendency to replace the human and philosophical reflection which has been presented here with one completely dependent upon theology. Interestingly enough, there are similar tendencies on the part of Catholics today.[17] The central thesis declares that the human person, who is a sinner, has no value whatever as his own; all his value lies outside himself, in the loving call made by the God of the covenant. It follows that a value possessed by the human person would play no role at all in the problem of the disposing of human life, one's own or that of others. Consequently, the prohibition against the disposal of human life could be based only in the will of God, from whom the dignity of being called is derived. This alone would provide the justification under certain circumstances of an affirmative and partial disposing of human life.

It is not possible for me to grasp such a thesis, whether from the standpoint of human philosophy or from that of creation theology. I do not see how it is possible, without the dignity which is given to the human person but is fully his own, to arrive at the encounter with the love of God which gives the basis of a final dignity; nor do I understand the dignity of the call of God that is not a dignity belonging to us, if this does not integrate in itself a dignity that belongs to the human person (and this is explicitly allowed, e.g., by Eberhard Jüngel and Helmut Thielicke[18]). And if this fundamental thesis does affirm occasional possibilities of the disposing of human life — as a permission or a command from God[19] — then I do not see how the divine permission or the divine command can be recognized by us, other than through the self-reflection of the human person with the dignity that is his. It seems to me that neither the high dignity of the human person, which is doubtless based in the relationship between God and man, nor this relationship's future promise of a life-to-come understood in a Christian sense, can bring the problem of the right of disposing of human life to concrete solutions. We shall have to discuss this point further.

(b) *Theological recourse to the Bible and its effective history.* Instead of continuing the preceding reflections immediately, let us first turn our attention to another theological approach. Some believe that beyond any theological reflection is a simpler and more direct way to a solution for the problem at hand. One endeavors to show that God himself in the tradition of the Old Testament and especially of the New (Sermon on the Mount) has already given the answer to the present question about the disposing of human life. One need only look in the handbooks of moral theology, even those of a quite recent period. In the same regard, one may read documents of the Church's magisterium, episcopal pastoral letters, and much religious-ethical literature. One who believes that he possesses the truth by attempting such a recourse is naturally convinced that he already has all, or at least most, of the answers. Consequently, one can do without further human reflection or recourse to philosophy. But are we not dealing with an uncritical and narrow theology?

In the holy books of the OT the statement occurs repeatedly that both life and death have their origin in the God worshiped by Israel. These words have not seldom been overinterpreted; some have wanted to read in them that the sovereign (and not only transcendental) right over life and death belonged to the Creator alone.[20] Man would therefore have no right over the disposing of human life. Basically, however, such biblical formulations are considered only the reverential expression of the transcendent superiority of the Creator, to whom even life and death are subject. The believing Israelite saw in such words no contradiction of the frequent killings that were lawful in the OT. It is thus that our theology and our Church must read and understand such texts today. Such an effort will not become contradicted when it finds that such words have been read and understood differently in the course of tradition and have had a corresponding effective history.

In this regard, the double account of the Ten Commandments and their origin in the OT becomes much more important. On this point, both the official ecclesiastical proclamation and the preaching in church, as well as much of the moral theology being done, should be more careful and speak with greater theological clarity and accuracy. Modern exegesis is universally agreed[21] that the two narratives of the Ten Commandments in the OT are not completely the same. The narrative of the origin of the Decalogue and of its relationship to a theophany in which God would have spoken and written is traced to a relatively late redactional event. The Decalogue (above all, the fourth through tenth commandments) is less a moral revelation than a short summary of some principles that were socially significant for Israel, through whose observance the people responded to the God of the covenant. One of these points is the "fifth commandment." This speaks not simply of "killing" (disposing of human life) but only of the arbitrary killing (murder) of a personal, especially defenseless, enemy. Moreover, the Decalogue as a whole knows in various ways a killing that is seen as justified — hence a human disposing of human life. Theologically speaking, therefore, it is wrong to appeal directly to the text of the narrative of the Decalogue against the death penalty, war, and self-defense, against prenatal or neonatal killing, against sacrificial death, suicide, and euthanasia. The immense effective history of the fifth commandment is to be traced in part to a later reading of the OT text, but also to a deeper understanding and evaluation of the reality of human life, of human existence, as the gift of the living God of creation and the covenant. It is theologically significant that the fifth commandment of the Decalogue has had such an enormous effective history under the efficacy of the Spirit of God at work in the salvific history of the OT and NT. This is seen, for instance, in the Sermon on the Mount. Nonetheless, one cannot simply deduce solutions for the many contemporary problems involving the possible disposing of human life from this effective history, especially since even it does not exclude all disposing of human life.[22]

(c) *Theological recourse to the Christian belief in creation.* Instead of appealing directly to the Bible, some appeal just as often or even more frequently to the Christian belief in creation. They hold that one can find in it a surer justification for the nondisposability of human life than they would through human or philosophical insight. The Christian faith speaks to us of a God whom the atheist or agnostic does not know, and who is different in part from the God believed in by Islam, Buddhism, or Hinduism. He is also somehow different from the God of Judaism who is confined to the OT. But the image of God that many Christians make for themselves, on the basis of the revealed God, likewise takes on various forms which are simply not reflective of the biblical faith in God.[23] This is true even of images of God that an occasional Christian, even official, proclamation sometimes transmits to us. The question of whether and to what extent they can be significant for the solution of the ethical question of the disposing of human life depends in large measure on one's faith in God and on one's image of God.

Probably the most widespread image of God is that which understands the Creator as the sole Lord over human life, over the earthly existence of man, and thus over life and death, whereas it consistently gives to the human person the right of disposing of other created realities. This is also the image of the God who wills human life to be a time of testing, in which, consequently, he and he alone has the right to determine the duration and the various circumstances of the test. It is the image of the God who has his plan for the life of each individual, a plan we, however, cannot know. It is, therefore, the image of a God to whom we must passively yield up our life, and still more our death. It is the image of a God whom humanists and atheists cannot grasp. The question arises: Is this the Christian image of God, on the basis of which we can or must solve the ethical problem of the disposing of human life?

Important difficulties stand in the way of this widespread image of God. Is the God of Christian faith really the God who understands the life span of man, with the conditions of his life, fundamentally and primarily as a time of testing that looks toward judgment? Is he truly the God who has created us as partners in the ordering of the world, exempting this partnership in regard to the disposing of human life, and above all over the method and point in time of our death? Is he really the God who works in every event of this world through secondary causes,[24] except in the determination of the duration and the circumstances of human dying, when the human person acts as the secondary cause? Is He a God who stands over against the human person as a rival with regard to a man's life and death?

Or is there not another image that better corresponds to the Christian faith: the image of a God who has created the human person in his own image as an "Other" to be his partner? This would mean that the person is responsible for all levels of human life, including health, life, and death. Understood as one created in God's image and standing as his partner in the world, the person cannot dispose of either his life or his death arbitrarily. Yet God has not informed the human person whether he really requires of him the full development of the whole potential of his life or under the circumstances expects of him a seemingly unwarrantable steadfastness. In accordance with Scripture, I believe that we should understand him rather as the God of love, who is present transcendently in the innermost depth of everything that happens on earth, and who charges the person-as-partner created in his own image with the duty of the appropriate and correct analysis and the execution of these events. God does not himself appear as the one who inflicts disaster and illness, who imposes dreadful destinies on human lives, who determines a sudden death or fatal accidents or a painful lingering infirmity or a mild death, so that the human person may only suffer them in humility. If he is the God who customarily works in this world through secondary causes, then on what theological grounds can we exclude that this should also be the case through responsible healing and nursing, or through keeping alive and letting die (letting oneself die), or through an artificial shortening of life — that is to say, by a curtailment of the dying process, therefore also by the free hastening of the end of life, which too is the hastened end of earthly freedom? Indeed, in this case the responsible theological judgment must consider that the freedom sacrificed for the sake of other values is not, as is sometimes said, a moral value but rather only a human value, i.e., the possibility of realizing moral values. Such would be the case in any sort of killing.

I do not judge here in favor of any one of the possibilities I have named; rather, I wish to make the point that the appeal to the

Christian God of creation as such and the solution of the problem of the disposing of human life do not open the door to a divinely given answer. The solution to the problem or the attempt at such solutions is entrusted to the person-as-partner who is created in God's image. Man and woman must, as far as possible, be constantly aware of the responsibility of their partnership, reflective of the image of God in which they were created, in the quest for tenable solutions. The believing Christian is ahead of many others in this regard.

(d) *Recourse to the God of the covenant.* As has already been said, the attempt (which I cannot copy) to understand human life and its dignity exclusively in the meeting of God and man that is bestowed from the outside by the God of the covenant does not seem to me able to produce any theological solution to the problem of the disposing of human life. It would doubtless follow from that consideration that it cannot be left to the human person to withdraw himself or others from this earthly encounter between God and man, and to determine the form of passage into the next life. Only where this interpersonal relationship on earth is utterly impossible would it be meaningful not to speak of human life, i.e., of the divine-human relationship on earth and human fidelity to it. But the possibilities mentioned above for a premature death or one painfully drawn out, of accidents and the artificial prolongation of life and death, would stand in the way of such a theological theory.

I cannot, therefore, see the reason for the nondisposability of human life being derived solely from the dignity of the graced relationship of God and man. Any reason for the prohibition lies in the created human person himself — in his own "truth". Accordingly, this is how he is integrated into the relationship that the God of creation and covenant has with humanity. This does not exclude but rather implies the fact that the dignity of human life, which as such is fundamentally non-disposable, is always set within that dignity which is experienced as a divine gift on the basis of the person's relationship to the God of creation and the covenant. This knowledge or faith may help him to remain ever aware of the obligations which arise from the dignity which is his own on the basis of creation.

(e) *Recourse to the death of Christ.* Karl Rahner once wrote: "The Christian — every Christian, at all periods — imitates Jesus in the concreteness of his life, by dying with him."[25] This is said not only of the duration of the life that is continually dying to itself, but above all of the final and definitive death. The eternal Logos entered our human situation even to the point of death; in this sense he imitates us. But since he has died our death, we have to die his death: we imitate him, our dying is a sharing in his dying. Does this mean that we have to die in the manner of his death, an unavoidable death in abandonment?[26]

Jesus' death was a violent annihilation. It was not the death that is known in most of the OT, a death ordained by God at the end of a fulfilled life. It was violent, therefore similar to death from a heart attack, from an epidemic, from a traffic accident, through the carrying out of the death penalty, and so on. It does not concern "an expression of the divine will . . . as a direct act of domination," but "through the mediation of secondary causes."[27] Cannot the same be said of the conflict situations that are "forced upon" us, ones in which many theologians (see below) would not dare to declare as absolutely unjustified sacrificial death, the taking of one's own life, or euthanasia? Then, however it would be a dying in the manner of Christ: the experience of total powerlessness, of the total necessity to give oneself up.

What, then, is death as an imitation of the dying Christ? The acceptance of the experience of the God who always fundamentally has a claim over us! The experience of death as the punishment of sin.[28] The total giving up of oneself as an earthly reality, the final gift of self, the ultimate act of confidence, entering into the resurrection and into the incomprehensibility of God. Thus it would remain true that "If we live, we live to the Lord; if we die, we die to the Lord. Whether we live or die, we belong to the Lord."[29] "Neither death nor life . . . can separate us from the love of God in Christ Jesus our Lord."[30] And lastly also, "for me to live is Christ, and to die is gain."[31]

The aim of the preceding discussion has been to show only this: we should not make excessive demands of faith and expect from faith declarations that it perhaps cannot make.

2. The Contribution of Christian Faith

(a) *A convergence on the basis of faith.* After what has been said, the Christian faith cannot be the authority that alone is able to make a prohibition of the disposing of human life understandable. That may at first sound very negative; but this seems to be the result of the preceding reflections. The fundamental problematic of this essay has been to reflect widely on faith insofar as it concerns normative ethics of behavior.

Yet something more can be added. The individual part of the arguments so far presented bear in themselves a converging positive statement: they point in a particular direction. The effective history of the words of the OT, which goes much further than their immediate content, shows that human life, human existence, as the gift of the Creator, absolutely claims respect. The reflections on the God who "creates" for himself in his omnipotence an "Other" as his partner, and chooses him for himself in the covenant as his beloved partner, lets us understand what a deep respect God must expect for the life and the existence of the "Other" whom he has created and chosen. Jesus' ready and confident handing over of his earthly existence, of his life, to the Father bears witness to the Father as the one who truly possesses life.

Does not a large part of mankind basically understand human life in a manner analogous to what is expressed more clearly and powerfully in the Christian faith?

(b) *Situations of conflict.* However, a demand for this respect for life in the sense of an absolute prohibition of the disposing of human life cannot be based on faith. This is why ethics speaks of situations of conflict, which do not absolutely exclude the disposing of human life, nor at the same time abandon the demand for reverence in the presence of human life.

It has always been seen, in faith and without faith, that the prohibition of killing and the right to life are not absolute. We know the examples of the death penalty, self-defense, and the just war, even if we have become somewhat more cautious on these questions today.

I have heard from soldiers of the Second World War, who could not take their seriously wounded comrades with them when they retreated, that they saw themselves faced with the alternative of leaving them to a certain, long, and painful death, or else of giving them a quick death out of merciful love. They held the latter to be their duty as Christians. Further, many, including Christian theologians, held the self-sacrifice of Jan Palach to be justified as a powerful act of witness. It follows that they must make a similar judgment in the case of similar self-sacrifices of Buddhist monks. In addition, a generally positive answer has been given to the question that has arisen in our time of the justification of self-sacrifice as the only possible way to preserve an important state secret. One could doubtlessly add many other examples of killing and taking one's own life under the presuppositions of other cultures. In the area of medical and biological capabilities, I have heard of justified interventions or "noninterventions" in terrible prenatal and neonatal situations. They were done in good faith by both religious and humanist doctors. Many theologians would not dare speak against those deciding in such situations.

Not only in the past has active euthanasia been practiced; it has become a "fashionable" problem openly discussed in our time. Not a few theologians have treated the problem openly, but usually very briefly. They see and lament a lack of human and Christian readiness to endure the process of dying, including suffering and pain. Rather than a concern with extreme cases in which it is doubtful whether God's will and human reason demand a prolonged death, they consider the human person with his dignity as an end in itself and see him as the "Other" created as the partner of the Creator and as the beloved in the covenant between God and man, who may under certain circumstances responsibly and actively determine the treatment needed in the remaining time of life, and correspondingly the duration of the approaching death. They hold that this is not an unjustified escape from suffering, nor a withdrawal from the full development of one's own possibilities in life, nor an unjustified autonomy vis-à-vis the plans of the God of creation and covenant. I could offer a list of well-known specialists in ethics and moral theology[32] for further consideration, but let this account suffice.

As has been explained, it is not my task in this essay to pass judgment on the disposing of human life. It has, nevertheless, been part of my task to draw attention to the concrete behavior of conscientious Christians in the light of their reflection on their faith. Likewise, it belongs to my task now to point to the theological justification that one believes justifies, by way of exception, a behavior in difficult situations of conflict that while departing from the universally normative formulation of the nondisposability of human life, does not diminish the respect that is commanded by the norm. It is now possible to reflect theologically on these justifications. I refer, broadly, to three such attempts at justification.

The first attempt is typical for many Protestant theologians. They uphold the absoluteness of the will of God, which admits of no exception. This will states: no human disposing of human life! To do so would contradict the sovereignty of the Creator. It would contradict the call of the God of the covenant, who alone determines the duration and circumstances of the concrete relationship between God and man in the covenant. According to some theologians, it would also contradict the God of creation as he is the ultimate foundation of any natural law.[33] Because the particular world in which we live, however, is marked by sin, they believe that it is possible to be in a conflict situation whose solution is judged to be too excessively demanding. One assumes that neither would God expect of the human person an overly demanding solution in these situations; hence, from the point of view of the human person, Christian love must override a kind of "natural law" and take on itself the corresponding guilt of disobedience of God's prohibition.[34] In such a situation of conflict, the act disposing of life would remain an act against God's commandment. God himself, however, and only he, could justify the human person in such a situation, or even command him despite the prohibition to do what is necessitated by our sinful world. Thus the agent (or sinner) would be justified by God, though not the act.

What are my difficulties with this attempt at a solution? First, I find excessively uncritical the assertion that is made of an absolute divine prohibition, admitting of no exceptions, against any disposing of human life; it is an assertion that is established neither in faith nor in human self-reflection. This applies both to the cases of the traditional so-called "divine delegation" in the death penalty, self-defense, and the just war, and also to special cases like that of Jan Palach or of one who bears a secret, or, finally, to the cases of euthanasia. Second, if one understands such "commands" or "norms" critically and not in this absolute and universally valid fashion, then the difficult distinction between the justification of the act and the justification of the agent becomes superfluous. Ultimately, we must arrive at the acceptance of a God-given justification or indeed of a divine commandment to act, appropriate to the necessities of the world that actually exists, by means of a process of human judgment in faith and in grace — not in accordance with an allegedly absolute prohibition. I understand this, however, to be simply the human discovery of the correct ordering of behavior, including the limits that are proper to this ordering — a human discovery which naturally is made in the light of faith and in the grace of the Spirit.

I encounter occasionally in Catholic theologians a second attempt at a solution of the situations of conflict.[35] In this view, it is presumed that in particular difficult cases absolute ethical norms of behavior come into conflict with each other. The Christian would, therefore, be condemned to do something morally incorrect (wrong) in order to be able to do something morally correct (right). In such a dilemma it would be the duty of the individual to discover which of the two demands of moral correctness (rightness) he must choose as the realization of what he judged to be most important. In this view toward a solution one cannot speak — unlike the case of the Protestant attempt — of an offense against the moral goodness of the person, because it is not a case of assuming guilt in the sense of personal morality, but of a readiness to make the free decision to do something that is morally incorrect (wrong), something that is understood to be forbidden by God. These considerations were frequently brought forward a few years ago in view of the problematic of *Humanae vitae*, [36] but they are also now heard, for example, in the area of euthanasia.

Already in the discussion about *Humanae vitae* it was pointed out that one would come nearer to the truth by speaking not of the conflict of ethical norms of behavior but of the conflict of human, not absolute, values or goods.[37] Such a conflict could be resolved by preferring the higher or more urgent good or value, and could lead in the concrete situation to the discovery of the single morally correct act as a moral demand. If, however, one remains with the formulation "conflict of norms" or "conflict of obligations," then I would point out that norms of correct behavior are discerned and formulated in a human manner (though also in the light of faith and in the power of the grace of the Spirit), so that an apparent case of conflict could demonstrate that our formulation has not been entirely successful, i.e., we have not observed certain inherent limitations to our inadequate statement of the norm. Paul shows in the First Letter to the Corinthians that such cases of conflict are possible, and shows how they can be resolved[38] with his decision concerning the so-called Pauline privilege. It could at first sight astonish us, coming as it does so closely after his allusion to Jesus' words about faithfulness in marriage.

The third attempt at a solution of conflict situations, which can certainly be maintained theologically and philosophically, has already been sufficiently indicated through the reference to my difficulties about the first and second attempts at a solution. This attempt knows neither the assumption of guilt nor behavior that is against moral correctness (rightness). This attempt does not specify in what cases it could *de facto* justify the disposing of human life, but that, again, is a question which arises outside the limits of this essay.

(c) *Attitudes of faith.* Although one cannot adequately justify or make comprehensible the nondisposability of human life specifically on the basis of the Christian faith, one's faith does not therefore remain simply without significance for the behavior of Christians. I have already spoken of a dynamic and converging power which does not merely draw attention maieutically to good human behavior vis-à-vis human life and death, but makes such behavior understandable as specifically congruent with the Christian faith.

On this basis one could see much of the behavior of Christians vis-à-vis human life and death as an expressive behavior. In it the simple acceptance of death and of the painful dying process is not the expression of a certain kind of fatalism; it is rather a gesture of thanksgiving for the gift of life and its giver. Such a Christian attitude makes possible or less burdensome a humble endurance in the process of dying. Such a quality becomes the expression of the relationship of the Christian to his Lord, who was not merely compelled to endure his suffering and death, but rather, despite his spontaneous unwillingness, was ready to endure it. In such a death there comes to expression at the same time the faith and the confident hope in the passage that permitted Jesus' death to become a dying into the resurrection.

In any case, it is clear that the Christians' attitudes of faith give a way of facing death that is not possible to the atheist or the agnostic humanist. The images of God from other religious communities, different from the Christian image of God, likewise determine a different behavior, or at least a different expressive behavior, when compared with the attitude of the believing Christian.

Moreover, we should not overlook the following: whoever as a Christian sees as justified an intervention or the omission of an act in an apparent conflict situation and behaves accordingly, can and must do so in such a way that his necessary death does not give up a Christian expressive behavior nor withdraw from a death with Christ, whose death was carried out in precisely the same way. This is the case for him just as much as for one who in the end consciously rejects the application of "disproportionate means" by artificial life support and so goes to his death.

The problem of Christian expressive behavior is different in cases where pain or weakness simply do not permit the realization of such an attitude. This problem becomes extreme when someone lies in a certainly irreversible coma. The question of an expressive behavior can only be addressed in such circumstances to those who care for the dying person. If one gives a positive answer in such situations to the controversial question of whether the justified act of letting a person die and active euthanasia are to be judged as equivalent and therefore morally similar,[39] one must still bear in mind that the justified act of letting a person die, as an expressive attitude, stands nearer to an attitude expressing respect vis-à-vis human life than does an active intervention.

One final remark on the theme of the attitudes of faith: in the cases of many Christians, another motive other than the attitudes of faith already named is at work in the humble and courageous endurance of a difficult process of dying, that is, many will be motivated by a sense of obedience, a willingness to go to the ultimate in the face of what a Christian proclamation has consistently emphasized as the unconditional will of God: no disposing of human life! The absoluteness, "in every case," of this proclamation, as has been said, will today sometimes have its validity questioned; when this happens, one would come again to the attitudes of faith which have been set out above, with their capacity to determine the expressive behavior of Christians.

(d) *Faith, fundamental experience, philosophy.* The faith of the Christian will not give him an unambiguous ethics with respect to the disposing or nondisposing of human life, but it will give him maieutic hints and empower him to determine particular attitudes of faith and corresponding expressive behavior.

Other images of God in other religions — for example, that of Islam or of Buddhism (insofar as this is theistic) — determine in part their own attitudes of faith and a corresponding ethical expressive behavior. This is equally true, if not indeed more so, in the case of the images of the human person held by atheistic or agnostic humanisms.

This does not mean that Christians and non-Christians, in the course of formulating and determining images of God and man, cannot have a deep fundamental experience of the dignity of human life and of its character as gift, or better, we should rather say that they in fact do. A certain ethical fundamental experience corresponds to such a fundamental experience. Such experiences can be richer than formulated convictions and systems, and can indeed stand in contra-distinction to these, at least in part, to the extent that the categorial and philosophical reflections are one-sided or false.

Therefore, the Christian faith gives birth to particular attitudes with-out determining an unambiguous ethics concerning the disposing of human life. Many Catholic theologians set a question mark over the philosophical reflections and arguments in this question. The con-junction of a Christian reflection on faith, of philosophical thinking, and of an original moral experience has developed a particular ethics in the Catholic church; it is one which goes into detail and tends to take itself rather absolutely, mediating not evident but concrete and often very useful orientations. When one maintains particular norms of behavior out of conviction, he believes himself to have moral certainty for the corresponding justificatory reasons; more is not possible. Nevertheless, differences of opinion on individual questions are possible within the church's fellowship. Indeed, we know such differences. The statements of the church's magisterium can be very helpful here; however, they too are no "moral dogma."

NOTES

1 Thomas Aquinas, *Sum. theol.* 2–2, 65, 5; cf. 1–2, 94, 2.

2 Pius XII, "Trois questions religieuses et morales concernant l'analgésie," *AAS* 49 (1957), 127 f. and 146.

3 E. Schillebeeckx, *Christ: The Experience of Jesus As Lord* (New York: Seabury, 1980) 590 f.

4 H. Thielicke, *Wer darf sterben? Grenzfragen der modernen Medizin* (Freiburg: Herder, 1979) 82.

5 G. Ebeling, *The Study of Theology* (Philadelphia: Fortress, 1978), 65.

6 P. Tillich, "Biblische Religion und die Frage nach dem Sein," in *Die Frage nach dem Unbedingten* (Gesammelte Werke 5; Stuttgart: Evangelisches Bibelwerk, 1964), 141 f.

7 E. Schillebeeckx, "Glaube und Moral," in *Ethik im Kontext des Glaubens*, ed. D. Mieth and F. Compagnoni (Freiburg: Herder, 1978), 17–45, at 29–31.

8 K. Rahner, *Praxis des Glaubens: Geistliches Lesebuch*, ed. K. Lehmann and A. Raffelt (Freiburg: Herder, 1982), 139; ET, *The Practice of Faith: A Handbook of Contemporary Spirituality* (New York: Crossroads, 1983).

9 Ibid.

10 A. Auer, "Die Unverfugbarkeit den Lebens und das Recht auf einen naturlichen Tod," in *Zwischen Heilauftrag und Sterbehilfe*, ed. A. Auer, A. Menzel, and A. Eser (Cologne: Heymann, 1977), 1–51, at 18.

11 A. Keller, "Lebensqualitat," *Stimmen der Zeit* 202 (1984), 33 f.

12 Cf. E. Jungel, *Death: The Riddle and the Mystery* (Philadelphia: Westminster, 1974), passim; Thielicke, see note 4 above; on the concept of *Glaubenssinn*, K. Rahner,

"The Problem of Genetic Manipulation," *Theological Investigations* 9 (New York: Herder and Herder, 1972), 225–52 esp. 238–45; on Christian inspiration and universalibility, Schillebeeckx, see note 3 above.

13 Cf. Vatican II, *Gaudium et Spes*, no. 46.

14 D. Bonheoffer, *Ethics*, ed. E Bethge (London: SCM, 1959), 209 f.

15 K. Barth, passim, quoted in U. Eibach, *Recht auf Leben − Recht auf Sterben: Anthropologische Grundlegung einer medizinischen Ethik* (Wuppertal: Brockhaus, 1974), 123–279. See also Eibach's *Medizin und Menschenwurde: Ethische Probleme in der Medizin aus christlicher Sicht* (Wuppertal: Brockhaus, 1976), 276.

16 See especially Eibach, *Medizin*.

17 See, e.g., Auer, "Die Unverfugbarkeit des Lebens" 20.

18 See, e.g., Jungel, *Death* 168, and Thielicke, *Wer darf sterben?* 82.

19 See, e.g., Eibach, *Recht auf Leben* 177, 204, 232.

20 See J. Fuchs, "Das Gottesbild und die Moral innerweltlichen Handelns," *Stimmen der Zeit* 202 (1984), 363–82, esp. 374 ff.

21 Cf., e.g., H. Schüngel-Straumann, *Der Dekalog − Gottes Gebot?* (Stuttgart: Katholisches Bibelwerk, 1973); F. L. Hossfeld, *Der Dekalog: Seine spatere Fassungen, die originale Komposition und seine Vorstufen* (Gottingen: Vandenhoeck & Ruprecht, 1982).

22 One could be tempted to have recourse to one or other text of the Bible to use in theological reflection. For example, it is related at the end of the First Book of Samuel (1 Sam 31:1–6) that Saul, badly wounded, asked his armor-bearer to kill him. Out of fear, the armor-bearer refused, and Saul killed himself with his own sword. In a different version at the beginning of the Second Book of Samuel (2 Sam 1:1–16), an Amalekite from Saul's camp confesses to David (perhaps lying, in the hope of gaining favor) that he acceded to Saul's request and slew him; David has the Amalekite executed for his action. But note that the explicit reason for the punishment is that the person killed by the Amalekite was Saul, the anointed king; neither the killing as such nor the request of Saul is censured.

23 See Fuchs, "Das Gottesbild," passim.

24 Cf. B. Weismahr, *Gottes Wirken in der Welt: Ein Diskussionsbeitrag zur Frage der Evolution und des Wunders* (Frankfurt: Knecht, 1973).

25 Rahner, *Praxis des Glaubens*, 224.

26 Is Jesus' behavior a command for all? See the question in G. Virt, "Sterben auf Verlangen," *Theologisch-Praktische Quartalschrift* 125 (1977), 129–43, at 136 f. On the whole topic, see also G. Greshake, "Bemuhungen um eine Theologie des Sterbens," in *Euthanasie oder Soll man auf Verlangen toten?* ed. V. Eid (Mainz: Matthias-Grunewald, 1975), 170–84.

27 So. O. Pesch, quoted by Virt, "Sterben" 137.

28 Rom 6:23.

29 Rom 14:8.

30 Rom 8:38f.

31 Phil 1:21.

32 Examples of those who would not absolutely exclude active euthanasia in borderline cases: P. Sporken, *Darf die Medizin, was sie kann?* (Dusseldorf: 1971), 36 f.; idem, "Euthanasie im Rahmen der Lebens- und Sterbehilfe," in *Suizid und Euthanasie als human- und sozialwissenschaftliches Problem*, ed. A. Eser (Stuttgart: Enke, 1976), 271–84; Auer, see note 10 above; J.F. Dedek, *Human Life: Some Moral Issues* (New York: Sheed & Ward, 1972), 130; very cautiously, Eid (see note 26 above), 89 f.; E. Drewermann, "Vom Problem des Selbstmords oder Von einer letzten Gnade der Natur," *Studia moralia* 21 (1983), 313–78, and 22 (1984), 17–54; H. van Oyen, "Grenzfalle in der medizinischen Ethik," *Zeitschrift für evangelische Ethik* 4 (1960), 139 ff.; Eibach, *Medizin und Menschenwurde* 203 f.; J. Wunderli, *Euthanasie oder die*

Wurde des Sterbens (Stuttgart: 1974), 156, 163 (174: "Seen from the doctor's viewpoint, euthanasia is lived, deep communication with the dying Thou of the patient"); see also the contribution of F.S. Cahill, J.P. Jossua, and A. Kuitert in the recent issue 3 of *Concilium* (1985). Here I should mention as well those who in certain circumstances make no ethical distinction between letting a person die and killing: cf. J.F. Keenan, "Toten oder Sterbenlassen?" *Stimmen der Zeit* 201 (1983), 825–37, with bibliography there (G. Hughes, J. Rachels, R. Ginters); also J. Fuchs, "Verfugen uber menschliches Leben? Fragen heutiger Bioethik," ibid, 203 (1985), 75–86, at 78 ff.

33 Especially Eibach, *Medizin und Menschenwurde.*

34 Cf. Eibach, ibid, 243 f., following in this Bonhoeffer, *Ethics,* 255 ff. Unlike Eibach, Wunderli sees the duty of love to be in contradiction here to the "natural law" (*Euthanasie* 156).

35 This question is formulated most clearly by Auer, see note 10 above.

36 On this see J. Fuchs, " 'Sünde der Welt' und normative Moral," in *Anspruch der Wirklichkeit und christlicher Glaube: Probleme und Wege theologischer Ethik heute,* ed. H. Weber and D. Mieth (Dusseldorf: Patmos, 1980), 135–54.

37 See, e.g., C. Robert, "La situation de 'conflit': Un thème dangereux de la théologie morale aujourd'hui," *Revue des sciences religieuses* 44 (1970), 190–213; J.–M. Aubert. "Hiérarchie des valeurs et histoire," ibid, 5–22.

38 1 Cor 7:12 ff.

39 Cf. Keenan, see note 32 above.

VI. Early Christianity in Search of a Christian Morality: 1 Cor 7

A Christian life corresponds to becoming and being a Christian. In this respect, early Christianity was found first of all in the word and way of life of Jesus and second in the tradition of the Old Testament, the latter being read in a hermeneutic corresponding to Jesus' position vis-à-vis the Old Testament. For Christians who came from paganism, their own traditions could create particular problems.

The question of how the early Christians slowly found a path to "their" morality must interest us as Christians of today. Without doubt, their teachers — the apostles and their helpers — were a strong conditioning force in this process, since they counted as an authority in questions concerning a lifestyle that accorded with being a Christian. In what follows, this will be demonstrated by means of one example, 1 Cor 7. How does the apostle Paul set about showing the young Christians in Corinth a way that leads to the solution of their moral questions? All the questions dealt with in 1 Cor 7 have to do with the problematic of marriage and virginity; but that is not what interests us here. Our question, rather, is formal and fundamental: how does Paul try to find moral solutions and make them comprehensible to the new Christians of Corinth? This must become clear in the treatment of the material-ethical questions about marriage and virginity.[1] We must always bear in mind that, in answering these questions, Paul is writing to new Christians in the largely pagan Corinth. The theme of "new Christians" makes its presence felt everywhere. It is the experience of newness, the new awareness that "You belong to Christ, and Christ belongs to God" (1 Cor 3, 23), that makes many Christians pose questions, and makes Paul reply.

A reading of 1 Cor 7 that looks at the questions that are of interest here (part A) will be followed by a modern reflection on questions of fundamental moral theology that can arise from a reading of 1 Cor 7 (second part B).

A. 1 COR 7

The new Christians in Corinth who have written to the apostle, or of whom he has heard, are of various kinds. Perhaps they are all enthusiasts, though in various ways. Some hold that because they are redeemed through baptism, or because of the law of freedom which Paul has proclaimed to them, they are free from further obligations: everything is "allowed" (1 Cor 6,12; cf. 1 Cor 10,23; Rom 6,1). Others, however, seem to accept in a rather spiritualizing fashion that the new belonging to Christ implies abstaining not only from sin, but also from normal human conduct (e.g., in marriage; 1 Cor 7,1). Paul shows the latter what matters really and "above all." The question is treated by Paul fundamentally in verses 17–24, and then further in his response to individual questions of the Christians of Corinth regarding problems of marriage (verses 1–16) and of marriage and virginity (verses 25–40).

1. What Matters: "Belonging to the Lord" (1 Cor 7, 17–24)

(a) *What matters "above all"*. If some Christians in Corinth believed that those who had become Christians and now belonged to Christ should change their normal lifestyle, Paul answers — three times: "For the rest, each one should live the life which the Lord has assigned to him, and in which God has called him. This is my rule in all the churches" (v. 17; cf. 20, 24). This means: such things are relatively unimportant vis-à-vis belonging to Christ. One who believes that, as a Christian, he must alter his lifestyle, has not yet grasped that it is belonging to Christ that matters, and that in comparison to this, any particular lifestyle is simply not important.

A first example is the question of circumcision, which was such an essential question for the Jewish past. Paul decides: "Neither circumcision counts for anything, nor uncircumcision" (19). This ritual question from the Old Testament has no significance for belonging to Christ. On the other hand, Paul adds immediately that there are other things which are absolutely essential for the life of the Christian, e.g., "keeping the commandments of God." Presumably, Paul is thinking of the commandments of the Decalogue, which he holds to be God's commandments, unlike the ritual ordering of circumcision.

A second example is the question of slaves. "Were you a slave when you were called (to Christianity)? Never mind. But if you can gain your freedom, make use of your present condition instead" (21; a less probable reading says, "avail yourself of the opportunity to become free"). The question of the injustice of slavery seems to Paul irrelevant for the social system of that time, and hence he says now: what matters is belonging to Christ, and not whether one is free or slave. Paul seeks to give a deeper reason for this (22–24): the slave who has become a Christian is "a freedman of the Lord" (i.e., free from every form of dominion that is opposed to belonging to Christ), "the Christian freedman is a slave of Christ." Of both it is true that "You were bought with a high price," and therefore: "Do not make yourselves slaves of men (living in a pagan manner)," be slaves of Christ!

(b) *What is "also" important.* Belonging to Christ matters "above all"; it is important to attach "also" to what follows from belonging to Christ with its freedom from everything that is improper. Paul counts among the things that "also" matter, among others, faithfulness to the "commandments of God" (19), the "commandment of the Lord" which he mentions in the case of marital fidelity (10), but also remaining free from those vices which Paul condemns with the catalogues of the Hellenistic popular philosophers: "Do you not know that the unrighteous will not inherit the kingdom of God? Do not be deceived: neither fornicators nor idolators, nor adulterers, nor boy-prostitutes *(malakoi)*, nor pederasts, nor thieves, nor the greedy, nor drunkards, nor revilers, nor robbers will inherit the kingdom of God" (1 Cor 6,9–11). In short, everything that contradicts the "freedom" which Christ has won for us (23; cf. 1 Cor 6,12) is also important for the Christian. And everyone who belongs to Christ will seek to understand the "Spirit," in order to follow him (40).

(c) *Christocentrism and theocentrism.* A strong christocentrism dominates the whole of the seventh chapter of 1 Corinthians; it is belonging to Christ that matters; Christ is the "Lord." But in this perspective we may not forget the words of 1 Cor 3,23 which have already been quoted: "... you belong to Christ, and Christ belongs to God." With this, we must compare other formulations of chapter 7: it is "God" who has called the new Christians (17), the commandments of the Decalogue are understood as "God's commandments" (19), each one is to remain in his lifestyle "before God" (24).

(d) *What matters: marriage, celibate life, virginity?* The problem of a change of lifestyle, treated in depth in verses 17–24, also seems to be the fundamental problem of those parts of the first letter to the Corinthians which deal with the Corinthians' questions about marriage and virginity. What matters above all is belonging to Christ; compared to this, even marriage and virginity are basically matters of only relative importance. The new Christians as such are called neither to celibacy nor to the task of living in the community of marriage. If practical questions in this perspective occur in Corinth, Paul only asks himself how the Christian vocation can be lived more securely and intensely. It is in accordance with this criterion that he makes requirements or gives advice, replies, and instructions.

2. "Belonging to the Lord" — Marriage (1 Cor 7,1–16)

(a) *Married life (1–9).* It seems that spiritualizing new Christians had written in their letter to Paul: "It is well for a man not to touch a woman" (1). They lived with the opinion that whoever now belonged to Christ must change his lifestyle. This could mean that Christians should not marry. But the context suggests a different understanding: whoever belongs to Christ, although married, should live in abstinence. Paul himself is very much inclined to the ideal of an abstinent life (7f); but even such a choice has only a relative value, because what matters above all is belonging to Christ, with all its consequences. Paul fears that this may be endangered in the case of the spiritualizing enthusiasts in Corinth. Therefore he warns: "Because of the danger of fornication; each man should have his own wife, and each woman her own husband ... Do not refuse one another except perhaps by agreement for a season, that you may devote yourselves to prayer; but then come together again, lest Satan tempt you through lack of self-control" (2,5).

This reflection could give the impression that Paul sees only the danger of fornication in the attempt at a life of abstinence endangering true adherence to Christ on the part of his new Christians in Corinth. But this is not so; he does not look on marriage only as a help against fornication. He points out that the marriage partners have mutual marital obligations, and that the individual may not dispose alone and arbitrarily of his "body" (*soma* = person), i.e., of himself (3f.). The failure to observe these interpersonal relationships would stand in contradiction to belonging to Christ. Paul warns the spiritualizing enthusiasts of Corinth on this point too.

Paul adds a limiting clause to his warning against the danger of the new Christians who wish to live in abstinence: "I say this as a concession, not as a command" (6), and he says this so that they may know in Corinth which lifestyle he prefers: "I wish that all were (unmarried) as I am. But each has his own special gift from God, one of one kind and one of another" (7). The exegesis of this text is not wholly certain. The phrase about the "concession" must in context refer less to the virginity which Paul recommends (and of which he speaks in verses 25–40) than to abstinence from "touching a woman."

Verse 6 has acquired a "notorious fame" with unforeseeable consequences, because of an arbitrary interpretation by St. Augustine. The great church Father read "I say this as a concession" in Latin as *per veniam* or *per indulgentiam*, and interpreted it to mean that where *venia/indulgentia* — understood by him not as "concession," but as "forgiveness" — is required, sin must exist. It follows that, when married people come together in order to escape the danger of fornication, rather than because of procreation — which was for Augustine the only aim of marital union — there necessarily exists (at least venial) sin. This understanding of St. Augustine determined the Christian teaching on marriage for many centuries. It gave relatively few married people the chance to belong wholly to the Lord.

After the "concession," Paul returns to his ideal and recommends it: "I say to the unmarried [perhaps better in context: *agamoi* = the new Christians who lead their married life in abstinence] and to the widows: it is good if they remain as I am" (8). The apostle sees — his personal evaluation, for which he gives no further reasons — a greater degree of coherence in belonging to the Lord in abstinence than in non-abstinence. But the presupposition, for the sake of sinless fidelity to adherence to Christ, is that "they can exercise self-control"; otherwise "they should marry. It is better to marry than to be aflame with passion" (9).

(b) *Separation, divorce, remarriage (10–16).* Up to this point, Paul as apostolic teacher has briefly shown the new Christians in Corinth what is important "above all" and what is "also" important, in order to use this as a measurement to relativize everything else, and to give, in accordance with this, good advice that can show a path which can be taken by Christians faced with the questions that are addressed to him. New elements now come in the further treatment of questions concerning marriage; but Paul no longer speaks only in the first person.

Not all marriages in Corinth were successful. What should one do then? "The wife should not separate from her husband . . . the husband should not divorce his wife" (10f). Paul observes that this solution is a commandment and comes not from himself, Paul, but from the Lord (10). If, in other questions, Paul himself argues or seeks to persuade his partners in dialogue, here the final instance is a word of Jesus that is known to him; since it is Jesus' commandment, it says the truth about conduct in unsuccessful marriages. Between the two sayings of Jesus addressed to the husband and wife, Paul (as the exegetes largely hold) adds an interpretation of Jesus' words. The interpretation of Jesus' words absolutely had to take place in the community; Jesus' words are by themselves, insufficient in the diverse circumstances of life. Perhaps it is an interpretation by Paul, perhaps a community rule of Corinth that Paul here adduces. The rule says: if — despite the words of Jesus — the woman separates, "let her remain single, or else be reconciled to her husband again" (11); remarriage would indeed exclude in practice any reconciliation of the two partners. Even in the irregular situation that exists in such a case — contrary to the words of Jesus — life must continue, and hence Paul and the community must find a defensible solution.

Paul likewise gives an interpretation of Jesus' word for a similar case in the Corinthian community: but because of a certain difference from the case that he has just handled, he believes that the words of Jesus cannot be applied in this case — Paul therefore does not understand Jesus' words legalistically. For this reason he explicitly emphasizes: "To the rest I say, not the Lord" (12). Paul knows that he is capable of discovering solutions for right conduct that are materially reasonable and correspond to the Spirit of Christ. In this second case, it is not a matter of a marriage between two Christians, but (it seems) an originally pagan marriage in which one of the partners has converted and hence now belongs to Christ, while the other partner remains a pagan. The apostle's decision is that, if the two partners in the marriage are able to live *peaceably* with each other, they should not separate (12f.), but if the pagan partner does not wish this, then the Christian partner should pose no opposition if the pagan partner wishes to leave (15). Paul undertakes here a teleological evaluation of goods: there is no way to reconcile with each other marital unity and fidelity lived fully, on the one hand, and the Christian partner's unhindered belonging to Christ, on the other hand; and the latter of the two values appears to the apostle to be the more significant. He believes that this solution can be defended before God, for God has called the Christian partner to peace, not to "slavery," as most exegetes interpret (15), and a continuation of life together would not in any case lead to the hope of a good outcome (16). (N.B. Paul speaks here of divorce. The Latin Church understands the possibility suggested by Paul also as the possibility of remarriage. It is difficult to say whether Paul meant not remarrying because of the ideal of abstinence, or remarrying because "it is better to marry than to be aflame with passion.")

3. "Belonging to the Lord" – Marriage and Virginity (1 Cor 7,25–40)

(a) *The virgins (25–35).* In the first part of chapter 7, the problem was the saying from Corinth, "It is good for a man not to touch a woman" (1); there is a different problem, that of marriage and virginity, in the part that begins with verse 25. Paul remains true to his fundamental principle that it is not appropriate to change one's state of life because of the new belonging to Christ: "Are you bound to a wife? Do not seek to be free. Are you free from a wife? Do not seek marriage" (27). The second half of this verse is basically already a plea for a life without marriage, and is as little a consequence of the fundamental principle as is the recommendation in the first part of the chapter "not to touch a woman." Paul explicitly says that he is here only giving advice. His concern in this is the richest and intensest adherence to Christ possible on the part of his new Christians. He explains this in detail: "in view of the impending distress it is well . . . to be so" (26), but whoever marries "will not escape earthly troubles, and I wish to spare you that" (28).

What are the troubles and "cares" of the married, from which Paul wants to know that his Christians are free (32)? Quite simply, the claims made by living together in marriage: the married must take care "to please" one another, and in general they must be taken up with "the things of this world" (33,35). Therefore, the apostle fears that the married will be excessively "divided" between the cares of marriage and care "for the affairs of the Lord, to be holy in body and spirit" (34), so that they can "always serve the Lord in the right way, undisturbed" (35). But, as in the case of sexual abstinence in the first part of the chapter, here too in the case of unmarried life Paul counsels caution: one should follow his recommendation (cf. verse 37) only if "one is under no necessity, but has one's desire under control."

Paul gives his advice, as he says, "because of the impending distress" (26). What is the impending distress? It could mean the necessary concentration on belonging to Christ in a pagan world — a theme that is more or less valid in all ages. But many exegetes, with good reason, believe that Paul is thinking here of an imminent eschatological return of the Lord. This can be suggested by Paul's warning: "For I tell you, brothers, the time is short" (29).

After these words, the apostle generalizes and strengthens his warning: "Therefore let those who have wives now live as though they had none, and those who mourn as though they were not mourning, and those who rejoice as though they were not rejoicing, and those who buy as though they had no goods, and those who deal with the world as though they had no dealings with it" (29–31). There follows again the appeal that motivates this: "For the form of this world is passing away" (31). This formulation can refer to the universal reality of the world, but it has its own especially urgent meaning if Paul is thinking of the near eschatological end. In any case, there takes place here an enormous relativization of earthly values over against the one thing that matters "above all," belonging to Christ: marriage is a relative value, as also is virginity, the lack of the use of this world is only a relative value, as is also the use of it; hence the repeated emphasis on the fact that he (Paul) is only giving advice, hence also his "as though" in the appeal that strengthens and generalizes his advice. The chief concern of the apostle is inner freedom and also the greatest possible external freedom to "belong to the Lord" in the situation that is thus described.

In his treatment of the problem of "marriage and single life," Paul gives a teaching that justifies marriage and at the same time, in an urgent manner, the advice to remain single for the sake of an undivided and undisturbed service of the Lord. He insists that this is only advice, emphasizing that he cannot appeal to a command of the Lord to back up this advice — i.e., it is only the advice of Paul, who, however, as an apostle, is one "who by the Lord's mercy is trustworthy" (25): not less, but also not more.

(b) *The engaged and widows (36–40)*. There is a dispute about the addressees of verses 36–38. Many exegetes today suppose that Paul wanted to give advice to Christians who were engaged. His reply is the same as to the virgins: "He who marries his virgin does well, and he who refrains from marriage will do better" (38).

Paul gives the Christian widow (39f.) the same charge he has given the virgins and the engaged, but adds that if she wishes to marry again, she can do so, "but only in the Lord" (39). The last remark could mean that the Christian woman should marry a Christian man; that would show how important belonging to Christ is for Paul in his reflections on conduct in the world. His advice, however, is to remain unmarried; though it is only "my advice." But he holds this advice to be significant: here too, similarly to verse 25, he adds: "And I think that I have the Spirit of God" (40) — thus it is not only the somewhat puffed-up letter-writers in Corinth who have the Spirit, but also not Paul alone, though he has the Spirit as an apostle.

4. "Belonging to the Lord" – Fornication and Christian Freedom (1Cor 6,12–20)

(a) *"Everything is allowed me — but not everything helps me."* The immediately preceding verses (12–20) of chapter 6 offer a certain parallel to Chapter 7. Here, too, the first saying, "Everything is allowed me," seems to come from the oversimple Christians in Corinth, who think that the Christian freedom attained in baptism makes everything permissible for them. They wish above all to justify fornication *(porneia)* thereby. Paul takes up the saying about freedom permitting everything, and does not contradict it, but rather deepens it. In some sense everything is allowed for the Christian, everything belongs to him, everything is for his use: "but not everything helps me . . . nothing is to have power over me." This is the same idea as in chapter 7, emphasizing the freedom that makes it possible for us to belong to Christ. If it is once again Corinthian letter-writers who reply to defend fornication – "Food is for the body *(koilia)*, the body for food" (13) – Paul picks up this saying too, but deepens it as in the seventh chapter: "God will destroy both" (7,31: "the form of this world is passing away"). And he shows what really matters. In order to explain this, he chooses the Greek word *soma* for the body, a word that means both "body" and "person" (that acts through the body). Then he replies: "The body [in the sense of *soma* = person] is not for fornication but for the Lord, and the Lord for the body [as *soma* = person]" (13).

In a similar manner, in 1 Cor 10,23, regarding sacrificial meat of the pagans, Paul replies to the Corinthians saying, "Everything is allowed": "Everything is allowed — but not everything helps... not everything builds up." He uses the same kind of slogan when he addresses the divided parties of the Christians at Corinth: " ... everything belongs to you, whether Paul of Apollos or Cephas or the world or life or death or the present or the future: everything belongs to you, but you belong to Christ and Christ belongs to God" (1 Cor 3,21–23). Thus, as in 1 Cor 7, he has relativized everything and brought everything to the one thing that matters above all. He has explained the meaning of Christian freedom: truly everything is subjected to you, but use it in such a way that *you* can belong to Christ; there is no need to set forth in a codex what this means in the individual spheres of life, for that is nothing new.

(b) *Fornication.* It is not entirely clear what is meant by fornication *(porneia)* in this Pauline text. Many exegetes believe that it covers all irregular sexual relationships, while others refer it to stable irregular relationships (because, in the context, Paul speaks only of stable relationships), others again refer it to the cultic prostitution which was widespread in Corinth (because, in the context, Paul continuously makes use of cultic terminology).

Paul warns the new Christians of Corinth to stay away from fornication. Here he appeals to their belonging to Christ: first, the Christian who unites himself (with his body) to a prostitute should reflect that God has raised up the Lord (and that includes his body) and will also raise up us Christians (and also our bodies) (14). Second, the Christians should reflect on the fact that our bodies (body here is *soma* = person = "we") are members of Christ (15). How can we make the members of Christ members of a prostitute, for according to Gen 2,24, the two become one flesh (16)? "But he who unites himself to the Lord is one spirit [*pneuma* = person] with him" (17). Third, the Christians should not forget that the one who commits fornication sins against his own body (*soma* = person) (18). But now "your body [*soma* = person] is a temple of the Holy Spirit... who dwells in you, and whom you have from God" (19). It follows that "You do not belong to yourselves; for you were bought at a high price" (19f.); formulated positively: "So glorify God in your body [*soma* = person]" (20). Thus Paul has explained Christian freedom, vis-à-vis fornication too: everything belongs to you, but you belong to Christ, and Christ belongs to God.

(c) *Moral argumentation and moral paranesis.* The text quoted in 1 Cor 6,16, "The two shall become one flesh" (Gen 2,24), holds not only for union with a prostitute, but also for married people — and for these above all — insofar as they become one flesh in the union of their marriage. It is not therefore a man's becoming one with a woman, as such, that is opposed to the union of the Christian with Christ. This becoming one is a contradiction of union with Christ only when it is a becoming one that is not allowed; but the reason why it is not allowed does not come fundamentally out of the relationship to Christ, but out of the circumstances of such an act of becoming one. It is only this kind of unpermitted bodily becoming one with a woman that is opposed to spiritual becoming one with Christ. Paul does not, therefore, prove the impermissibility of fornication by his "Christian" arguments — he presupposes this impermissibility; if this were not so, then marital becoming one in the body would contradict being one with Christ in spirit. Paul also establishes moral norms by his argumentation in 1 Cor 7, but in 1 Cor 6,12–20 he only exhorts them (paranesis) to avoid as Christians what is in any case immoral. In this paranesis, however, he employs a specifically Christian motivation to show a specific unfittingness of fornication — the moral wrongness of which is presupposed — for Christians.

We have briefly alluded above to verses 9f., which precede verses 12–20. Here we should add that in this text too Paul does not establish moral norms by his argumentation; rather, he presupposes that the modes of conduct condemned as vices in this catalogue are truly contrary to morality. It is precisely for this reason that he warns the Christians against such vices and points out to them as Christians that whoever does such things cannot inherit the kingdom of God. In this "neighboring text" too, therefore, we have paranesis and not normative moral theology.

B. THEMES OF A CHRISTIAN FUNDAMENTAL MORAL THEOLOGY IN LINE WITH 1 COR 7

The reading of 1 Cor 7 was able to show by means of one example how early Christianity, and in particular the apostle Paul, went about the search for a right and practicable way of daily living as Christians, and how they arrived at concrete results. The insight into this process of seeking and finding could appropriately shed light on the process of seeking and finding a Christian way of life, with the themes implied in the process, under today's conditions, including theological and philosophical conditions.

1. The Call to Belong to Christ

(a) *What matters above all: "belonging to Christ."* Until recently, the central theme of Paul's direction on the Christian way of life was not strongly accentuated as the central theme of common Christian fundamental moral theology. Vatican II's directive in *Optatam totius* (no. 16) brought about a change here. Explicit importance is attached in this passage to the fact that, *above all*, the high vocation in Christ has to be the theme of moral theology, while it is also true that obligatory forms of living in this world arise out of this.

Paul's "belonging to the Lord" has the quite simple positive meaning that we belong to the Lord, we have been "ransomed" (at a high price) and in this sense are "slaves" of Christ; and as Christ belongs to God, so do we belong to God. As "those who belong to Christ," we have not lost ourselves, but have rather gained ourselves: "to belong to God" is our salvation. This is the great freedom of those who do not allow themselves to be dominated by anyone or anything, i.e. by anything that could stand in contradiction to "belonging to Christ." It is freedom for God's commandments, for the good life that is appropriate for the heirs of God's kingdom, for right social conduct, e.g., with respect to marriage, for everything that is "useful" and "builds up" and lets us be "one spirit with Christ," hence lets us have a life that, like his life, exists entirely and solely for God (cf. 1 Cor 3,23; Rom 6,10).

(b) *The function of Christian requirements.* The Council and 1 Cor 7 agree that belonging to Christ also determines definite concrete conduct in this world. It is likewise interesting that both documents agree that it is not obedience to what can be understood as God's or Christ's requirement that determines belonging to Christ; it is rather genuine "belonging to Christ" which of itself generates corresponding conduct. Right conduct is indeed also obedience, but it is less obedience than the *fruit* of belonging to Christ. The terminology of "fruit" (cf. Rom 6,22; Gal 5,22; Jn 15) is certainly more in keeping with the New Testament and more theological than the terminology of obedience.

The traditional theological teaching on "law and grace" is in keeping with this observation. This formulation conveys both the function of grace (of "belonging to Christ"), hence of all that constitutes the graced "interior" of the one who belongs to Christ, and also the function of law, i.e., of all that does not make up the graced "interior" of belonging to Christ, but comes to man from outside and makes requirements of him, and yet "also" matters: the "commandments," the book of the Bible, the church, the sacraments, etc. This famous theme, found in Paul and John and later handled with emphasis by Augustine and Thomas, tends to be treated today (after the Reformation), because of a slight displacement of emphasis, under the title "law and gospel" or "proclamation of the law and proclamation of the gospel."

2. What is "also" Important even if not "Above All".

(a) *Various models of what matters "above all"*. Alongside the model of belonging to Christ, there are other models in the New Testament, even in Paul, that aim at expressing what matters above all, e.g., "being reconciled to God" (2 Cor 5), "being buried and risen with Christ through baptism" (Rom 6), "being spiritual in the Spirit (rather than carnal)" (Rom 8), etc. These models too should be dealt with in moral theology. Here we shall not pay further attention to them but shall turn instead to what is "also" important and its relationship to what matters "above all."

(b) *The manifold requirements which "also" matter for the Christian*. One can attempt to determine whether someone truly "belongs to Christ" by means of signs that are the manifold fruits — i.e., the observance of the commandments, the avoidance of vices, the realization of what "is useful" and "builds up," protection against what should not have dominion over us, etc. To this extent, the fruits truly matter. Like belonging to Christ, they are absolute necessities, and yet they are necessary in a different way, as an "also" rather than as an "above all." They are related to each other; yet the things that are "also" necessary have an independent source of existence, and hence are also valid for non-Christians and are independent of what is "above all" necessary for the Christian.

What is the relationship between what is important "above all" and what is "also" important? Here we make two points. (a) In the context of belonging to Christ, the many things that are "also" necessary receive a deeper and richer meaning. Paul makes this very clear when he speaks to the Christians of Corinth about fornication. (b) The various things that are "also" required have their meaning for every human life, not only for Christians. We may ask whether the requirements that are "also" made would have a truly absolute meaning, if life in its entirety did not have a positive, definite and absolute future. The question also has a philosophical significance. Christian theology would say that, without Christ and belonging to him, there is no true, meaningful and absolute future for the human being as he in fact exists. Even the carrying-out of the things that are "also" required would be very partial and full of egotisms. So we can formulate as follows: without "belonging to Christ" as the absolute "above all," the things that are "also" absolute lack their final and full character as absolutes — a theme that is demanded by 1 Cor 7.

3. The Person that Belongs to Christ and His Acts

(a) *A necessary distinction.* The reading of 1 Cor 7 and the two themes
that have been set out above point to an important distinction in
Christian moral theology. Belonging to Christ, which matters "above
all," signifies that the Christian is a person by reason of his freedom
and his calling. What is "also" important are the many acts through
which the Christian — as one would expect — expresses and demons-
trates his belonging to Christ. The principal work of the philosopher
Karol Wojtyla (John Paul II) bears this distinction as its title: *The
Acting Person.*[2] The acts, therefore, as individual acts and in their entirety, are in themselves a sign of what the person is in his belonging to
Christ. Nevertheless, the person as such in his belonging to Christ
transcends both the signs as individual acts and also as an entirety.

Moreover, the categorial acts are signs of the personal reality only "in
themselves," hence presumptively; for acts can derive partly or wholly
from sources other than personal freedom.

(b) *The transcendent "morality" of the person of the Christian.* When
one does this or that particular thing in his various free acts, he clearly
reveals not only this or that particular thing, but also himself, himself
as a person in his entirety as subject; i.e., in the freedom that he *is* as
person, he transcends his deeds that have been carried out in categorial freedom. This self-realization of the person as such and as a
whole is also the free realization of the inmost free reality of the
person, hence also of his "belonging to Christ." It is also the realization
of what the person has already made of himself as a person — in his
past, together with his free orientation toward his future. "Belonging to
Christ" therefore qualifies and directs the self-realization of the
person with his past and his future.

(c) *The self-realization of the person and his deeds.* When it is a case of
the person *as a whole,* it is clear that free self-realization takes place,
not as a particular "categorial" act, but as the realization of the self in
different categorial acts. An act of faith, a religious act, an act of repen-
tance are also, as such, only categorial acts. The self-realization of the
one who belongs to Christ can penetrate such acts either through and
through or only superficially; the personal morality that characterizes
the acts lies ultimately in this penetration by the free belonging to
Christ. The acts are the fruit of the personal belonging to Christ that is
alive in them (and hence does not only precede them). The personal
belonging to Christ of the person and the free acts of the person are
therefore "a unity," but must be distinguished from one another.

The reflection presented here leads us to pose the following
questions: (a) What acts can be the fruit of belonging to Christ — acts

adjudicated by moral norms or the judgments of competent authorities (this seems to be the point the apostle Paul makes in his letter to the new Christians of Corinth), or such acts as are responsibly found to be right in the conscience of the individual Christian? (b) How can the individual acts be the expression of belonging to Christ on the part of the person who decides in freedom — very deeply, superficially, or even not at all? (c) The same questions occur in the case of the acts of one who closes himself as a person in freedom against belonging to Christ, i.e., in the case of the acts of the sinner.

(d) *Moral goodness and moral rightness — what matters "above all" and what "also" matters.* The apostle's distinction between what matters "above all" and what "also" matters corresponds not only to our customary distinction between person and act, but also to the distinction between moral goodness and moral rightness. Moral goodness can be predicated only of persons and their inner attitudes and decisions; they are what matter "above all." Paul understands personal goodness especially as free "belonging to the Lord," and this is likewise the characteristic tendency of Jesus when he speaks of conversion and the kingdom of God, and also in the Sermon on the Mount.

"Rightness" can be predicated of acts — i.e., whether they are in accord with the shaping of the horizontal reality of the human world as a human reality, or do not contradict it. One thinks here of the reality of individuals, of interpersonal relationships, of human groups and societies, and of the material world. This reality should be such as to serve the human person[3] and thus be in accordance with the will of the Creator. This is "also" important, even for the one who belongs to Christ; therefore, the "rightness" of the realization of the world, desired and sought by man, is always at the same time "moral" rightness. Its morality, however, is due ultimately not to itself but to the personal goodness of the one who seeks it. This is why Paul, along with the new Christians of Corinth, seeks how they should behave "rightly" — in respect to the rite of circumcision, in respect to conduct in marriage, in the realm of what is required by God's commandments and of what is rejected in the catalogues of vices. It is "rightness," understood thus, in the shaping of the human world that "also" matters, when one is "good" in belonging to Christ — the thing that matters "above all" for Paul.

In 1 Cor 7, Paul does not show that one who lacks moral goodness can under certain circumstances do what is right, and that, on the other hand, one who — belonging to Christ — is good can mistakenly do what is not right; he does this in the following eighth chapter, regarding the question of eating meat that has been sacrificed to idols (cf. also Rom 14).

(e) *Moral goodness as a question of salvation.* Active belonging to Christ, as moral goodness, is a "question of salvation." Salvation is the positive relationship between God and the personally good person. Questions of moral "rightness," on the other hand, as questions of the rightness of action, are fundamentally not questions of salvation; purely as such, they are questions of innerworldly rightness. But although questions of innerworldly rightness — i.e., more or less concrete norms and judgments of conduct — do not directly touch personal goodness and (according to Paul) active belonging to Christ, they are nonetheless very frequently termed, less precisely, questions of salvation: this is because moral goodness, or active belonging to Christ, cannot forget concern for the world of men that Christ loves and for the mission of creation. One who forgets this concern shows thereby that personal moral goodness, and correspondingly salvation, are not in him.

(f) *Salvation morality and social morality.* The morality of "what matters above all" is salvation morality; it is the morality of personal ethics. Personal morality does not mean individual morality. Personal morality deals with moral goodness; problems of individual morality, just like those of social morality, are concerned with the innerworldly rightness of human action. Both the individual and social morality of innerworldly behavior are moral questions only in an indirect sense, i.e., because of their relationship to personal goodness. To insist on the alternatives "personal morality"/"social morality," terming the first of these "privatistic," is to fail to see the distinction between person and individual; an alternative would be the distinction between "individual morality" and "social morality." Morality in the true sense always means personal morality, whether this is individual or social morality. Thus, in 1 Cor 7, Paul speaks primarily of personal morality — what matters "above all" — but does not forget many questions of individual and social morality — what also matters: giving up and making use of innerworldly goods, marriage and celibacy, marital fidelity and slavery. But in the background there stands for Paul what is supremely important to him: moral goodness as belonging to Christ, and thus salvation.

4. Presuppositions of Free Belonging to Christ and of its Categorial Realization

(a) *The conscience.* The moral endeavors of the early Christians in 1 Cor 7 imply presuppositions which are not explicitly stated by Paul in this chapter. The problem of conscience has first place.

An attempt was recently made to write a moral theology without dealing with the problem of "conscience." The explicit reason given for this was that the conscience was a psychological phenomenon and so must be left to psychology. However, the psychological problem of the conscience is also a problem of moral theology; for one who does not know the experience of conscience and thus of the problem of morality is unable to speak about morality, just as a blind man cannot speak about the distinction between various colors.

Paul knows the problem of conscience, and deals with it in various places, but not explicitly in 1 Cor 7; hence it can be present here only implicitly, and must be discussed as an implicit problem. The apostle presupposes that the new Christians in Corinth are aware of the moral justification and requirement of belonging to Christ; otherwise, their belonging to Christ, together with its ethical consequences, would have no ethical justification. This awareness must logically (though not necessarily chronologically) precede free acceptance of belonging to Christ; it is, however, quite possible, psychologically, that ethical judgment and the call of Christ occur simultaneously and that each makes the other possible; and this is because both realities are real at the same depth in the one person.

(b) *Metaethical, metaphysical and epistemological problems.* Apart from the problem of "conscience," other problems are present, though they are not directly expressed and remain implicit, in the moral-theological reflections of the apostle in 1 Cor 7: (a) Is there any sense at all in speaking of morality? (b) How can one explain the phenomenon of what is moral (of conscience)? (c) What are the criteria that permit us to make judgments about what is "good" and "right," and what is the source of these criteria?

5. Categorial Norms of Conduct of the Christian

(a) *The problematic of a normative morality of conduct.* The new Christians of Corinth, and Paul with them, display great interest in the question of which forms of conduct should be understood in practice as the "fruit" of "belonging to Christ." This is the question of the moral norms of conduct of the Christian.

A first criterion for the apostle and for the new Christians is the "commandments of God" (19). It is obvious that the apostle understands the words of the Decalogue to be such; today's problematic concerning the sense in which the ten words can be considered as God's commandments is unknown to Paul. But one thing is clear, according to Paul: where there is a revelation of God about morally right conduct, it is a case of right and hence obligatory requirements for the one who belongs to Christ.

Paul thinks in the same way in the case of a directive that goes back to Jesus as Lord (10f.). In the presence of this directive, there is no discussion; yet Paul does not believe that he must interpret it verbalistically or fundamentalistically or legalistically (13–16). Nor does he believe that such a logion cannot be open to adaptation for factual situations in the community with its various situations (11f.).

When the new Christians confront the apostle with problems for which he knows no commandment of God and no logion of the Lord, he believes that he himself can find a prudent and Christian answer. The answer is "Christian," inasmuch as he believes he is able to find a solution that is in line with the Spirit of Christ. He is sure that he as apostle, though not he alone, possesses this "Spirit." Thus he gives "his" directives and "his" counsels; Paul himself insists that he does not then have a word of Christ or of the Spirit to impart. In context, many Christians today ask themselves whether Paul did not speak one-sidedly when he expressed himself so clearly in favor of "not touching a woman" and "not marrying," whether he is not here too much influenced by the idea of the imminent eschatological return of the Lord. They wonder whether he is not inconsistent when on the one hand, he emphasizes the equality of rights and duties of the married partners while on the other hand, he is not disturbed by the unequal legal situation of free men and slaves. They wonder also whether in fact his requirement that one remain in the situation in which one was called to Christ must be seen as the moral will of God, or should be seen fundamentally only as a powerful sign that the calling to the Lord does not necessarily signify a change in social situation.

The apostle does not shrink from associating himself with the sincere moral catalogues of pagan philosophers, provided that he can discover no contradiction with the Spirit of Christ; he makes use of such catalogues (e.g., 1 Cor 6,9f.). He does not know the idea that Christians have a behavioral morality which is different from that of other sincere men. Even the "good" pagans do not want to be dominated by worthless men and by passions; fundamentally, they too know how to distinguish between good and evil, between right and wrong.

(b) *Consequences for a Christian normative morality of behavior today.* What can the search for categorial moral norms of behavior by the new Christians of Corinth, and above all by the apostle Paul in 1 Cor 7 teach us Christians of today?

Paul's undertaking shows clearly that one may not proceed in a verbalistic, fundamentalistic or legalistic manner when one appeals to the words of Jesus. One must try in all seriousness to understand both the context and the genuine meaning, the "truth" of his words (and actions). The directive of the Lord is never arbitrary; it is a "truth" and hence has its inner justification. This is precisely how Paul proceeds in 1 Cor 7,10–16.

How should one appeal to Paul himself in the formulation of an ethical morality of behavior, when he for his part appeals to the Spirit whom he (too) has received? It would certainly be false to take his directives and counsels as directives and counsels of Jesus or of his Spirit; Paul himself explicitly contradicts such a temptation. He insists that it is a matter of *his* help, not of a special revelation. It is, however, the case that the Bible is inspired; must one not, as happened once a few years ago, speak of an "inspired authority" *(forza ispiratrice)*? Must one then say that the inspiration of the Bible guarantees the truth of everything that Paul has written in the Bible, although he insists that it is a case of his personal reflections? What do the corresponding professional theologians say to this? In the meantime, we can be impressed by the very idea of the apostle who has his mission, who has received mercy from the Lord, who in a special way possesses "the Spirit of God" and therefore deserves our "trust" (1 Cor 7, 25–40).

And in general, what is the result of reading the Pauline text for our appeal back to the New Testament in our reflection on ethical norms of conduct? First of all, it is necessary to be clear about the true sense of the words, which in many cases cannot be achieved without taking historical circumstances into account. Paul's use of the word *porneia* (fornication) in 1 Cor 6 draws attention to this necessity: against what is he in fact warning the new Christians of Corinth? A few verses earlier (9f.), the *malakoi (molles)* are excluded from the kingdom of God. For centuries, the rejection of *mollities* was understood to mean the rejection of masturbation; today we know that this translation is false. (Even the Vatican document *Persona humana* of 1975 no longer adduces this text as an argument against masturbation.)

Is not Paul also perhaps occasionally indebted in his reflections to particular ideas of his time? Perhaps one must ask, how could he not have been so? After Paul, Christianity needed centuries in order to free itself from some time-conditioned ideas upheld by Paul, e.g. regarding the injustice of slavery or the relative under-evaluation of woman in social life. And did not Paul perhaps — along with other contemporaries of his — reckon with the early eschatological return of the Lord and give corresponding counsels to the community in Corinth? Christians may never consider themselves free from the need to reflect on the presuppositions implied in particular counsels and requirements, in order to arrive at their inner truth.

It must be at least equally important to take account of the distinction in Paul between normative discourse and paranetic discourse. Paranetic discourse (cf. the texts in 1 Cor 6 which were read above) does not establish ethical norms but presupposes them, and often presupposes that they are known to the reader and other people. In such texts, then, no specifically Christian norms are taught.

Finally, Paul has made clear in 1 Cor 7 that Christians are always bound to seek and to find in their communities the solution to ethical problems that arise. The new Christians, including Paul, did not receive a "morality of the church" from somewhere; they had to seek and find the "morality of their church" in Corinth. What happened in Corinth and through Paul must necessarily continue in the church of today.

NOTES

1 The present contribution is intended to be moral theology, not exegesis. However, it presupposes knowledge of exegetical studies of the Pauline text; occasionally, attention is drawn to differences in exegetical research. When he wrote the first draft of the present text, the author did not have any knowledge of a dissertation which was just about to be published: Werner Wolbert, "Ethische Argumentation und Paränese in 1 Kor 7", *Moralth. Studien*, Syst. Abt 8, Düsseldorf (1981). This dissertation is also intended to be moral theology, although it deals with a subject which is quite different from that of the present contribution. In his dissertation, Wolbert also explicitly examines different exegetical studies.

2 Karol Wojtyla, *The Acting Person*, Dordrecht, Netherlands (1981), the final text of *Person und Tat, Endgültige Textfassung*... Miteinem Nachwort... v.A. Poltaweski, Freiburg i. Br., Basel, Wien 1981.

3. Cf. Thomas Aquinas, *S.C.G.* 3, 122, beginning.

PART 2

The Moral Self of the Christian

VII. Morality: Person and Acts

1. The Problem

This essay concerns two word-pairs: good and evil, person and acts. At first sight, it could appear that the meaning of the two word-pairs is clear and well known; two facts, however, could make us suspect that this is not really the case. First, in the Lord's Prayer, we pray at the close, "But deliver us from evil." Does this perhaps mean, "Deliver us from every kind of evil"? It seems to me difficult to believe that this was the intention of Jesus when he told us to pray thus. Did he not rather intend the deliverance from the evil that we are accustomed to call "sin," i.e., *moral evil*? In fact, in German we have two different terms for the word "evil": *Übel*, which means "evil" without distinguishing among the various kinds of evil, and *Böse*, which means moral evil; it is for this reason that the German bishops some years ago changed the traditional wording, "Deliver us from *Übel* (evil)," to "Deliver us from *Bösen* (moral evil)."[1] The title of this chapter implies that I am to speak of *moral* good and evil.

But there is more to be said in accordance with this line of thinking. Karol Wojtyla chose as the title of his most important book *The Acting Person*. When we pray, "Deliver us from evil (i.e., from moral evil)," do we mean freedom of the *person* from evil, that is, from being personally wicked (a sinner), or freedom of the person's various *acts* from evil? I think that all would agree that we mean the moral goodness of the self, i.e., of the person, hence that the person may be free from being wicked, in order to be what is humanly "worthy" and acceptable to God. But how does one distinguish the evil of the acts of the person from the evil of the person in the Lord's Prayer, according to the distinction made by the philosopher Wojtyla and so many other philosophers and theologians today? Let us suppose that a person newly converted to Catholicism (perhaps with little instruction) considers regular sexual relations with his fiancée to be perfectly normal and right behavior with no evil content. Our bishop would say that, while our new convert is not personally evil or a sinner, and hence is without the moral evil from which the Lord's Prayer asks deliverance, his behavior — i.e. the acts of sexual relations that have been mentioned — cannot as such be considered morally right and acceptable: and the Lord's Prayer does not ask for deliverance from such non-rightness of behavior and acts.

In fact, morality in the strict sense belongs to the person, to the self and to his internal attitudes; only the free person can be moral or immoral, in the strict sense of the word — the self with its free attitudes (what German calls *Gesinnung*). The acts are not morally good or evil in the strict sense of the word, but rather right or wrong insofar as they can be judged suited or unsuited to the reality of the human person and his world, or tending to lead to or away from the good of the human individual, of mankind, of humanity. We are accustomed by a long tradition to call such acts morally good or evil, and indeed to call unfitting acts "sins" — adding, however, that they can be called "sins" only "objectively speaking," precisely because it is only the person with his or her free attitudes, plans, decisions, desires, virtues, etc., who can be morally good or evil (a sinner) in the strict sense.

Precisely for this reason, that is, to make the clear distinction between what can be predicated of the person as such and what can be predicated of the person's acts as such, a trend developed some time ago to keep the words "good" and "evil" (in the sense of the Lord's Prayer) for the person in his or her attitude, and to call the acts as such right or wrong. It is clear, on the one hand, that a person who is aware of the wrongness of a certain act and nevertheless decides to behave thus is morally evil in this decision and action; on the other hand, certain acts share in the "moral evil" of the person and are a part of the person's sin if they are carried out freely in spite of being considered wrong according to a moral judgment on our part.

2. Problems of the Twelfth Century

To explain better this distinction between the moral good of the person and the moral rightness of the acts of the person, and also to show that these kinds of problems are not exclusively the concern of the moral theologians of our "modern" period, I should like to draw attention briefly to a similar problematic in the twelfth and thirteenth centuries.

1. The famous *Peter Abelard* (+ 1142) was a genius in philosophy and theology, but his works were considered a provocation in his own period, and some of his theses were condemned. Abelard has his own theory concerning morality, which he viewed (thinking especially of sin) as being solely in the interior of the human being, in his soul.[2] For

him, sin consists exclusively in the consent to what, according to the will of God, should not be done; the action and the deed itself would add nothing, from a moral point of view, to the sin. It is only in a broader sense[3] that one could call sexual relations outside marriage a sin, when compared to relations within marriage. In the following century, St. Thomas would say more clearly that, while it is certainly true that sin consists in the internal consent of the sinner, the act of the sinner which incarnates the personal interior sin also bears within itself an evil of its own that is contrary to morality, i.e., an evil that is contrary to the true good of the person.[4] Thus an element that is not human is introduced into the world of the person and the act is therefore one that is opposed not only to the will of God. One might think today, for example, of the discussion about the moral character of *in vitro* fertilization, of the use of atomic energy, of the various modes of living out sexuality, etc.

Many today make a terminological distinction between the *moral goodness* (or *moral wickedness*) of the person and the *moral rightness* (or *moral wrongness*) of acts. As we have said, only the interior morality of the person is morality in the proper sense of the word. The morality of the acts as such is, rather, morality in an analogous sense — because it is measured not by the attitudes of the person but by the fittingness of the acts to the good of the person and of his world. The rightness (or wrongness) of the acts is, however, analogously termed moral, because the person, in order to be morally good, must endeavour to become incarnate only in right acts in the human world. Such a distinction is not very visible in the teachings of Peter Abelard, but is more clearly seen in those of St. Thomas.

2. St. Bernard of Clairvaux, Abelard's theological contemporary, was his decided adversary. Among his teachings we find a thesis which is incomprehensible to us today: he asserts that one who acts contrary to what ought to be done — today we should say against what is "right" — commits a sin, even if he acts in good faith.[5] How could the holy Doctor arrive at this judgment? It seems that the reply to this question must be that he was not yet able to distinguish sufficiently between the moral goodness of the person (in good faith) and the lack of rightness of his conduct. When he saw the lack of rightness in the act, the saint did not feel entitled to call the person who carried out such a morally wrong act, a non-sinner, even if the person was in good faith.

Peter Abelard could not accept that his adversary St. Bernard was right, and the great theologian Aquinas in the following century was obliged to take up Abelard's position rather than St. Bernard's. But even Aquinas still had a difficulty: he was prepared to say that one who carried out a wrong act in good faith did not sin, but seeing the wrong act of the subject, he was not yet prepared to call this morally good. In other words, he made a greater distinction than St. Bernard between the moral goodness of the person and the rightness of the acts — (in short, between person and acts) — but he did not yet do this in a satisfactory manner, as does Karol Wojtyla, for example.

3. Peter Lombard, the author of the famous *Sentences* (+ 1160), taught that when the church lays an obligation on us under pain of excommunication, we must always fulfill such an obligation, even if we are convinced that what is enjoined is morally illicit.[6] St. Thomas Aquinas comments dryly on this in the following century, despite his great respect for the author of the *Sentences:* here the master is wrong; and he adds clearly that one must rather agree to die excommunicated than act against one's own conscience.[7] The Master of Lombardy had not yet understood sufficiently that personal moral goodness is interior and that it therefore consists in free adherence to the internal light of the conscience and not in the relationship to a rightness of conduct that is required and imposed from without. In the time that had elapsed, however, Aquinas had better understood such a distinction.

4. The result of our brief excursus in the history of moral theology may be formulated as follows. It has always been known that a person's moral goodness is basically an interior reality, an attitude and disposition of not being closed in on oneself but of being open to what one knows of God, of the human person, and of right behavior in the world of human persons. It proved difficult, however, to perceive that rightness of conduct is not directly related to the personal morality of the human person, i.e., to his moral goodness, but refers as such to the good of the human being (of mankind) in his horizontal dimension. Only slowly did it come to be understood that right or wrong behavior, purely as such, does not affect personal morality (goodness). Personal morality (goodness) is concerned with moral rightness of conduct only to the extent that personal goodness makes us internally and sincerely disposed to seek to identify — together with others and with moral authorities — what is right behavior in the various fields and situations of human reality, and to behave in accordance with what has thus been found and has therefore become an interior light and guide for the moral decision (which is always interior) of the personal human being. We are left thus with this clear distinction: only personal (interior) moral goodness is morality in the more proper sense of the word, and the moral rightness of behavior is "moral" only in an analogous sense; finally, personal moral goodness is interested in and cares for the rightness of human behavior in this world of human beings. This is how personal goodness and rightness of conduct, per se and ideally, ought to coincide in the person who is an individual and is the subject both of his free moral goodness and of his right conduct in the world; but unfortunately, this is not and will not always be the case in a being with such great limitations as the human person. Personal moral goodness

is always possible. Not so the identification of the rightness of conduct in our world, and the realization of such rightness.

3. Jesus

It might be interesting to see if the masters of the past (and of today) could not have found some sign or suggestion in the attitude, behavior and teaching of Jesus. The fundamental question would be this: are Jesus and his mission to be understood in the first place as a teaching about how better to realize and structure the world, human society, interpersonal relationships, and the life of the individual? All these things can undeniably have a certain influence on the personal morality of human beings and thus on their situation vis-à-vis salvation. Or should Jesus rather be understood as the one sent by the Father for the redemption or liberation of human beings from their intimate self-alienation, in which they have enclosed themselves to a profound extent within themselves, so that they may open themselves up to God and man, i.e., to their own true good and that of humanity — with a consequent availability to confront the true needs of the human world as well? Such a grace of redemption and liberation is salvation.

It cannot be doubted that the principal aim of the mission of Jesus is the work of redemption and liberation of the personal human being in the sense indicated here, and with this comes the grace of salvation. Briefly, Jesus aims in the first place at the moral goodness and salvation of the person, and only as a consequence of this, rather indirectly, does he aim to teach about the rightness of the behavior of the person in his world. And in fact we do not find in the life of Jesus a genuine endeavor to teach us how to administer and structure the human world rightly. He takes it for granted that this is well known, and admonishes us to be personally and morally good and consequently not to forget or rather, not to betray — the due rightness of human social, interpersonal and individual life.

One may, for example, think of the first preaching of Jesus, as this is recounted to us in a few words in the Gospel of St. Mark (Mk 1:15). The Lord insists on the need for conversion of the person, i.e., of the person as such in his interior, where we are dealing truly with the person himself and not merely with some wrong activity of the person. This presupposes that the person needs such a conversion, i.e. that he is, unfortunately, closed in upon himself and not open before his God (and hence also before the eyes of men), and that, in accepting the good news of Jesus, one can receive the grace of a personal conversion and so be saved. Jesus' preaching therefore aims at the moral and personal goodness of the human person; the question of the rightness of the realization of the reality of the human world does not directly interest him.

One may think of the Sermon on the Mount (Mt 5–7). Despite what is sometimes said or written, the teachings and exhortations of Jesus do not refer directly to the rightness of the structuring of human life on earth, nor to the personal morality of his disciples in the kingdom of God as different from, or antithetical to, a morality that is merely human: the reference is rather to the fundamental distinction between a disciple of Jesus (and this means all of us) and the intimate attitude of those whom Jesus here explicitly calls sinners ("even the sinners do this"), among whom he sees also the Pharisees and tax-collectors. It is obvious that Jesus criticizes those who, as sinners, are not right in their behavior in the world; but instead of teaching the commandments of correct behavior in the human world, he insists on the difference between the morally and personally good man and the one who is not so, the sinner, who precisely for this reason is often also not right in his behavior in the world.

Although his primary concern is the personal morality of the person who belongs to the kingdom, Jesus does not forget the problem of the rightness of behavior in the human world. But instead of discussing this, he presupposes it and insists that personal morality, i.e., the good-ness of the disciple, will be seen in concern for the rightness of life in the world of human persons. He frequently laments the oppression of the poor by the rich. He pardons the penitent adulteress, but insists that she does not continue in her wrong praxis. On occasion, he cor-rects the erroneous opinions of those who are egotistically closed in upon themselves and consider as right what is not so — for example, the opinions of his contemporaries about divorce. Not a few scholars (e.g., Pinchas Lapide) think that in such cases, Jesus does not so much wish to hand down a word "from on high," as to recall his hearers to the opinions of the best spirits of his period, in order to thus give indications about a right "human" morality.

For Jesus, therefore, it is clear that a person who is morally good will seek to identify what is right in life in the human world, so that he or she can realize it.

4. Reflections

After having looked at the person/acts problem from the point of view of what is morally good/morally right both in a period of uncer-tainty in the Middle Ages and in the words of Jesus, I should now like to begin a similar reflection from another point of view. A frequent preoccupation today is the question: what has become of Christian morality, what is still good and what is not good, what has become of the certainty that once existed? Further, is the morality of the Bible no longer valid? And are the church's magisterium and the moral theologians no longer able to say clearly what is good and what is not? One should pose a question in response to such questions: do they refer to what is "good" in the sense of the moral goodness of the person, or to what is "good" in the sense of rightness of conduct in the human world — with regard to justice, peace and nuclear weapons, marriage and sexuality, etc.?

If the question intends to refer to what is "good" in the sense of personal moral goodness, i.e. to morality in the proper sense of the word, the question of the salvation of the human person is involved, because it is clear that whoever as a person — i.e., in his interior attitudes — is not good, does not seriously intend what is good, has not accepted the interior grace of conversion that is offered by God to everyone in his inmost self and thus remains outside the grace of salvation. If, however, the question refers to "good" in the sense of right behavior in the world of human persons — what is right or permissible and what is not — the question directly involves neither the moral goodness of the person nor his salvation: for, as has already been seen, one who does what is unfitting, but does this in error or in good faith, can be morally good and can be saved in his relationship with God.

It would therefore be a very serious matter if there were doubts in the teachings of moral theologians, in the church's magisterium, or among the people of God about what is relevant to morality and to personal moral goodness. We have seen that Jesus' primary concern was directed at the personal moral goodness of mankind: it is precisely here that it is decided whether one is a true disciple of the Lord and whether one belongs to the kingdom. There may have been some discussion among the medieval theologians about this point, but that is not the case today. Everyone admits that, if one is morally and personally good, one tends toward the good, both the morally good and the human good that is not necessarily moral good; that such a person, in his decisions and consequently in his conduct, follows what is said to him by the light of a responsibly formed conscience and thus also by the Spirit; that he has the attitude of a man who is just, faithful, truthful, chaste, generous etc., and therefore seeks to know what such an attitude implies in practice for a correct realization of his life in this human world; indeed, he seeks to create in himself strong tendencies and virtues in order to be more easily inclined and able to do what is demanded by a correct human life.

If, on the other hand, the question about the "good" refers (as seems generally to be the case) to correct behavior in the human world, i.e. to what is morally acceptable and what is not, one cannot deny that there are uncertainties, doubts and discussions here. Although it is true that such a question does not directly touch the problem of the salvation of the human person (as has already been said), and that it does not deal with truths that are distinctively Christian, and that the Bible does not give us many answers regarding these truths, it remains the case that the situation of uncertainty and the divergence of opinions are felt by many to be particularly painful. It also seems true, however, that many lament such a situation not because they feel the lack of a true answer to so many questions of right behavior in the human world, but rather because they personally need certainty and security about questions of right daily behavior. Moreover, while some fear that the traditional truths may be lost, others would like to be assured that what they wish to do, and see others do without scruples, is truly right and permissible, and that consequently it is not necessary for such behavior to be rejected by personal moral goodness and by a good conscience. One could perhaps say that both groups are defending interests that are justified up to a point; but this would have to be verified in each individual case.

It is undeniable that such questions can have great practical importance, and it is not without reason that study commissions and congresses are convoked on the local, national and international levels to shed some light on the great moral questions of the world of industry, commerce, international affairs, and social questions. The bishops were right in feeling constrained in recent years to speak publicly in order to help find a morally acceptable solution to the problems of peace, war and armaments. The whole range of bioethical problems born of the continual progress being made today, for example, in the field of genetic engineering, calls for continuing studies both on an individual scale and also on governmental and international levels. It is already clear from this list of some of the problems of moral rightness in human behavior that one should not be surprised if clear solutions that absolutely exclude uncertainties and doubts do not exist in any case. The Second Vatican Council, in *Gaudium et Spes* (no. 43), taught that those who share a deep faith and the same sense of responsibility may "legitimately" arrive at contrary answers. At various times in the past, Catholic moral theology recognized and accepted that there are no unanimously accepted answers to questions which, even today, moral theologians cannot resolve. Also moral theology taught for centuries through different moral systems, e.g. probabilism, how one should behave when there are no universally communicable and acceptable solutions.

I am aware of the objection that what I have said is perhaps applicable to such questions, but that the same cannot be said regarding questions which have rather an individual or interpersonal character, and especially if the past thought it had the solutions to such questions. In principle, however, it is not obvious why it should be possible to reflect, as has been done above, on one question regarding the moral rightness of human behavior, but not on another type of moral question of behavior in this world.

What is to be said when it is insisted that we have had for a long time accepted solutions for certain questions (although not precisely for the great human problems of today)? First, I would like to point out that perhaps many consider the last group of questions to be moral questions of right human behavior, but do not take the first type of question to be equally so: such an assertion would certainly indicate a defective concept of what is "moral" in this context. Second, it is easily forgotten that certain solutions of moral rightness in behavior had sources that cannot be authoritative for us today — although it was otherwise in the Christian past — and that the church too has recognized this in certain questions, with the passage of time. I am thinking, for example, of the influence of Stoic philosophy or of gnosticism and Manicheism. Third, human realities can be judged under the aspect of moral rightness only within the limits of our knowledge of these realities. When experience or the sciences — e.g., medicine, biology, psychology, sociology, chemistry, etc. — bring us new knowledge, it is not very objective to refuse to review the judgments of moral rightness that have been made previously, to see if they can be upheld in confrontation with such new knowledge. It would certainly be unjustifiable to resist such new reflections a priori, from fear that they might perhaps give rise to some moral "novelty"; if such a resistance existed, it would have to be eliminated. Fourth, we must also remember that the human person as such is a historical being, i.e., that it is not only the circumstances of his environment and of his physical reality that can slowly show some alteration, but also the personal human being as such; his history and the history of his vital and moral experiences can lead him to see and evaluate certain things in a somewhat different manner.

Anyone who may feel a little perplexed by these last explanations of mine should remember that the history of Christian morality knows examples of certain alterations in moral evaluation. Some of us have lived through Vatican II's handling of the problem of what is called religious liberty — i.e., the secular power, as such, must not interfere with religious choices and praxis — or with the lack of positive religious choices — of individuals or of particular groups; the state should instead guarantee freedom of such choices and praxis. The Council's decree on religious liberty changed a tendency that had endured for centuries, right up to the time of the Council itself. To take another example: the evaluation of matrimonial love, in that this love is also erotic, was very negative for many centuries, not only in the case of some pessimistic theologies, but also in the commonly accepted teaching of the church; a kind of pluralism existed not only in one particular period (in the twelfth century, as I have written elsewhere), but for a long time afterward. Anyone who insists that we Christians must only bear witness to the Christian wisdom of the centuries in questions of moral conduct forgets that a certain pluralism has existed in the church, and shows that he or she is not very well acquainted with the history of moral theology in Christianity.

We must not, I repeat, hide from ourselves the fact and the knowledge that what concerns fitting and right acting and behaving in the human world (not necessarily excluding every correction of a moral idea from the past or even every innovation in the present) contains in itself a great danger for man in his weakness and egotism — the danger of convincing himself that acts which he likes or desires are also justifiable and justified. This danger should not, however, exclude the reflections made above. What can effectively reduce such a danger and such a temptation is the authentic and deeply rooted moral goodness of the person, the true morality of the interior man, which coincides with the grace of salvation.

5. Consequences

The wish — indeed, the demand — is often expressed by a certain type of believer that the magisterium of the church intervene with an authoritative word to bring fresh certainty, or at least a little more certainty, regarding the rightness or wrongness of certain acts and behavior in the human world, from a moral point of view. Such a desire or demand would surely be erroneous if one wished to view the church's principal task as consisting in such interventions about the moral rightness of behavior in the human world, for the principal task of the church and her magisterium (just as for Jesus) is not the good functioning of the world of men and of human society, and hence the question of right and best conduct in this world, but the salvation of mankind, of persons as such. From a moral viewpoint, this means that the church is not interested primarily in acts and their moral rightness but in the person and his moral goodness. To fail to see this is to misunderstand the true mission of the church and of its authority. The church must insist above all that people accept the grace that is offered of a continuous true personal conversion, that they not be so closed within themselves but that they be open to what is good, to their neighbor, to God. This personal opening, which is the church's primary concern, includes a free interior opening to the search for right human behavior in mankind's world and a personal decision to realize such a world as far as is possible.

It follows that the competence of the church and of her magisterium is not in the first place the way of life of individuals, or interpersonal and societal relationships. This does not mean that the church has no competence with regard to human conduct in the world, but that this competence is only secondary when compared with the primary com-

petence. One should also bear in mind that questions of human conduct in the world are not resolved directly by Christian faith; and that
problems of right behavior in the world, on the part of individuals and
groups, throughout so many centuries, are innumerable and cannot
therefore all have their solution from the faith; neither the words of the
Decalogue nor the words of the Sermon on the Mount can be even
minimally sufficient here. One should consider, furthermore, as we
have already said, that some individual solutions regarding what is
morally right behavior can possibly undergo certain alterations; faith
does not and cannot foresee all this.

It is true, on the other hand, that the faith and likewise the apostolic
preaching of St. Paul do not merely offer us some indications for
conduct in the world, although all these indications require not only a
simple pious reading, but also an exact hermeneutical reading.
Moreover, many things bearing on the conduct of the human person
presuppose situations and mentalities of many centuries ago, and cannot therefore be applied in a simple manner to the world of today: they
have, however, a maieutic value for us in that we learn how to seek
correct solutions for ourselves. First of all, faith gives us what the
Council calls "the light of the gospel" which illuminates us so that we
may know better what and who the person is — every person — and
what his dignity is, above all in the eyes of the God of love. All this
can help us and the church and her magisterium to find appropriate
solutions for behavior in the world somewhat more easily.

It remains true, however, that in order to discover appropriate
solutions for the realization of human life and human society, we need
competence with regard to the realities whose human realization is in
question. Anyone who wishes to teach right behavior in international
politics, change in tribal marriages, the correct realization of human
sexuality in different phases, situations and cultures, etc., must be
very competent in all these matters of human reality. It is clear that
Christians as such, and the people involved in the church's magisterium as such, have no privileged competence with regard to such
questions, which per se are neither Christian nor religious nor moral. If
one wishes to give moral instructions and teachings concerning such
human realities, inasmuch as they are human, one must acquire sufficient competence, receiving information from others who are more
competent. One can thus attempt to make a pronouncement against
the background of one's Christian knowledge of what it is "to be man,"
and in the light of the gospel and with the aid (not, per se, the
instruction) of the Spirit.

It is obvious that there is a clear distinction between statements of
the church's magisterium on questions regarding faith, revelation and
the *depositum fidei* on the one hand, and the many moral questions of

right behavior by the human person in the world on the other hand — questions that, at least as such, are not elements of the faith, of revelation, or of the *depositum fidei*. It follows that so-called infallible statements, which under certain conditions are considered possible, are not easily to be thought of with regard to right behavior in the world and the right shaping of the human world. This was formulated in a certain way at Vatican I and Vatican II, despite the generic formula (which has never been explained) about the power of the church in questions of faith and morals. I could not, indeed, identify a single infallible statement proposed by the magisterium in all the history of the church regarding questions of right behavior in the world (unless this behavior is also part of revelation). I should not say the same about questions of the moral goodness of the person; it seems to me that these are sufficiently contained in the faith that has been revealed to us.

What has been set out here should not lead to the conclusion that the word of the church has no authority in questions of conduct in the human world. Indeed, it is my opinion that a religious authority must also give a hand as guide to the people of this church, and that the Spirit is with this authority in a special way — without, however, always promising us an irrevocable answer or statement. This means that while we devoutly accept the presumption that a statement of the church is true, we do not wish to exclude the possibility of withholding consent where the reasons for contrary solutions become convincing for truly responsible persons who are competent in such moral matters. This personal openness, although limited to a certain degree, belongs precisely to the moral goodness of the Christian person, i.e. of the disciple of Jesus.

6. What is Morality?

A first reply could be that morality is a gift of God, a grace. This reply leaves no doubts, if one has understood the word of Jesus, about the conversion that is involved in accepting God's good news that is brought to us by the one he has sent. Conversion, and hence moral goodness, are personal life and true morality, but, as such, they are a gift of God, and therefore at the same time the "salvation" of the person. Salvation, which is already present in us during our earthly pilgrimage, is experienced as the interior and profound morality of the person. Such a life, however, cannot be lived only in the depths of the person, but must also be lived in the whole life and activity of the world in which the morality of the human agent is present and active: thus it incarnates itself, expresses itself, shows itself and is manifest in the horizontal world, which is different from the depth of personal morality as such.

But the person with his moral goodness can never present himself as he is in his entirety; he manifests himself only in particular acts which, for their part, never touch more than a rather small area of the full horizontal reality of the individual, or of humanity, or of the subhuman world. And precisely when a personal human being is morally good and, therefore, a man of the grace of salvation, he accordingly takes care that his particular self-manifestation in its effect in the world can be integrated into the entirety of this whole world, i.e., into the world of the human person and of humanity; it is in this that rightness of behavior in this world consists. Such rightness shares by analogy in the moral goodness of the person and is therefore also called, by analogy, moral.

NOTES

1 Cf. A. Delp, *Der Herrgott*, ed. R. Bleistein (Frankfurt/Main 1985), 92f.: "It follows that the evil that we here ask to be turned away from us is not what is oppressive in life, need, care, what is harsh, what is difficult, deprivation, pain, injustice, violence, etc. Rather, it is the oppression that leads us into temptation, that displaces the emphases, relocates the midpoint, corrupts the perspective. We sense at once that the so-called 'good things' of life belong here just as much as the difficult and harsh realities. In all of them, there is the possibility of reducing us or of leading us into temptation. This includes everything that can place itself between us and the Lord God; and this can be ourselves too.

"This petition reveals life's character as a struggle, even more than the earlier petitions. The dialectic of existence can repeatedly intensify to the point of agony, not only the agony of the Mount of Olives, but that of the Lord when he was tempted in the wilderness."

2 Peter Abelard, *Ethica seu scito teipsum, PL* 178, 636.

3 Ibid., 657.

4 St. Thomas Aquinas, *S.C.G.* 3, 122, beginning.

5 The theses of St. Bernard against Abelard are found in the nineteen propositions of Abelard condemned by the Council of Sens in 1140 (1141?); especially interesting here are propositions 9, 10, 19 and 13: H. Denzinger and A. Schönmetzer, *Enchiridion*, nos. 729, 730, 739, 733.

6 Cf. the texts (discussed) *Ver.* 17, 4 and ad 5, *S.Th.* I-II, 19, 6.

7 *In 4 sent.* 38, 2, 4 q.a 3: *"Hic magister falsum dicit"*, and he explains that one who would be constrained under pain of excommunication to enter an illegal marriage: *"potius debet excommunicatus mori quam..."* Likewise: *In 4 sent.* 27, 3, 3 *expos. textus: "sed quantum ad forum conscientiae non est verum quod Magister hic dicit;"* further: *In 4 sent.* 27, 1, 2 q.a. 4 ad 3: *"Deberet potius mori excommunicatus."*

VIII. The Phenomenon of Conscience: Subject-Orientation and Object-Orientation

There is no doubt that conscience is connected with the sphere of ethics; a closer study of the phenomenon of conscience leads into the field of psychology as well. Now that I, as a Catholic moral theologian, am to say something about the conscience-phenomenon, I would like first to refer to two extremely diverging statements made recently by two Catholic moral theologians. In the foreword to his *Fundamentalmoral* (1977)[1] Franz Böckle says that he is dispensing with a chapter on conscience as he cedes this subject to the competency of the psychologists and will apply himself to problems concerning justified ethical judgment. Contrary to this, Amicato Molinaro identifies moral conscience and moral norm in his 1983 article on conscience[2] and understands them as being "the constitution of the ethical subject or person." In the following, an attempt will first be made at grasping the conscience-phenomenon to a certain extent[3] in order to be able to study the primary subject-orientation and the merely secondary object-orientation more closely afterward.

1. The Phenomenon of Conscience: Various Aspects

It is not possible here to expound and analyze the extremely complex phenomenon of conscience in its entirety. The aim is rather to call attention to only a few aspects of this phenomenon in order to come to some sort of common understanding and so prepare the ground for discussion.

(a) *Conscience and orientation for the conduct of life.* One generally tends to look upon conscience somehow as an authority of the personal ego and as one which strictly governs the good and correct conduct of life: *in abstracto* it passes judgment on human values, good personal behavior and the correct way of leading a worldly life; *in concreto* it determines personal obligation and, thereby, the goodness and correctness of actual behavior and of a freely lived life. The conscience is consequently understood throughout as being an authority governing the conduct of life.

Today we are more aware than in the past of the fact that the conscience is not the only authority governing the way life is conducted. There are other authorities which determine our conduct in life and which do not call on the freedom of the human being. Behavioral research shows, for instance, that certain behavior in humans and animals is based on biological factors[4] which pretend to be something of an ethical order but which are not ethical orientation; astonishing cases of "selfless" behavior within personal relationships and society are not necessarily ethical and conscientious acts — certainly not with animals, nor with human beings. Social conduct and personal behavior can be spontaneous reaction prompted by accepted rules of social behavior and are, therefore, not necessarily caused by morality. Psychology investigates how certain types of psychological motivation determine the behavior of young children, who undoubtedly lack moral conscience, and also often that of juveniles and adults. The Freudian superego can play a predominant part in the way we conduct our lives and is far too often in danger of being mistaken for moral conscience. Kohlberg's studies on moral maturity and immaturity clearly show that not all orientation for life is the call of moral conscience. We usually consider the adult and mature person — contrary to animals — as that living being who is able to reflect on himself and his behavior: he has a moral conscience which affords an orientation for his life.[5] He is also able, at least partly, to reflect on biological, sociological and psychological impulses and orientation and to evaluate their goodness and correctness, and eventually either to accept or reject them at will. It can be supposed that people's good and correct conduct is sometimes based on both ethical and nonethical orientation simultaneously. Who can judge to what extent their conduct is based on spontaneous reaction or on moral motivation and decision?

(b) *Conscience and practical reason.* Morality thus presupposes that human action is not a spontaneous reaction but follows decision based on insight of conscience. Such insight is, in a formal sense, the result of that which is generally termed practical reason. As already mentioned, Böckle emphasizes the fact that he is exclusively interested in the problem relating to practical reason which determines, *in abstracto* and *in concreto*, the ruling as to good and correct conduct, and so attempts to by-pass the question of the conscience-phenomenon in his considerations. It is true that practical reason and conscience are not one and the same. The question as to whether one can separate the two, be it only theoretically, remains problematic. In other words, is there such a thing as practical reason outside conscience or not?

This question has a double meaning parallel with the double meaning of the concept of "conscience." Conscience means — particularly in Catholic moral theology — in a narrower sense, the authority which determines good and correct conduct in a concrete situation. Another conception of conscience, on the other hand, does not limit the authority of conscience to the assessment of a concrete situation, but extends its competency to include theoretical moral evaluation and formulation of norms.

It should not be overlooked that in both meanings, and most importantly in the first, narrower meaning, the issue is never one of "pure" practical reason. What is that supposed to mean? Owing to the many facets of human existence, practical reason is subject to diverse influences; it does not, however, lose its own identity. For moral judgment based on practical reason is carried out under the powerful influence exercised by tradition, custom and environment, and also under biological, sociological and psychological influences as well as individual tendencies, interests and dispositions. Judgment based on practical reason is truly its own judgment and is, nevertheless, a result of influences exercised by the diverse elements comprised in human reality as a whole. In this sense, it is true that practical reason proves itself to be not pure a priori speculation, and that it comes closer to the much richer concept of conscience, which always pervades man in his personal entirety.

This becomes even clearer if one asks on what grounds and with what justification judgments that are based on practical reason are termed "moral judgments"? This indeed presupposes that when making such judgments, one knows what morality means; young children, for instance, do not know this. Whoever talks about morality, even with respect to judgments based on practical reason, is only justified in doing so if he has personal experience of the phenomenon of morality, which is, in fact, nothing other than the irreducible phenomenon of moral conscience. And this means: the valuing and driving experience of the human person, which stems from the innermost self-consciousness, is the participation in absolute freedom; one's own freedom is not, therefore, in itself original and absolute, but bound by obligation. Here freedom is understood as freedom of the *person as such* and for the means of self-realization, and not necessarily as freedom for all concrete, particular action. This phenomenon cannot be explained in psychological categories nor does the free recognition by the personal subject, or even a definite theoretical explanation of the deepest self, force this phenomenon onto reflection. It is not only considered and declared to be a primary phenomenon by Christian philosophers but also by humanist and Marxist ones; compare, for instance, corresponding thoughts in Polish philosophical circles.

Judgment of good and correct conduct based on practical reason, therefore, always takes place as part of existential basic moral experience and deepest moral conviction. Moral judgment and personal moral experience are always intertwined. This becomes clearest when it is not only a case of abstract values and standards, but of a concrete decision made by the subject in a concrete situation. Judgment based on practical reason qualifies as being "moral" exclusively on account of the interconnected and evermanifest conscience. Indeed, it may sometimes appear in the case of judgment based on practical reason that it is first a matter concerning only particular ethical questions, whereas it is, in the last analysis, a matter concerning the human being as such and its meaningful self-realization. This then makes it understandable that judgment based on practical reason, being judgment in the conscience, has above all else, but not exclusively, the characteristics of insight, and simultaneously, to a certain extent, those of decision.

(c) *Conscience and religious experience.* According to what has already been mentioned, conscientious experience is of an absolute nature. This is not meant in the sense that the particular contents of judgment based on conscience guarantee absolute moral truths but in the other sense that moral judgments, as long as they hold good, imply absolute personal commitment on the part of the subject. This then leads to the question of whether awareness of conscience is not basically a religious experience and, furthermore, whether an awareness of conscience lacking religious sense is possible at all.

Many agnostic and atheist humanists would answer this question in the negative. They would explain the experience of morality and with it the experience of conscience as an *absolutum* and, perhaps, as a mystery. They would, hence, reject the explanation of the conscience-phenomenon as being a religious one and, at the same time, as being a purely psychological or social phenomenon. Is one not obliged to say that the human being at his deepest level experiences himself as he in reality *is*: that is, as a being with obligations, not an *absolutum*? He is not able to free himself from this experience, not even by way of explicit reflection on the matter or by either denying it or trying to explain it as a pure fact, or as a purely psychological phenomenon – at any rate, not as a religious one. The religious person might possibly understand the awareness of conscience, as it has just been described and discussed, as an *implicitly* or *virtually* religious experience *without* an explicit belief in God.

A creationist interpretation of the experience of conscience can talk of the deepest experience of the true relationship between, and in, the created person and his ever-present God of creation. And this is done in the sense that the person, every person, is at his deepest level always conscious of his own being and thus of his true reality as being related to God, and accordingly, is conscious of the ultimate significance of his reality: this applies even when the person, on considering the matter, is not able to define this relationship. It may particularly be pointed out that a God who "imposes" demands is neither expressly nor implicitly experienced within the conscience, but rather as a "God" in whom everything has its base and on whom, therefore, everything is dependent and who provides a meaning to life. In accordance with this, one can then define morality as an implicit religious dialogue. However, the religious person comprehends these facts according to his specific belief, be it Hinduism, Mohammedanism, Judaism, Christianity or his own individual religion. Belief of this sort qualifies the experience of conscience, even when it has not been reached by way of reflection.

The question of the possible significance of a particular sort of belief determining the moral content of conscience has not been broached.

(d) *Conscience — superego — ethical maturity (immaturity)*. It has already been mentioned that there is also an orientation for the conduct of life which does not in the least represent ethical judgment based on practical reason in the conscience. Additionally, it should be remarked that there is also a true moral orientation coming from the conscience which has no reference to actual values, but to ones which are nevertheless true, even though more obvious: the necessity of self-integration in a specific society, for instance. The question arises as to which *moral* significance should be bestowed on this kind of orientation for the conduct of life.

Several years ago (in 1971),[6] John W. Glaser investigated the question of the moral significance of decisions which are not or have not obviously been based on true judgment stemming from the conscience, but on the authority of the superego. Glaser is primarily interested in whether decisions concerning the future, such as those that are taken for life (e.g., celibacy and priesthood), which, however, unconsciously, are clearly made on account, not of genuine morality but of the superego, represent a moral commitment once they are revealed as what in reality they are.

According to Lawrence Kohlberg, the question as to the significance of moral maturity and immaturity lies partly elsewhere, as relatively few people attain the full maturity necessary to arrive at moral valuations. There are many variations between these relatively few, on the one side, and young children, who lack any sort of moral maturity, on the other side. Is it really true that all these variations are moral judgment? Should these decisions made according to such "immature" motivation be considered "moral" decisions? This question must be answered in the positive. Whoever demands more than this does not recognize the peculiar manner in which human beings find their way and how they arrive at moral judgments; humans are social beings and not isolated islands. Judgment so reached is to be considered as true judgment stemming from the conscience and, likewise, as a binding authority. Nevertheless, this does not exclude the possibility of further experience of life and deeper insight into the true meaning of humanity leading to new and different moral judgments, which will then have binding validity. Again, such possibilities for improvement are also not excluded in the case where moral judgment has been reached at a high level of moral maturity.

2. The Subject-Orientation of the Conscience

The foregoing thoughts on various aspects of the conscience-phenomenon should now lead to reflection on the fundamental difference between the conscience's primary subject-orientation and the secondary object-orientation. In earlier centuries too, distinctions were made between the various functions of the conscience but the distinction at stake was not always arrived at by thorough methods and, above all, was not applied permanently. This led occasionally to long-standing vehement discussion and friction, which up to now has not been fully resolved.

(a) *The problem.* In the history of moral theology (and also of the problems connected with conscience in other sciences), emphasis has been placed on the object-orientation of the conscience. This tells one *what* one has to do, providing ethical evaluations and formulations of ethical norms, and indicating the solution to problematic situations. In theology these elements are often considered as being "the voice of God"; hence, there is a general tendency in many cases to identify the conscience with practical reason. The fact that the conscience, understood in such terms, can also make mistakes — *per accidens* — has consequently been the cause of harsh discussion through the centuries.

Occasional passages are to be found also in the New Testament in which the conscience is understood as being object-related, e.g. Rom 2, 14 f., Rom 14, 1 Cor 8 and 10. However, in the two latter texts, the fundamental subject-orientation of the conscience also gains in importance. In other passages conscience is considered to be, above all, subject-related, as, for instance, in parts where the conscience is understood as having inner knowledge of the moral goodness of the Christian, and as standing before God, and Christ, and in the Holy Spirit; or where it is emphatically stated that it is only on account of belief in the works of Christ, and of the Holy Spirit which acts within us, that there is such a thing as a "good conscience," e.g. Rom 13, 15; Rom 9, 1; 2 Cor 1, 12; Rom 2, 15; Heb 9, 14; 1 Pt 3, 21.

The expression "follow your conscience," often heard in connection with morality and pastoral matters, is basically subject-related. Nevertheless, it is frequently concerned with object-orientation; it is, after all, about correct conduct in the world of the human being — the object. That is to say, it is not possible to learn about objective and morally correct behavior and conduct in the world from external norms only but also from one's own convictions embedded in the conscience.

Object-orientation is basically the tendency more or less to identify conscience with practical reason. Conversely, the formulation which grants that the moral subject is constituted in the conscience is clearly subject-orientated. This subject-orientation logically precedes the object-orientation.

(b) *Subject-orientated conscience — the basic phenomenon.* In order to comprehend the true essence of the conscience-phenomenon, one is obliged, as indicated above, to return to the matter of the human being's deep-seated self-consciousness. Fundamentally, this consciousness is always present in every human self-realization, so that it concerns not simply the realization of one deed or another, but also, at the same time and very profoundly, the realization of one's very self. This is not intended to be taken as solely a psychological observation but rather in a deeper sense as a transcendental philosophical and theological reflection. This is also valid with regard to morality. A moral decision concerning conduct in any situation is at the same time decidedly — even if unreflectedly — a decision made by the ego about itself. Decisions about concrete actions can only be understood as an expression and symbol of an ethical decision about oneself (Martin Luther: "*Persona facit opera*"; Karol Wojtyla: *The Acting Person*).

It has already been implied that the human being, at his deepest level of consciousness, which is never fully accessible by way of objective reflection, is aware of himself; he therefore is also aware of himself as an existence bound by obligations, a moral being. This is the deepest core of the conscience as personal subject. This deepest experience of conscience is at the same time, and to a certain extent, experienced as part of the person's categorial existence, even in the case of this having been reflected upon and denied; a considered denial is unable to suppress the existential experience.

The existential experience of the person at a reflected level is expressed in various ways: someone considers himself to be bound by obligations; he is aware of the personal responsibility for his self-realization — in a state of freedom both granted and claimed; he holds himself responsible for the furtherance of the "good"; he professes faithfulness to true insight gained through the conscience; he feels required to remain receptive to all things that prove themselves to be either true or good, and also as obliged to be open to his neighbor, etc. All these definitions concern the moral reality of the personal subject. In accordance with this concept of oneself, morality basically deems that the personal subject should accept itself as it is and realize itself as this self. This is the genuine imperative made by the conscience in its fundamental subject-orientation.

In other words, the conscience's genuine and therefore primary interest is the moral goodness of the personal subject as such. And it is solely this personal morality that is morality in the true and original meaning of the word. Every other use of the word is analogous, e.g. "moral rectitude" in life, moral norms for acting, etc.

It is true, on the other hand, that the subject always fulfills itself only when it emerges from itself, steps into the categorial object world and becomes responsibly active there. For this reason, then, the conscience has to be object-oriented.

This is only so because the personal subject expresses itself symbolically in the realization of the object world. Therefore on account of one's goodness one must seek in personal responsibility to act according to the appropriate call of the human objective world. Grounded in one's own personal goodness one strives for right behavior in this world, acting in the interests of the well-being of the human global community as an extension of the core of one's very self. It is precisely because of this relationship between personal moral goodness and the correctness of conduct in the world that this correctness is defined analogously as "moral." For the same reason one is obliged to refer to "primary" subject-orientation and "secondary" object-orientation of the conscience.

It will then be clearly understood that the personal subject's own decisions are either moral or immoral not on account of the subject either actually accepting or rejecting the "morally correct" conduct of the object world, but because he either takes the necessary pains or fails to do so. Personal moral goodness is not a case of someone acting in a morally correct way in our human world, but of acting according to what the conscience recognizes as being right. Moral goodness, being personal, is exclusively something existing within the subject (conscience), as is likewise the "moral truth" and the "moral decision" which exist and take place internally; the latter refers not to a truth "in itself" but to a truth "in myself." Thomas Aquinas agrees with

Aristotle[7] when he says that the "moral truth" with reference to personal decisions is not determined by the objective correctness of the action but by the correct moral orientation applied by the acting subject (*"appetitus rectus"*). It is obvious that here Aquinas has in mind the concept "moral truth" as personal goodness which exists exclusively in the person, i.e., in the decisions made in accordance with the conscience.

It is, therefore, understandable why there is a tendency in present-day moral theology to view conscience as being exclusively subject-orientated and purely concerned with personal moral goodness. The object-orientated "knowledge within conscience" is thus eliminated from the concept "conscience" and banished to the area of practical reason. It then follows, accordingly, that the psychological question concerning moral maturity and immaturity (Kohlberg) in its proper sense does not primarily concern morality and conscience in a narrower sense. There is, of course, no obligation to acknowledge this concept of conscience as implied here. But in a broader sense of the concept "conscience" a fundamental distinction (not separation) between moral goodness as the primary element and moral correctness as the merely secondary element belonging to conscience is imperative.

(c) *Problems of moral theology in history.* An insufficient, or at least an inadequately accurate, differentiation between primary subject-orientated and secondary object-orientated conscience, and the likewise insufficient or inadequate differentiation between personal moral goodness and moral correctness has caused considerable friction and debate in the history of theology. And today it is not in the least as if these difficulties have been simply overridden. A few brief examples will suffice here as illustration.[8]

An allusion has already been made to the concept of "moral truth" in regard to the concrete personal situation as understood by Thomas Aquinas. As already mentioned, Aquinas relates this definition to personal moral goodness, the primary interest of conscience, above all else. It is, of course, possible to interpret this same terminology in another way by relating it to moral correctness, thereby leading the way to judgment of moral rightness *in concreto* as opposed to general norms.[9] There is certainly a danger of not adequately differentiating the two concepts, which is the case if, on the one side, one accepts strictly universal norms of moral correctness while, however, allowing *in situatione* a "moral truth," which is different in content, and without defining it as moral truth and as belonging to the sphere of moral goodness.[10]

It is well known that even as late as the twelfth century St. Bernard of Clairvaux's opinion on so-called "erring conscience" considered it still to be a sin (the contrary of moral goodness) if one acts morally in-correctly even though one is acting in good faith. This opinion was in opposition to that of his contemporary, Abélard. A century later, Thomas Aquinas refuted the opinion held by Bernard but did not go so far as to say that whoever acts in this way is consequently morally good. It is obvious that neither Bernard nor Thomas made a sufficiently clear distinction between primary subject-orientation and secondary object-orientation of conscience. Moral goodness exclusively corresponds with subject-orientation, whereas the "conscience's error," which occurs unintentionally, emerges from the sphere of the conscience's object-orientation and consequently is not concerned with personal good-ness, but with the correctness of moral judgment in the conscience.

Discussion on the problematic nature of "erring conscience" has never been brought to a conclusion. Not only is the emphasis con-stantly placed on the primacy of the "objective" moral norm as against the merely "subjective" and, consequently, its occasional erroneous application in the matter of concrete conscience, although in both cases the individual subject strives for objective correctness, be it *in abstracto* or *in concreto*; but, on the contrary, it also sometimes happens that an erroneous judgment made by the conscience is represented as justified only *per accidens*. Here one overlooks the fact that justified compliance with the conscience's erroneous judgment has nothing to do with either correctness or incorrectness of the object-orientated function of conscience but only concerns the conscience's judgment as such and as an inner element of the conscience; com-pliance with that is assigned to the personal moral goodness and thus to the subject-orientated and, correspondingly, to the primary function of conscience. Fear is unfortunately often expressed that this leads to primacy being granted to the "subjective" conscience instead of the "objective" moral norm; here one overlooks the fact that it has nothing to do with the correctness of a moral norm and the correctness of the content of judgment reached by conscience, but rather with the dis-tinction between moral goodness and moral correctness. One should say that morally good — in an objective sense — is personal fidelity to the conscience's judgment. The judgment which is morally correct — in an objective sense — is that which corresponds to concrete human reality. The relationship between the abstract norm and the concrete judgment made by the conscience is in both cases a matter concerning the object; this will be discussed later.

3. The Object-Orientation of the Conscience
Even if the conscience's subject-orientation is also its primary characteristic, it would be impermissible not to speak here about its object-orientation, especially as the object-orientation is the one more

likely to be dealt with in discussions on conscience. And even if this is referred to as "merely" secondary, it is of considerable and crucial importance for the conscience-phenomenon as a whole. The question here is how conscience provides orientation for a correct human behavior and conduct in this world; this means that it concerns the material content of the function of the conscience.

(a) *The evaluative and normative function of the conscience.* The evaluative and normative function of the conscience is also part of the broader sense of the concept of conscience as the evaluative and normative authority for the human being, and also in the narrower sense of this concept as the authority which expresses an orientation — with regard to content — at times when a concrete decision is to be made.

The individual is certainly not an isolated island within his object-orientated conscience. The pure a priori reason does not exist here. What one in a particular epoch, and what an individual in his life considers to be humanly and morally justifiable is also determined by long-standing traditions and accepted valuations. Whether one as a member of a certain cultural society considers that to take loving care of an aged person up till his very last breath satisfies the demands of piety, or whether in another culture one considers that it is not permissible according to the rules of piety to allow an aged person, on his own account as well as on that of others, to suffer the burdens of old age, is in both cases understood as being explicitly based on practical reason. Differing moral convictions, even when they are the honest result of practical reasoning, are nevertheless to a great extent influenced by upbringing, family traditions, political affiliations and existing trends in particular groups and movements, etc. They are nonetheless often the result of rational insight within conscience and therefore partake of the conscience's subject-orientated and absolute nature.

The individual is thus in the object-orientation of his conscience also not "pure" reason. It is possible that someone, on account of his moral immaturity, quite simply orientates himself according to "convention," and consequently, not morally and in accordance with conscience. But it can also be the case that the decision in favor of conventional behavior is grounded on rational insight and the corresponding fidelity to conscience. Not only the reasons advanced to justify conduct grounded on traditional convention, but also the fact that one advocates and adjusts oneself to convention, can be understood as being rationally justified and, therefore, morally correct and consequently, as being unconditional demands made by the conscience's subject-orientation. Moreover, it is possible that what someone considers and declares to be morally correct is dependent on his personal interests (good or bad) or on his moral disposition and readiness to accept abstract norms and concrete insight; his interests and his disposition can lead him to judge that what suits his interests and readiness really is morally correct.

Nevertheless, one should not too readily subscribe on account of such considerations to the opinion that nothing is practically definite and that nothing in human society is adequately equipped for a consensus. It is indeed true that there is nothing of metaphysical insight as regards practical judgment; but even so, a general skepticism would contradict broader experience. Where there is a possibility of discussing and considering differences of opinion and values, the hope of arriving at practically certain moral truths has not and should not be abandoned. The human being is fundamentally able to get insights of the practical reason.

(b) *Conscience in a specific situation.* Judgment made by conscience in a specific situation, that is, with respect to the person in a concrete situation, is exclusively judgment by the subject who has to reach some decision on the spot. Conscience's judgment on moral correctness, the conscience's subject-orientated assessment and the personal moral decision all take place simultaneously. There is neither a preceding nor a subsequent situation from the point of view of time, only from a logical point of view. This is why the moral subject is quite alone with its conscientious decision, theologically speaking, with and before God.[11]

The statement as formulated above is extremely important for the forming of moral judgment in the conscience, since in the personal situation it is not a matter of academic questions on the subject of moral correctness and not even only a matter of the personal interest afforded to the considerations which slowly lead up to the judgment in the conscience. The moment the conscience reaches an actual decision, it becomes clear that it is also a matter concerning the moral person as a whole — not only a particular action, but also the person's meaning of life and his fate as a person. This is, in any case, valid in those situations in which demands are made on a person's entire being and innermost existence.

How does concrete judgment — judgment about moral correctness — made by the conscience *in situatione* "ensue"? The case of someone completely understanding himself in his concrete situation and directly — that is, without referring to norms of moral acting, making a moral judgment on the correct handling of a concrete situation — is not an impossibility in itself.[12] Why should that be less possible than theoretical judgment of realities and, hence, assessment of moral norms by way of the human ratio? In fact, however, it is true that one does not begin making a concrete judgment in the conscience without any moral insight into the human way of acting. One lives permanently in contact with moral orientation and moral judgments, either assumed or self-formulated, and with moral experience and moral guidance. All this can influence moral rational judgment in the conscience. Nevertheless, this judgment is unique and one which has never been made before by the subject in this particular situation. It contains elements that have never before formed and defined the human being in exactly this way. It is in this sense that judgment in the conscience on concrete moral correctness must be considered as unique and as having been arrived at in a state of isolation.

(c) *The problem of "universal norms and the conscience in a concrete situation."* As a result of what has just been said, the question arises as to the significance of general, normative authorities with regard to the contents of the subject-orientated conscience's judgments in concrete situations. Such normative authorities can possibly be so-called objective norms, which are perhaps advocated by authoritative sources such as acknowledged moralists or authorities in the church, and which are perhaps also accepted in principle by the subject. Normative authorities can also, for example, be the habits of certain societies which are looked upon as being unalterable, or pieces of advice offered by people competent to do so, etc.

According to a long and not yet overcome tradition, it was taught that universal norms point to solutions in concrete situations, whereby the situation is obviously considered as being just a numerical case. The norms were considered "simply applicable" to the case in question. It would seem that it is in fact possible to handle many concrete situations in this way; only "seemingly," however, since the suggested solution overlooks the fact that there are perhaps morally relevant qualitative peculiarities involved in concrete situations and not just quantitative ones. This has been admitted indirectly by several moralists who advocate the principle of a simple "application" of norms to a single case. The formulation that deems the norms are to be "applied, of course, in accordance with the concrete circumstances" makes it clear that the way in which the application is made *in situatione*, in respect of the particular circumstances, is still a matter for moral judgment, since this cannot be deduced from the "objective norms" alone.

This means, briefly, that there are still moral judgments to be made that have not been pronounced so far. This may concern new problems which were overlooked by the community of moralists, or it may concern judgments of conscience that are absolutely determined by the situation. Thus it follows for the object-orientated conscience that moral norms of correct conduct and other normative authorities coming from outside offer basically nothing more than assistance –

real assistance, but nonetheless merely assistance — in the assessment of morally correct decisions made in the conscience.

All this concerns the hermeneutic problems involved in the sphere of moral norms;[13] for wherever concrete norms present themselves, be it in the conscience or elsewhere, the question arises as to the actual truth (in the singular) of the moral correctness. On account of this, one must ask the following questions: whence do such norms come, which facts of human nature are being presupposed in them, which ethical problems (from a historical point of view) are supposed to be thus solved, and under what sort of human self-awareness of a particular period or culture were these norms formulated? Possibly some of the conditions referred to are, at least partly, different from those in which the person who is searching for answers here and now finds himself? It is a matter of course that one who is confronted with existing norms brings along his or her own interests and personal questions and, obviously, the self-awareness that is imparted by them. These norms are then challenged: What is their meaning from the viewpoint of the enquiring subject? Do they offer him help in understanding and, also, can they somehow be modified by the interested subject according to his response to them? Thus a process of mutual questioning and understanding begins, and this can definitely yield a valuable concrete answer to the question on moral behavior. Need it be emphatically stated by the theologian that the described hermeneutic problems also exist with regard to biblical formulations and those of the church?

(d) *Compromise and the conscience.* The group of problems connected with "norm and conscience" is closely related to that of "compromise and the conscience." As it is, the word "compromise" does not have only one meaning. Here it is not used in its actual meaning of a moral compromise. It would concern this meaning if one were convinced of the correctness of a judgment made by the object-orientated conscience and, consequently, knew oneself to be absolutely bound by the subject-orientated conscience; however, and perhaps in order to avoid a possibly significant difficulty, one believes one should decide contrarily to the judgment made by the conscience. That this is morally not right is supported by both Protestant and Catholic theology. Nevertheless, there is a difference in that Protestant theologians very often rely on the incompatibility of divine commandments with the actual world; whoever decides to follow one prescription as opposed to another in a situation where the commandments are incompatible should know that God will not approve of this but nonetheless offers forgiveness in view of this predicament.

Catholic theologians think differently in this respect. Many of them would not refer so readily to divine commandments as unconditional (universal) norms, but would rather consider such norms as being interpretations formulated by human beings about the reality of creation and, therefore, as possibly very inadequate, if not altogether false. Seemingly incompatible norms may possibly be in reality not incompatible at all. In a situation which may appear impossible, one might be reminded of the possibility of a limited moral norm, even if the validity of the one or other norm is not formulated as being limited. This sort of recall not only comes to pass in the course of reflection on difficult situations in life which precedes the concrete situations themselves, but also in the conscience in individual cases *in situatione*. It would then accordingly be a case not of a real moral compromise but only of an apparent one.

According to some moralists (the author included), closer examination of the problems to be solved would show that norms regarding correct conduct within the world always reflect the earthly, and therefore, the limited good/values possessed by human beings. Such limited good/values can, of course, prove themselves incompatible in a concrete and confined situation. The question is then which of the qualities/values that are under consideration in a situation of incompatibility are to be given precedence by reason of their hierarchical order or their concrete urgency. A solution to a problematic situation arrived at in such a way, perhaps in the conscience alone, would at any rate be a compromise, but not a moral compromise in respect of a demand which is considered to be absolutely binding; it would be a compromise made within the limited sphere of human beings' good/values that are not necessarily demanding.

4. Conclusion

The fact that the conscience exists as a phenomenon is doubted by no one; whether it is an ethical phenomenon in the true sense is doubted by some. Even where there is no doubt about this, there are, nevertheless, great differences regarding the explanation and interpretation of the ethical phenomenon. And even in Christian ethics, where there is largely a consensus of opinion, there have been some problems and these are still under discussion. I believed that within the sphere of Christian ethics the focus should be placed, above all, on the primacy of moral goodness as opposed to moral correctness in the world, and that proportionate focus should be placed on the primacy of the conscience's subject-orientation as compared with its object-orientation.

NOTES
   1 Franz Böckle, *Fundamental Moral Theology* (Dublin: Gill and Macmillan 1980. Original German 1977), xii.
   2 A. Molinaro, "Coscienza e norma etica," in T. Goffi and G. Piana, eds., *Corso di*

Morale, I (Brescia, 1983), 449 and especially 453.

3 Cf. also K. Golser, *Gewissen und objektive Sittenordnung. Zum Begriff des Gewissens in der neueren katholischen Moraltheologie* (Vienna 1975).

4 Cf. H. Preuschoft, "Angeborene Verhaltensmuster, Konflikt, Norm, Gewissen: Wie frei sind Entschlüsse?," in J. Fuchs, ed., *Das Gewissen. Vorgegebene Norm verantwortlichen Handelns oder Produkt gesellschaftlicher Zwänge?* (Düsseldorf, 1979), 9–18.

5 Cf. J. Fuchs, *Das Gewissen*, Foreword.

6 J.W. Glaser, "Conscience and Superego: A Key Distinction," *Theological Studies* 32 (1971), 30–47.

7 Thomas Aquinas, *In Eth. Nic.*, L VI, l.1, n. 1131. C. also the essay by D. Capone, *Intorno alla verità morale*, excerpt of dissertation, Pont. Univ. Greg., Naples 1951.

8 Cf. also the essay by K. Golser, note 3 above.

9 Cf. J. Fuchs, "Sittliche Wahrheitem — Heilswahrheiten?," *Stimmen der Zeit* 200 (1982), 662–76.

10 This is how I believe D. Capone's interpretation of *Persona humana* (1975) with regard to homosexuality (*L'Osservature Romano*, 28 January 1976) and also his interpretation of *Humanae vitae* (in *Lateranum* 44 (1978), 195–227) should be understood.

11 Cf. Vat. II, *Gaudium et Spes*, no. 16.

12 Cf. J. Fuchs, The Question Addressed to Conscience, in *Personal Responsibility and Christian Morality* (Washington, D.C.: Georgetown University Press: Dublin: Gill and Macmillan, 1983), 216–28.

13 Cf. also J. Fuchs, Moral Truth – between Objectivism and Subjectivism, in *Christian Ethics in a Secular Arena* (Washington, D.C.: Georgetown University Press: Dublin: Gill and Macmillan, 1984), 29–47 and Hermeneutics in Ethics and Law, ib. 42–47.

IX. Conscience
in a Pluralistic Society

In the Constitution *Gaudium et Spes*, the Second Vatican Council warns us not to expect that all Christians, though equally believing and conscientious, should necessarily arrive at the same solution to all questions regarding life and humanity (no. 43). In his letter on the eightieth anniversary of the encyclical *Rerum Novarum*, Pope Paul VI emphasized the fact that it is not possible, even for the church, to offer solutions to many social problems that are valid in advance for all times and situations (no. 4). When the North American bishops set down their reflections two years ago, in a document that attracted much attention, on the ethical problem of peace and war in the atomic age, they explicitly admitted the possibility that many men of goodwill, including Catholics, might — perhaps even justifiably — refuse their assent with regard to individual questions. For this reason, the German bishops preferred not to offer solutions to concrete questions of detail, and were content to indicate criteria for the discovery of solutions. The Christian church (together with its authorities) has not given the same answer in every era to individual questions regarding the ethics of marriage and sexuality. In today's church, there are moral answers for the various spheres of life that are accepted by many without problems, although many of their non-Christian contemporaries are unable to perceive the rightness of these answers. However, like these latter, many Catholics — including ones who take their Catholicism very seriously — are perplexed at such answers of their church. While some suffer because of this situation, and others infer a radical "arbitrariness," others again calmly and simply disregard the problematic of such a situation. They feel confirmed in this attitude by the fact that a great many non-Catholic Christians, and even more non-Christians, take a path that contradicts the answer of the church's teaching authority and do so not "thoughtlessly," but nevertheless unhesitatingly and confidently.

There are, then, ethical questions that certainly permit a plurality of answers in the church. There are other questions in which the church's teaching authority believes that it must absolutely reject answers that diverge from the positions it has taught. There are Christians who are unwilling or unable to convince themselves of the rightness of traditional or official moral standpoints, and in fact take alternative paths in their lifestyle; they hold one of the other plural models of the moral structuring of life to be more in keeping with human reality. How can these Christians manage their decision? What help can be offered them in their situation, which is so delicate and full of responsibility? The first presupposition for a reply to these questions is a correct understanding of what we are accustomed to call conscience.

1. Conscience

A widespread viewpoint among Catholics holds that the conscience's function is to transmit concrete moral instructions, or general moral norms, to the individual. Clearly, this opinion must not be taken to mean that the conscience is a prefabricated moral information service; otherwise, how could different consciences give mutually contradictory information? And how is it possible for such a diverse pluralism in ethical questions as we actually find today to exist, if we do not wish to assume that human beings are generally irresponsible? It is a fact that we do not simply discover precepts and instructions in the conscience in a passive manner; we ourselves are active in search and discovery, in the acceptance and rejection of moral standpoints. Since this activity takes place in freedom, our awareness of responsibility is very important in shaping the contents of the conscience's affirmations. This is seen precisely in the attempt to instruct consciences in the midst of a widespread pluralism that makes its influence felt. We must, however, consider whether the influence of moral pluralism on individuals and groups is exerted exclusively by means of personal responsibility or whether it partly works without the personal responsibility of forming one's conscience.

From the fact that personal responsibility plays a significant role in the formation of our conscience with respect to questions of right human behavior, we see that the function of the conscience in transmitting to us the mode of right behavior is not its only or even characteristic fundamental function. Rather, the conscience is above all the awareness (a very deep inner insight) that we are free beings — with a freedom that is "given" to us — and that hence demands are made of us and we are morally responsible beings. This freedom, given to us as a participation in absolute freedom, requires that we accept ourselves instead of absolutizing ourselves: it therefore requires an openness and readiness for what the realization of the self that has been entrusted to us demands, in its status before God and in the world. This personal openness and readiness is the deepest and most original requirement of the conscience; we call it the requirement of *personal moral goodness.*

Since the conscience absolutely desires this personal moral goodness, it also demands absolutely that we endeavour conscientiously to seek and discover the moral rightness of behavior in the world of the human being. This means that conduct is not to be abandoned arbitrarily, but must be submitted to the criterion of human, and hence moral, rightness.

One who wishes to correspond to the original moral requirement of moral goodness cannot behave arbitrarily in the realm of the moral pluralism of our society, but must aim at moral rightness in his conduct.

There is in our society more than one single choice with regard to our conduct, and also with regard to right conduct in the various spheres of life. Given this plurality, one must reflect conscientiously on the various choices and on their internal and external authority, in order to strive with the will to arrive at true insight. What is thus grasped as the manner of morally correct conduct becomes the requirement spoken by one's conscience; if one has sought it in moral goodness, one must also follow it with a view to moral goodness. The word spoken by the conscience about morally right behavior is the only word of the inner man about such behavior, and is therefore the only norm in him that is able to guide his decision, which is likewise inner and personal. It is the observance of this norm — and thus not the observance of norms, as such, that are offered from outside one's own self — that achieves inner unity of the self (instead of division), and this determines personal moral goodness on the path that must always be sought afresh in a world that offers a plurality of such choices.

2. Pluralism

Moral pluralism becomes incomprehensible or unacceptable when one understands right behavior to be laid down by God's commandments and directives. For many Christians, it is not just a way of speaking but a genuinely held conviction that all right behavior is regulated by God's instruction (commandment, prohibition, directive); they are unable to understand moral pluralism either in the church or outside it. One may read in this sense certain pious books, serious sermons and also official ecclesiastical documents. These have not yet understood that God's act of commanding and prohibiting does not take place by means of divine legislation: rather, God is the origin of the human being and entrusts his free responsibility to the one who has thus "come forth" from him; so it is humanity itself in its history that must seek to discover, by means of reason, which modes of conduct correspond to humanity, and which do not. Not even the "human nature" that derives from the Creator declares this, although such a formulation is often made. This nature does permit us to "read" what the Creator created as human existence, and thus what he wanted and still wants; but it does not tell us God's will for our free conduct in the realm of what is created: whether this is a case, for example, of international relations between peoples or of marriage and sexuality. It is up to the human being to interpret, to understand, and to evaluate as "human" humanity, the human realities and possibilities and their meaning. Such understanding and evaluating takes place in changing historical and cultural circumstances; we should not therefore be surprised that various (and thus plural) moral norms have been found not only in the course of history and in various cultures, but also today on the basis of the different origins, orientations, interests, viewpoints, etc., of various individuals and groups or societies. During a period when there is a strong tendency to understand freedom and self-determination (as opposed to rule by authorities) as one of the highest values of the human person, one must reckon all the more with a plurality of viewpoints that are not easily guided from outside.

Human self-interpretation with regard to morality is fundamentally possible for all persons, even for those who have no links with a Christian community or who are unable to acknowledge a God, and even for those who do not wish to bother about the inmost experience of moral responsibility. But this experience must be our starting-point: the deep experiential insight that an inmost moral awareness of a required non-arbitrariness belongs to all persons, together with the fundamental possibility of grasping what this non-arbitrariness concretely demands. Nevertheless, not only those attempts that are less than serious, but even very serious attempts to discover moral norms can lead to very different results; moral norms and solutions do not impose themselves in an obvious way on the person in his or her thinking. Thus pluralism cannot be excluded. Many who can believe in God will understand and proclaim their mutually different attempts at solutions as "God's will" or compatible with "God's will."

There is no lawgiver-God who confronts the human possibility of pluralism, and thus of error: neither the commandment of Sinai nor the Sermon on the Mount, nor other biblical texts, are to be understood simply as the revelation of the divinely willed ordering of the morally right conduct of the human being in his world. Faced with widespread pluralism, one cannot appeal to such biblical documents in order to overcome it, for although the Bible's statements about God and man shed much light on the moral understanding of the human person, and the grace promised in the Bible effects an opening of the self to the truth, the ordering of right conduct itself is not disclosed in this way and thus wrested from the human person's endeavor.

It is frequently held that the church can exclude all pluralism from its community and thus from its believers. It is true that a certain moral order has crystallized in the church in the light of faith and under the working of the Holy Spirit, in connection with historically given moral understandings, and that this process of crystallization continues. But since the faith itself does not give the moral answers, and God's Spirit does not occupy the place of the community or the individual believer seeking the moral truth, it is likewise true that a historical search for moral truth, and hence also mistakes and alteration, are not excluded – both in the community and in the individual. To speak about the church's competence to teach and, under certain circumstances, about infallibility "in questions of faith and morals" requires a specific clarification; because the broad realm of all concrete right behavior in the world does *not* belong to the divine and ecclesiastical "deposit" to which the church's search for truth refers directly. This realm of right behavior in the world is fundamentally accessible outside and inside the church – though also in the light of the gospel and under grace – but, as has been said, it does not absolutely exclude varieties of opinion and, indeed, error. The church's teaching authority can and should be active in the realm of truth concerning morally right behavior, and can be certain in this of the support of the Spirit who is present in the church, and hence of special authority; but where the teaching authority insufficiently heeds the inherent boundaries of its competence and authority, its teaching becomes indoctrination and the exercise of power over human beings, for it does not possess unconditional absoluteness. In such a case, one must reckon with justifiable lack of understanding, contradiction and pluralism in laity, priests and bishops.

3. Conscience and Moral Pluralism

Christians must confront the fact of moral pluralism in society and also in the church, and this confrontation is a question of conscience. Different Christians resolve it in different ways. The "more severe" (or "narrower") among them feel very strongly and one-sidedly the obligation of conscience to lead a life that accords with the truth, and only with the truth. In the face of moral pluralism, they easily become unsure and anxious. Instead of obeying the obligation to seek calmly, they attempt to find their path by having recourse to various authoritative instances, such as, for example, the commandments of God, Christian tradition, the church's authority, the word of bishop and priest, the theologian. Certain sermons and episcopal statements fortify them in this attempt, which is often dictated, moreover, by a great personal need for security — "in the conscience." They are often unaware that the various instances to which they appeal are authoritative only in a particular sense and within determined boundaries, and they do not know where, according to the church's teaching, these boundaries lie; they often regard such knowledge as a danger that must be rejected on the obligatory path to the truth and to the carrying out of the truth.

Another path is taken by those who tend rather to an assimilation of plural opinions, or even to a certain wide-reaching arbitrariness; they are quite pleased with the pluralism in society. Why should not the alternative solutions, different from those of tradition or those preached today, possess validity and have good reasons? May not Christians with good intentions — laypeople, priests, theologians —who do not exclude the alternative solutions, or indeed live them as something taken for granted, have good or certainly sufficient reasons for their viewpoints? The inherent boundaries of the instances to which appeal is made by the "more severe" are perhaps known to these people, so that they feel no obstacle from that quarter. Indeed, occasionally one speaks of an explicit tendency consciously and intentionally "to infiltrate the church" — her official teaching — on the basis of the pluralism which in fact exists.

Both of these attempts by Christians to find the correct attitude vis-à-vis pluralism in society are one-sided and therefore unsuccessful. Both somehow lack a clear orientation to the truth that self-evidently and simply opens itself to the truth, and a lifestyle that corresponds to it. This orientation permits neither a one-sided need for security nor an unlimited desire for arbitrariness. The Christian with such an orientation knows that he is absolutely bound to God's will, but he does not find this will positively formulated as a commandment, nor is it "to be read" in nature as the work of God's creation. He takes so seriously what he has discovered within human and Christian society — and in the light of the faith and under grace — to be acquired human insight into morally right conduct guaranteed by good reasons, that he understands himself to be addressed by God therein. He must therefore take with equal seriousness alternative solutions that have been discovered with the same seriousness, and thus he will not easily be intolerant. As a matter of course, he adheres to the moral formation of conscience that has taken place through past centuries, as well as to the church's official word on moral questions. But since insight and the word of the church are also human insight and human word (though certainly also supported by the Spirit of God) he is not disturbed by the fact that in the church's history, changes have occurred in individual moral questions, and that change must occur. He is not anxious about the fact that it was possible in the past, and correspondingly can sometimes be possible in the present, to arrive at a reasonable doubt about individual statements of the church; in certain circumstances, indeed, this can "free" him for alternatives that are well founded. This was also the intention of the Second Vatican Council (in an explanation of the rather "narrow" formulation of no. 25 of *Gaudium et Spes: Acta Synodalia . . .*, vol. III, part VIII, 88). What the Council finally said explicitly regarding possible pluralism in questions posed to mankind applies legitimately, for the believer, to all moral questions: i.e., that even in the church the answer to all questions is not known, and that alternative solutions by conscientious Christians are possible (*Gaudium et Spes*, no. 43). This, then, is the church of Christ, the church that is led by the Spirit and yet lived by human persons themselves: as such, the church is the guide to conscientious, morally right behavior in our world of human persons.

4. Pastoral Aids

The preceding reflections permit us to understand what direction must be taken by catechetical and other pastoral aids, and what central points should be their aim. It is obvious that decisive weight attaches to the elaboration of a clear notion of conscience. The distinction of the conscience with regard to the personal moral goodness of the person and the moral rightness of the person's behavior should be clarified. It is true that the rightness or wrongness of behavior does not as such determine personal moral goodness, but moral goodness — if it is to be itself — requires a serious endeavor to attain true insight into right behavior. Moral goodness, therefore, allows no arbitrariness vis-à-vis a moral pluralism of behavioral models; it requires, in this endeavor, that one honestly take into account the help offered by Christian resources for the attaining of true insights, without closing oneself to possible correct insights of alternative solutions. Such an attitude in the conscience presupposes a willing openness to the working of the Spirit, who always works to bring about personal moral goodness and thereby, secondarily, moral rightness that is to be striven for in behavior.

Believers who attach importance, in the midst of pluralism, to the rightness of their conduct in this world often lack an understanding of the manner in which we can arrive at insight into such rightness. Above all, they often lack the knowledge that we owe moral insights to the active intellectual activity of the human being and of human society. It is therefore important to state clearly the *human* character of moral insights into right behavior — one's own insights, those of others, and those of the church; for it is only by knowing this that one can properly carry out the task of finding one's path in a pluralistic world. This also requires an open introduction to the true or falsely presupposed significance of "Christian" instances like God, the nature of the human person, the Holy Spirit, ecclesiastical tradition and community, the church's teaching authority, theology, etc., as has been indicated above. Human alternative solutions always confront human solutions, even in the church; their value must be discerned, in order to arrive at correct formation of the conscience by means of a conscientious weighing of one against the other.

In leading people to such an endeavor by the conscience in a pluralistic world, special attention must be paid to some specific problems.

First, there exists in the church a tradition that has grown up and a teaching that is proclaimed. In the people of God, these have the privileged status of a presumption (no less and no more) of truth, and thus signify an irreplaceable aid for the Christian path in the world. It is therefore also true that whenever, in the course of time, a change in individual points is discernible in the church, a new path of responsible behavior opens up on each occasion; similarly, when at any period serious reasons against something proposed by the church can be indicated, then the presumption may have to yield, in certain circumstances, to a new and sufficiently well-founded insight.

Second, concrete moral norms of behavior, because they are formulated by human persons (even in the church), run the risk of failing to consider all possible circumstances of human behavior and hence of formulating as a norm with no exceptions, something that is perhaps not at all so absolute. Naturally,. this would have to be demonstrated in each case; and it remains true that there are norms of behavior that permit no exceptions.

Third, a pluralism that arises within the church must be thoroughly discussed within the church. Not every opinion that arises is to be considered acceptable merely because it arises. Believers must be led to the ability to understand, on the basis of the acknowledged conscientiousness and competence of those who uphold alternatives, whether or not such alternatives can find their place in the realm of Christian morality.

Fourth, confronted by the reality of a pluralism of opinion that is arising outside or inside the church, a Christian leadership should opt neither for personal security nor for arbitrariness, for only in that way can healthy reflection in the church be attained. It is clear that what has already been said about the presumption vis-à-vis the church's teaching and about the conscientiousness and competence of discourse in the church is relevant here too. Thus it is possible to discover laboriously a path between security and arbitrariness — as a human attempt in the church to discover the truth about correct behavior in the world.

Fifth, a significant aid could consist in leading believers more and more to see the values that are in question in various modes of conduct, rather than the formulated norms which seek in their fashion to bring recognition to such values. In the case of a choice between "classical" and "alternative" moral conduct, it frequently happens that the challenge to reflect on the values that are emphasized or preserved in one or other solution, rather than on particular normative statements, helps one to arrive at a good and defensible decision. This is true above all in cases in which the subject is clearly unable to reach a positive relationship to the given norms as such. It is, however, true that the act of evaluation does not take place without a relationship to those who evaluate likewise. It would be necessary in certain circumstances to indicate their relationship, or given link, and the responsibility to make the choice of such links in accordance with objectively defensible criteria.

X. Self-Realization and Self-Alienation

Before his death Rabbi Sussja said, "In the world to come, I will not be asked, 'Why were you not Moses?' I will be asked, 'Why were you not Sussja?' " This Hassidic legend[1] makes only one demand of the human person, but this is an absolute demand: self-realization. Rabbi Sussja need not and should not be Moses; the attempt to be Moses would be self-alienation, the realization of what is neither given nor imposed as a task. As long as Sussja fails to bring Sussja to the development of the possibilities that are given him and imposed on him as a task, he lacks final self-realization and lives to a certain extent in self-alienation.

It is occasionally objected that to speak of self-realization is unchristian. The reason for this objection is seen to lie in the requirement of conversion, i.e., the requirement that one should not remain in the self that is actually present, but should bring it to ever greater perfection by continually rising above oneself. It is clear that such an affirmation presupposes a concept of the self different from that of the legend, either understanding the self as self-seeking, or else identifying it with one particular element of the self in its entirety, e.g., with concrete psychological data. There is no doubt that self-realization in the sense of yielding to the self-seeking self, or in the sense of the exclusively psychological realization of self, would not be true human and Christian self-realization in the full sense of this word. We perceive already that an interdisciplinary discussion of themes like "self-realization" and "self-alienation" requires a clarification of the terminology used.

1. Psychology or Ethics?

"Self-realization" is understood to be a fundamental normative principle of human and Christian morality, and in this sense the principle of self-realization finds its place in Christian ethics. But many philosophers use it too; and psychologists, especially representatives of so-called humanistic psychology, take it to be fundamental. We must, however, inquire whether the concept of self-realization is always used by all in the sense set out above.

Several years ago, an American friend of mine, Isaac Franck, expressed his opinion critically as a philosopher about a normative concept of self-realization in "Self-realization as Ethical Norm."[2] Franck deals especially with the representatives of humanistic psychology, but also with certain philosophers. His essay may serve here as a starting-point.[3]

(a) *Psychological or human self-realization?* The chief representatives of humanistic psychology are well-known: A.H. Maslow, C.R. Rogers and Erich Fromm. They have taken over the concept of "self-realization" or "self-actualization" from K. Goldstein, although Franck believes he can show that Goldstein never understood this concept in the sense of humanistic psychology. The chief representatives of humanistic psychology are active above all in the United States of America, but are well known in Europe too. Their psychology enjoys a certain esteem among Christian ethicists.[4] In this psychology, every act that helps to build up and fulfill the human self, and also the self of others, is evaluated positively and is promoted. Every act that has a destructive effect is rejected. Self-realization is thus declared to be the principle and criterion of correct human conduct.

In his essay, Franck establishes that the self to be realized in this psychology is the psychological self that is capable of being experienced. Various developmental possibilities in this self lead to a "fulfilled" and "healthy" self, while the prevention of their development determines symptoms of frustration. Self-realization is fundamentally a descriptive concept here. Nevertheless, the psychologists named above see self-realization, so described, as rooted in the inmost nature of the human person; self-realization is the inmost drive and will of the human person, the motive that sets everything in motion. When self-realization is traced back to the "nature" of the human person, realization of the self is proposed as a requirement, and indeed explicitly as an "ethical" requirement in the understanding of humanistic psychology.

Franck points out that humanistic psychologists do not consider all the tendencies that derive from the interior of the human person to be good and deserving of realization, and he consequently holds that fundamentally it is not self-realization (the realization of the self that actually exists at present) that is the criterion for the goodness (or undesirability) of particular needs or tendencies; for otherwise, all tendencies present in the self, without distinction, would have to be brought to fulfillment. The criterion, therefore, must lie somewhere other than in self-realization. Franck is certainly right, inasmuch as the expression self-realization is understood in terms of its definition to be a selective form of psychological "fulfillment," and only this. This reduces the scope of the term enormously.

(b) *Philosophical reflections.* Franck holds the representatives of humanistic psychology to be "philosophers *manqués*," because they make the move from establishing the presence of psychological facts to ethical requirements. He points out, however, that some philosophers also consider self-realization to be an ethical principle; he refers especially to Stephen C. Pepper and C.A. Campbell for recent times.[5] Their concept of self-realization is strikingly different, however, from that of humanistic psychologists, because the starting-point of their understanding of self-realization is not, one-sidedly, the givenness of psychological experience. Rather, they aim at as broad an integration of human realities as possible, especially those of an interpersonal and social kind. To this extent, Franck sees the ethical criterion of these philosophers too, despite their explicit formulation, not in the realization of the self that actually exists, but in the integration of everything that — independently of "self-realization" — can be considered good and right human conduct in the various spheres of life.

Franck pays more attention to the position of his colleague F.H. Bradley[6] and, in connection with Bradley, the philosophy also of Aristotle. These philosophers too are concerned with self-realization, but this is a goal for them, not a norm. For them, however, the norm is not a part of nature that can be experienced (as in humanistic psychology) and that as such seeks its realization, but rather the value and the dignity of particular partial aspects of the human being, which justify or demand their realization. For Aristotle, the selective criterion for the choice of these aspects is their correspondence with human reason, inasmuch as it is through reason that the human being distinguishes himself/herself from other earthly realities; for Bradley, it is the social self-transcendence of the ego that is the criterion.

In the cases of Aristotle and Bradley, Franck signals philosophical reservations. In the case of Aristotle, he asks whether it is only reason, and not other realities too, that distinguishes us from animals and thus establishes what, humanly considered, is worthy of being realized; and he doubts whether reason (alone) always finds out what is actually worthy of being realized by the human being. Franck understands Bradley to say that, despite his ethical criterion, "morality" is rather a contradiction, since the self that is to be realized experiences in itself goodness and evil as simultaneous but irreconcilable tendencies which both demand to be realized; therefore morality has a necessary reference to religion, which says which self, or what in the contradictory self, is to be realized.

(c) *Which self-realization?* It is obvious that the concept of self-realization is not used in the same sense by all those who apply it or reject it as an ethical concept. The distinction is determined by an antecedent philosophical or theological decision. This is unmistakably clear in the understanding of self-realization found in humanistic psychology, in which the human self is unequivocally reduced to psychological health and integration; the other manifold aspects of human reality, including culture, ethics and religion, are not included in the realization of the self that is demanded. Christian ethicists are correct in acknowledging that many insights of this psychology can be helpful for the discovery of moral judgments in concrete life; one cannot deny, however, that absolutizing an exclusively psychological self-realization ignores other higher values of human reality, and can consequently lead to forms of a fundamentally reduced self-realization that are ethically indefensible.

Instead of this, the philosophers who have been drawn into the discussion seek to bring the human person in his manifold aspects to a harmonious self-realization. It is, of course, significant how each philosopher understands the human person in his dignity and in his values. Despite the reservations expressed by Franck, it appears also to be true that these philosophers do not simply judge individual spheres of human value to deserve realization independently of the concept of self-realization. For how can these values be recognized as deserving realization, unless they are seen in their correspondence to the ethical requirement of the self-realization of the human person *as human person*, i.e. in his totality and taking evaluative account of all aspects of his reality?

The evaluating and judging reason (cf. Aristotle) may not be seen only as an element that distinguishes the human person from the animal, as Franck sees it. It is not precisely the fact that the reason makes us *different* from other creatures that is significant, but rather the (fundamental) capacity given to man by reason to understand himself in all aspects, and especially also from a moral point of view. Thereby, self-realization in the full sense is fundamentally possible. The self-understanding of the human person that is made possible by reason makes it also possible, at least in principle, to judge which of the contradictory tendencies that are present together in the human person should be nurtured or preferred, and which should rather be opposed. For self-realization does not mean the − impossible − realization of all tendencies, even those that are incompatible and even contradictory (cf. Bradley), but distinction and choice with a view to the best realization possible of the *hu·nanum*. This also involves a negative selection which is in reality not self-alienation, but serves a better self-realization. To this extent, morality as self-realization is anything but "self-contradiction."[7]

In this sense, self-realization is not, as Franck thinks, a "morally vacuous concept." Rather, it is precisely and only on the basis of the self-understanding of the human person as such – i.e., the understanding that he tends essentially to self-realization and therefore to progressive humanization – that it is possible to discover and judge which of the manifold possible forms of behavior and attitudes in the entirety of the human person and *in concreto* serve the better self-realization of the human person and are thereby morally valuable or even commanded.

2. Which Image of Man?

Which image of man determines the various stances on the problem of self-realization and self-alienation? Let us attempt to say something about the image of man that understands self-realization as the meaning and task of human existence. Thereby we shall at the same time make clear what self-realization in this context basically means.

(a) *Responsible self-realization*. Self-realization is seen to be the basic and all-inclusive task of each individual self. If the self is understood, not as the author of its own being, but as something objectively existing and given, then the acceptance of the self will be understood as the self-affirmation that is required, rejecting every self-alienation and demanding a positive self-realization that proceeds from the significance of the given self.

Self-realization must take place categorially in the enormously varied reality that is the horizontal "expansion" of the self and its meaningful and correct ordering. The individual varied reality of the self includes in each case body and spirit, the relationship to others and to society, the creation of culture and technology, the experience of joy and sorrow, the experience of tendencies in one's own ego that are humanly constructive and humanly destructive (alienating), etc. This entire reality of the self is to be realized through the progressive humanization of what is given. For this reason, self-realization can be aligned only with the good of the self, understood in its totality. The well-known formulation of Aquinas, that God is hurt only by deeds that contradict the good of the human person, is excellent.[8]

One must therefore search responsibly to discover what serves the good of the self and is thereby genuine self-realization. The criterion is the insight of evaluating reason: "Bonum hominis est secundum rationem esse," "the good of the human person consists in his being in accord with reason," says Thomas Aquinas.[9] Because reason has the possibility of arriving at self-understanding, and also at an understanding of individual realities, it can attempt to evaluate and discover which of the manifold possibilities of action best corresponds to the true good of the human person and to his development.

Self-realization, understood in this way, is not at all selfish. The understanding that a particular choice or renunciation promotes genuine self-realization, is a psychological presupposition and condition (*condicio sine qua non*) of the possibility of such choice and renunciation; this proceeds therefore from the inmost essence of self-realization and is therefore in no way selfish. If, however, self-realization is essentially not selfish, it follows that the conscious non-realization of the self is self-alienation.

(b) *Self-realization as radical openness.* Responsible self-realization will always bear in mind that the self (including its own horizontal "expansion") is a self that discovers itself existing objectively and receives itself. Self-realization therefore demands the exclusion of arbitrary decisions; it remains open vis-à-vis the objectively existing reality that is received. Self-realization always involves this openness. Let us briefly discuss openness in three areas of human reality: openness to the facts and the human meaning of the horizontal reality that belongs to our self; openness to what is unconditioned in conditioned human reality; openness to the other in interpersonal relationships.

The world that belongs to the self (including the world of the earthly reality that incarnates the person) is often called nature.[10] Nature is discovered as something given, and as something that belongs to the self as the expansion of its being as person. It is discovered as already existing, though always in a manner already interpreted and simultaneously transformed by others and by ourselves; and the continuing relation with this reality of "nature" that exists here and now in this way takes place continually in further interpretation and transformation. It is decisively important that the self open itself to reality and to the meaning of this reality for the human person; in other words, the self must not make use of or arbitrarily misuse this reality, but must let itself be measured and determined by it, for otherwise it would no longer have genuine self-realization. This, however, does not mean pure passivity; rather, the self that is informed by letting itself be determined must keep itself open to a realization measured by reason within the whole of reality, as well as in relation to its personal self. This double attitude of openness is the condition for self-realization through the transformation of nature into culture.

Within the pre-existing entire reality of the self that it accepts, there is a remarkable experience that characterizes the human person in its personal-intellectual nature — the experience of the unconditional in the midst of the human reality which is essentially conditional.[11] The self must open itself to this, unless it wishes to live in self-alienation rather than in self-realization. The truth makes an unconditional claim upon the personal man — not in the sense that we cannot err — i.e., mistakenly hold what is false to be true, but rather in the sense that we see what we take to be true with a certain conviction as standing on the horizon of unconditional value: if it is true, then it is always true for everyone.

We must say the same for the unconditional claim of what is good. The experience of the absolute validity of what is good is an original experience of the conscience that is not to be attributed to anything else, irrespective of whatever explanation of this phenomenon may be occasionally proposed. It may be the case that in some questions the evaluative judgment of what is morally good or morally right may turn out to be quite varied; but if someone believes that he has discovered what is morally good or morally right, even if he is materially mistaken, this implies an unconditional personal requirement.

Even when we do not reflect upon this, we always live within the horizon of the absolute validity of what is true and what is good. Even one who explicitly attacks the absoluteness of the true and the good does so while at the same time experiencng in the most interior manner and necessarily (though not explicitly) affirming the absolute validity of the true and the good: consequently, his action is self-contradiction instead of self-realization.

Openness vis-à-vis the givenness of nature and reason, and openness vis-à-vis the unconditional in the conditional reality of the human person, are surpassed by openness vis-à-vis the other. Like one's own self, the other is grasped as a freedom that is not absolute, but bestowed, and thus as a freedom that participates in absolute freedom. This signifies the dignity of the other, like the dignity of one's own self. Openness to the other as the one called and loved by God is the reverent acknowledgment of the inmost dignity of the other, and is our own participation in the love of God for the other. This is true self-realization, since the God who loves the other is present in my own self as the reason for my own dignity. The unselfish self-renunciation in the generous transcending of oneself toward the other is thus seen to be self-realization in one of the deepest dimensions of the human self.

(c) *Vertical self-transcendence as self-realization.* The inner orientation of the human self to innerworldly transcendence is based on the fact that it has received itself. Behind this inmost orientation there necessarily stands something absolutely transcendent, in which every act of transcendence has its meaning and its origin. It is the ground of our self that is ever present in us; we are accustomed to call it God.

Therefore ultimate self-realization consists in transcendence toward what is absolutely transcendent.

It is, therefore, in this vertical self-transcendence that the perfection of the self-realization that transcends the narrow self lies; it is, however, a condition of this, that the ultimate aim of this self-transcendence be not a selfish fulfillment, but absolute transcendence, God. Then we have a self that goes out from itself in its entirety and transfers itself to God.

The transcendent God who is present in our inmost depths imparts himself to us in a particular way in Jesus Christ. He who can believe this sees in Christ the salvation and the kingdom that come to us from God. Jesus Christ, his call, his kingdom of God, his word, his grace, his Sermon on the Mount form an existential factor of our self: and thus the realization of this existential factor belongs essentially, for the believing Christian, to his self-realization. That is why the Christian understands all true self-realization to be ultimately self-realization in Jesus Christ.

3. Conversion and Self-realization

True self-realization means the willing acceptance of the self, the radical openness of the self, horizontal and vertical transcendence of the self. The human person and Christian, moved by contradictory tendencies, will try to live such a self-realization, instead of self-alienation, in the power of grace. This implies a continuous conversion from real and threatening self-alienation to self-realization. Even when fundamental conversion is given in the inmost basic decision, the self-alienating tendency will continually try to wrest small or great victories, and will succeed in doing so. Even the one who is converted needs a continuous conversion that is a renewed turning back and a deepening of the conversion that has already taken place. Self-realization will never perfectly succeed before the promised and then definitive gift of the eschatological realization of the self.

(a) *Conversion to the true self.* The requirement of conversion is found in Jesus' sermon at the beginning of his public activity, as Mark 1:15 relates. Jesus proclaims the coming of the lordship of God, already begun and present in him, i.e., the realization of the love of God in this world. If it is in Jesus, as he himself says, that this lordship of God dawns, then it is obvious that it is not effectively present or accepted without him. Men alienate themselves from the true relationship to God, and thus alienate themselves from the deepest meaning of their self: they refuse the openness and self-transcendence that are demanded by their very being, and shut themselves up in their own closed self. By turning to Jesus and to his message, they can emerge from the narrow closedness and absolutizing of their narrow self, and come to their true self, which opens up and transcends itself. Jesus' call is a call to conversion from self-alienation to self-realization.

In a similar way, Paul shows in the first chapter of the letter to the Romans (18–32), perhaps in a certain generalization, how the human person without Christ (thinking certainly here above all of the pagans) has indeed an inmost experience of God and of the relationship of the human person to God that is thus required of him, yet rejects this relationship and thereby rejects true self-realization. He shows how the human person arrives at this basis, at a reflex self-decision, at a categorial self-actualization in this world which without any doubt means categorial self-alienation. Paul's message is that it is possible to overcome this transcendental and categorial self-alienation only in Jesus Christ, who calls one to, and makes one capable of, such a conversion of self-realization.

In the fifth chapter of the second letter to the Corinthians (16–21), the explicit theme becomes the reshaping and conversion of the "old" creature, the human person alienated from God and from himself, to the "new creation" through the work of Jesus Christ, including reconciliation with God and thereby liberation to the true self. It is God himself who effects such a reconciliation; but the reconciliation does not come into effect unless the human person who is alienated from himself accepts it; if he shuts himself up in himself, he does not come to conversion.

The apostle develops similar thoughts in the sixth chapter of the letter to the Romans, using the sacramental model of baptism here. Dying and rising into Christ's death and resurrection through the effective sign of baptism means the conversion God brings about from a selfish and thus self-alienated, sinful life to a self-realizing life without sin.

In the well-known canticle of love in the thirteenth chapter of the first letter to the Corinthians (1–8), Paul teaches how deeply a conversion that leads to true self-realization must penetrate. To turn to holy and great works as categorial self-realization is insufficient proof of a true conversion and hence of true self-realization, for such works could also have a selfish motivation.

In its deepest essence, the refusal of openness to God is "the sin" in all "sins," insofar as these are sins in the full sense of the word (mortal sin). John says in his first letter (3:4) that all sin is *anomia*, i.e., the act of shutting oneself up in oneself and hence the self-absolutization of the human person, who fundamentally refuses to accept his salvation from God because he wishes to bring it about out of himself.[12] Sin means self-alienation and hence the arrogant refusal of true self-realization.

(b) *The self in contradiction.* The conversion that is required for self-realization presupposes that there is a strong tendency to self-alienation in the human person — even in the converted Christian. To the extent that the Christian lives "in the Spirit," he lives his true self. But to the extent that he also discovers existing in himself the tendency of the "flesh," i.e., of the selfish self, he feels a power at work in him that makes for self-alienation. As Paul teaches in his terminology of "spirit and flesh," we experience ourselves in this era of the world simultaneously as "spiritual" and "carnal," and so we are a "self in contradiction" (cf. Rom 6–8). Paul gives the reason for this in the passages in which he exults and professes that we have been given the Spirit as a power that works against the selfish self, while on the other hand he repeatedly teaches that the Spirit is given to us only pro-visionally, as a down payment, hence not yet in its fullness and definitiveness (cf. 2 Cor 1:22, 5:5; Rom 8:23; cf. also Eph 1:14). It remains the case, therefore, that true self-realization is in a struggle with the tendency to self-alienation.

Self-realization succeeds only to the extent that one accepts in each particular case the grace of the Spirit. He who lives out of the Spirit does the works that are the "fruit" of the Spirit. "To bear fruit" is the deeper terminology of the New Testament, as opposed to speaking about observing the commandments (cf. Gal 5:22; Rom 6:22; Jn 15). Self-realization is the fruit of the Spirit in us.

Another very significant formulation of the New Testament ex-presses continuous conversion as the path to complete self-realization. Both Paul and John speak of their conviction that the believer who is "baptized" and thus "born of God" does not sin, i.e, does not live self-alienation instead of self-realization. "If we have already (in baptism) died to sin, how can we still live in sin?" (Rom 6:2). "We know that the one who is born of God does not sin" (1 Jn 5:18). It seems, accordingly, that the problem of sin has fundamentally found its solution. And yet, beside this Christian conviction, there continually stands the apostle's word of warning: "Let the one who thinks that he stands, take heed lest he fall" (1 Cor 10:12), i.e., lest he fall back, to a greater or lesser degree, from the gift of self-realization into self-alienation.

(c) *Instructions.* It is above all Jesus' Sermon on the Mount that gives, among other things, instructions on true self-realization (Mt chapters 5–7). The first beatitude (5:3) is for the "poor"; it includes basically all the other beatitudes. It is not poverty as such that is praised, for that is a manifestation of need: it is only the poor who are truly poor that are praised. For there are poor people who, like some rich people, put their trust completely in themselves and in their (hoped for) riches. The truly poor are those who, whether poor or rich in the eyes of the world, understand themselves to be poor and weak in their depths, and there-fore honestly put their ultimate hope in God. They are not closed in on themselves, but are open to the source of true riches and true humanity. They do not seek selfishly and one-sidedly the achievement of their own interests, but endeavor to live "the truth" in this world. They are "blessed": they realize in their genuine endeavor what is required of them by the truth of their being. That is self-realization.

The one who knows that he is "poor" in this sense is rich in the hope he has in the God of promises. He will not entrench himself behind selfish interests in the search for the right actualization of his self and his world. Such self-interests — self-alienation — played a role in partly determining certain self-limiting normative formulations of the Old Testament for "correct" behavior in this world, such as the directive of Moses about divorce from a woman by her husband. We are all in danger of entrenching ourselves behind our own interests and of using these as the starting-point for sketching rules of conduct in our life and in our human world — rules that do not express the whole truth. Jesus' antitheses in the Sermon on the Mount oppose this permanent danger of self-alienation.

In this sense, Jesus' radicalisms are the radical requirement made of everyone to be truly himself in each individual case: in the Spirit, in truth, without selfish self-limitation, i.e., without self-alienation. Denial of the selfish self sets one free for realization of the true self, in which true imitation of Jesus consists: "If anyone wishes to go with me, he must deny himself, . . . and he should follow after me in this way" (Mk 8:34).

NOTES

1 M. Buber, *Die Erzählungen der Chassidim* (Zurich, 1949), 394.

2 I. Franck, "Self-realization as Ethical Norm. A Critique," *The Philosophical Forum* 9,1 (Fall 1977), 1–25. Franck was a (Jewish) Professor of the (Catholic) Georgetown University in Washington, D.C.

3 I could have referred to the shorter criticism by B.M. Kiely, *Psychology and Moral Theology: Lines of Convergence* (Rome, 1980), 71 f., who explicitly quotes C. Rogers and understands the "self-fulfillment" of the philosophers referred to explicitly in the sense of "happiness."

4 One may consult, e.g., the moral-psychological dissertation by H. Stich, *Kernstrukturen menschlicher Begegnung. Ethische Implikationen der Kommunikationspsychologie* (Munich, 1977).

5 Stephen C. Pepper, *Ethics* (New York, 1960); C.A. Campbell, *In Defence of Free Will* (Oxford University Press, 1967).

6 F.H. Bradley, *Ethical Studies* (Oxford: Clarendon Press, 1935).

7 Ibid., 313; quoted by Franck, 12.

8 Thomas Aquinas, *S.C.G.* 3, 122.

9 Idem, *S.T.* I–II, 18c.

10 On the following, cf. the reflections: "Nature and Culture — in Bioethics," in J. Fuchs, *Christian Ethics in a Secular Arena* (Washington, D.C.: Georgetown University Press; Dublin: Gill and Macmillan, 1984).

11 On the following arguments, cf. E. Coreth, "Der Mensch ist Transzendenz," in *Herderkorrespondenz* 36 (1982), 442–46.

12 On the exegesis, cf. I. de la Potterie, "Le péché c'est l'iniquité," in *Nouv. Revue Théol.* 78 (1956), 785–97.

PART 3

Christian Moral Life

Continuity in the Church's Moral Teaching?
Religious Liberty as an Example

Married Love: Christian Pluralism in the
Twelfth Century

Disposing of Human Life: Recent Problems in
Bioethics

"Catholic" Medical Moral Theology?

XI. Continuity in the Church's Moral Teaching? Religious Liberty as an Example

1. Introduction to the Problem

In 1985, much attention was paid to an article that appeared in the Roman periodical *La Civiltà Cattolica* (which is not published by the Vatican, but is nevertheless more or less official), under the title: "Il ministero del Papa dopo i due Conilii del Vaticano" ("The ministry of the pope after the two Vatican Councils").[1] The author of the article (the editorial team of the periodical!) makes a distinction between the doctrine of papal infallibility and a certain "infallibilism." The first asserts that a papal teaching can be infallibly true under certain extremely narrowly defined circumstances; infallibilism, on the other hand, means the phenomenon that can at times be observed of not limiting reflection on almost every papal teaching, or indeed almost every word of the popes, to the consideration of its particular meaning and importance, but of approximating it closely — or even very closely indeed — to infallibility, with all the consequences of undesirable and extreme personal attitudes vis-à-vis the person of the popes.

The article under discussion is directed against this phenomenon of infallibilism. The mistaken evaluation of papal statements and words easily implies for many people the equally mistaken opinion that such statements and words correspond to a traditional and constant doctrine in the church, and are therefore true and immutable. Behind this understanding there often lies hidden the opinion, explicit or not, that every phenomenon of tradition, and correspondingly every papal statement, is to be understood without nuances as the manifestation of the Holy Spirit, and not as merely a proclamation that has its origin in human beings, under the assistance of the Holy Spirit, and is attributable to human responsibility. That is the spiritualizing of a church of human beings.

One would have to say the same about non-papal statements of the ecclesiastical magisterium, e.g., about pronouncements of the Congregation for the Doctrine of the Faith or of bishops — whether they are teaching or proposing a particular doctrine, or censuring assertions that depart from such doctrines. When the magisterium acts thus, this does not necessarily mean that the doctrine proposed or defended by it is a proposition of faith; nor does it mean that the doctrine has taken precisely this form in all periods, and that one is therefore absolutely obliged to adhere to the teaching that has been handed on. It means therefore only that the church's magisterium today believes that it has weighty reasons for making a decision thus and not otherwise; and precisely in questions of moral theology, which cannot be decided on the basis of faith alone, one can reckon with such a possibility in certain circumstances. New knowledge and new insights can lead to such a development within the church.

A few years ago, a moral theologian published an essay in which he asks whether the church has ever changed a doctrine of moral theology that it had previously defended: his own answer was in the negative.[2] A church historian praised him in a discussion for his apologetic endeavor, but went on to affirm that this was an endeavor undertaken without sufficient knowledge of history. Likewise, the rather frequent use of the formulation "the constant teaching of the church" in ecclesiastical documents is often more an apologetic than a historical statement. Many Catholics, including theologians, react allergically when the supposition or statement is expressed that some questions of moral theology did not always find the answer in the church that is the official answer today. The essay previously mentioned (*La Civiltà Cattolica*) deals with the problem that sometimes arises, of the continuity and discontinuity of statements about moral theology in the history of the church.

This chapter deals with the problem of continuity and discontinuity in questions of moral theology in the church, not in a theoretical manner, but by substantiating the fact that both continuity and discontinuity exist. We shall do this by means of an example that brought much disquiet to the church during the Second Vatican Council — perhaps the greatest upheaval during the entire Council. Nevertheless, after long discussions the Council found an almost unanimous solution in the decree *Dignitatis Humanae*. The question was that of religious liberty.

When the right to religious liberty was approved at the Council, the problem of the significance of doctrinal tradition (continuity and discontinuity) in moral questions had been thought through and brought to an acceptable solution. We shall now reflect on this fact.

It is clear that in what follows we are not concerned with the problem of religious liberty, or a detailed exposition of the history of the Council with regard to religious liberty, or with the history of religious liberty in different centuries, but only with the question of how the Council coped with the problem of an apparently non-continuous tradition of moral theology; the decisive word here is "coped."

2. The Theme of the Council's Declaration

The theme of religious liberty can pose numerous very delicate questions. For the Council to arrive at a conclusion, the direction of the Council had to delimit the theme exactly, in order to avoid a super-fluous flood of opposition "bound to tradition." It was not only the theme of religious liberty by itself that had to be considered, but also the delicate and controversial problem of the tradition of centuries with regard to religious liberty; and this consideration had to be kept within due limits. Indeed, the theme of religious liberty had to be made more precise and to be clearly defined, because of the problem of tradition. This is what interests us here.

Religious liberty can have various meanings. (1) Is the choice of religious commitment or the adoption of a religious position left to the free choice of the individual or of a society; or is there the one true religion to which one must adhere when one discovers it in an honest search? Here, we are obviously dealing with the problem of indiffer-entism, which undoubtedly contradicts Christian tradition. Some Council fathers feared that the intended declaration of the right to religious liberty implied the thesis of indifferentism, which is con-trary to tradition. From this viewpoint, the theme of religious liberty had to be formulated and defined in such a way that concern for fidelity to tradition could find nothing objectionable coming from the problem of indifferentism.

(2) It was also necessary to exclude from the theme of religious liberty the traditional question, discussed or formulated above all from the last century onwards, about whether the right to existence, public character and propaganda belonged only to the truth and not also to error, i.e., only to the single true religion (the Catholic religion) or also to other religions and *Weltanschauungen*. It had to be made explicit that it was not a case of an objective right on the part of truth or error, but a case of an objective right on the part of persons — viz., their right to religious liberty. The discussions at the Council showed how dif-ficult it was for some Council fathers to understand this distinction, because of a particular teaching that had been handed on.

(3) The Council's declaration does not deal with the problem felt by many, but equally feared by many others as foreign to tradition, of

the rights of individuals and of groups to freedom within the church itself. It was necessary to formulate clearly that this question was not open to discussion.

(4) Even the fundamental question of the positive right of each human person to free, responsible development of his own possibilities in the sphere of religious reality could not be posed, still less affirmed, for many Council fathers would have suspected that such a formulation hid the denial of traditionally emphasized limits to Christian freedom. It is for this reason that religious liberty is always understood only negatively, as freedom from constraint and hindrance in religious desires in the societal and civic sphere.

(5) Likewise, the full problematic of the relationship of church and state does not belong to the theme of the Council's declaration, even though the problem of religious liberty first appeared at the Council in the ninth chapter of the scheme of the Constitution on the Church,[3] precisely in the discussion about the relationship between church and state. Although the problem of religious liberty was separated entirely from this sphere, the problem of religious liberty and the state remained, causing many to be concerned about fidelity to tradition, because of traditional opinions about the task and competence of the state in its relationship to the church and to religion.

In accordance with these clarifications and limitations, the theme of the Council's declaration on religious freedom is, briefly, as follows. (1) The dignity of the human person has its profound roots in the Gospel, but slowly became more and more acknowledged in the course of the centuries, and finally reached its fuller acknowledgment in our times. (2) Fuller attention is paid to the religious liberty which has its ultimate basis in this dignity. (3) This liberty is then defined in the sense of religious liberty in the societal, civic and political field. The Council's declaration about religious liberty therefore received, in its fifth and final draft, the explanatory and limiting subtitle: "The right of the person and of societies to societal and civic liberty in religious matters."

The introduction of these clarifications and limitations meant the elimination of many possible problems concerning sufficient, necessary fidelity to the church's teaching tradition when the declaration was drawn up. But some of the elements eliminated at the Council had played a significant role through the centuries in the understanding of religious liberty; they had conditioned and determined the teaching and the praxis of the church, even in part up to the time of the Council — and this, to a large extent, in a different sense from that of the final declaration of the Council. It is therefore easy to understand how these elements occurred again and again in the course of the Council discussions as an exhortation to fidelity to the tradition that had to be preserved. There was a fear of an anti-traditional innovation.

Thus, despite all clarifications and limitations, loyalty to tradition is repeatedly used as an argument against the declaration of the Council. But more is at stake than this. If the Council's declaration goes beyond the previous understanding of religious liberty, and does this in a way that does not simply correspond to the officially valid teaching of the church in the period up to the Council, the Council fathers must have been aware of this, and this must have been seen by them as necessary and justified. The conciliar declaration is therefore a step that says something about the real significance of tradition and of continuity and discontinuity in moral questions.

3. Tradition and Innovation in the Council's Consciousness

As has already been said, the first attempt at a conciliar statement about religious liberty is found in the ninth chapter of the schema of the Constitution on the Church (1962). In terms of content, this draft corresponds to what was said officially in more or less the same terms in the church in the hundred years that led up to the Council. The Council's final statement about religious liberty (1965) is different from this in various points. This difference cannot have escaped the notice of the Council, and thus, the problem of "tradition" must have been present in the consciousness of the Council fathers.

A first draft of a possible conciliar statement was proposed in 1963 by the Secretariat for Unity as the fifth chapter of the Decree on Ecumenism. An independent document followed this in 1964, a second draft that was likewise proposed by the Secretariat for Unity.[4] The Secretariat for Unity attempted to show that there was no difference between the traditional understanding of religious liberty, as this had been expressed in the ninth chapter of the schema of the Constitution on the Church, and the present declaration (which was in fundamental agreement with the definitive document); the difference which did in fact exist had to be explained away. Archbishop Garrone of Toulouse showed in the discussion that he did not agree with this procedure.[5] He pleaded that one should say honestly and openly that the church's teaching and praxis in the past were certainly not in full harmony with the text of the document that now lay before the Council; a judicious explanation of this should be added to the text. In fact, the text of the declaration, produced by the Secretariat for Unity with a clearly apologetic intention, did not reappear in later conciliar drafts of the text. The Council was therefore aware of a certain difference, a discontinuity, in the understanding of religious liberty. The later conciliar drafts of the text are exceedingly careful when they touch on the problem of this awareness.

Thus, the definitive text of the conciliar declaration says (no. 1), on the one hand, that the Council wished to consult "holy tradition and the doctrine of the church", but adds that it does this in order to bring forth "what is new" from these, although "in harmony with what is old." This is a cautious formulation, admitting that something "new" is being said, but adding that this is "drawn forth" from tradition and the doctrine of the church and "is in harmony with what is old." How this is so, is not said; obviously the Council fathers, even the "opposition," were almost unanimously in agreement with the careful balance of this affirmation.

The other cautious formulation is also found in programmatic form at the beginning of the conciliar statement. Bishops had repeatedly said that they feared that the new declaration contradicted the teaching of earlier popes; here, they were thinking above all of the popes of the nineteenth century, up to Leo XIII. The Council statement now says that it intends to "take further" the "teaching of the *more recent* popes" on religious liberty. In an earlier draft, this reads "popes," instead of "the more recent popes." The new formulation makes it clear that it is not only the teaching of the popes of the last century, but also the teaching of the popes of this century — above all John XXIII (the encyclical *Pacem in Terris*) — that is to be taken into account in this development. "Taking further" here clearly means more than mere "repetition": there is a development here that goes beyond the teaching of the previous popes.

In parentheses: in the same context, in the preceding sentence, the Council observes that religious liberty does not (as many opponents feared) abolish the doctrine of the moral obligation to venerate God, but that on this question the Council stands by "traditional Catholic teaching." When this "traditional" teaching, which the Council upholds, was described more closely, and with apologetic intention, a slip was overlooked in the editing. The text speaks of the traditional, and also conciliar (!), teaching about the moral obligation of human persons "and of societies" with regard to the true religion and the unique church of Christ; but such an obligation on the part of "societies" is denied precisely by the declaration about the religious liberty of human *persons*.

Archbishop Garrone's call to avoid an apologetic cover-up in the conciliar text, and to speak openly and honestly about the position of the church in earlier centuries on the problem of religious liberty, was heeded in a certain manner in the second part of the conciliar declaration. At one point it is said clearly that the teaching on the dignity of the human person belongs unambiguously to the teaching of the gospel: although the same is not true of the explicit teaching about religious liberty, it is in harmony with the first teaching. Since religious liberty is not understood to be the explicit teaching of the gospel, it could have been appropriately possible here to say something about a difference that could not be excluded in the manner of thinking or teaching in the various situations in the course of church history. There was undoubtedly an awareness of the difficulty with regard to tradition, and this is touched upon (in no. 12), although with the following distinction: in the case of the *teaching* of the church, it is only emphasized that all periods have insisted "that no one may be forced to believe." In all other problems of religious liberty, it is not the teaching of the church that is spoken of, but its praxis on its pilgrim journey through the ages in the changes of human history. Delicate but frank words are used in speaking of this praxis, for a way of behaving came about "that was little in accord with the spirit of the Gospel, and indeed was in opposition to it." Nevertheless, if one supposes that all this happened in good faith, then the praxis also implies a teaching that was little in accord with the spirit of the gospel, and indeed was in opposition to it. A cautious explanation adds that it is clear that the leaven of the gospel takes a long time to pervade the spirit of human persons, and that it made its contribution to the deeper conviction regarding the dignity of the human person, and correspondingly regarding the right to religious liberty (no. 13).

The Council's task to find the words to speak about the teaching of a long tradition in comparison to the text of the conciliar declaration was exceedingly delicate and difficult because of the different attitudes of the Council fathers, who would have to support the Council's declaration by a wide majority. And yet the formulations are so transparent that the Council's declaration about religious liberty is not simply to be called a continuation of tradition's teaching and praxis, with no break in continuity. We shall now discuss this.

4. The Council's Change-around

It is possible to distinguish the change in the understanding of religious liberty at the Council from a change that took place outside the Council, although a relationship exists between the two.

(1) The conciliar change can be demonstrated by means of two different documents, both dealt with by the Council. The first is the already mentioned ninth chapter (about the relationship between church and state) of the schema of the Constitution on the Church, produced by the theological commission; in terms of content, this schema generally corresponded to the ecclesiastical teaching that went back to the previous century. Many Council fathers felt that it was not possible to speak in this way at the Council today, especially in the age of a recognized secular autonomy of the state, of ecclesiastical ecumenism and of awareness of the dignity and rights of the human person. However, since this schema was never discussed in its entirety

at the Council, the ninth chapter dealing with religious liberty did not come before the Council. The Secretariat for Unity, more than others, was sensitive to the impossibility of tackling the theme of religious liberty today in the manner of this ninth chapter (and hence in the manner of the teaching of a certain past period). The Secretariat proposed to the Council a schema that was conceived in a substantially different way, and this finally became the definitive conciliar declaration about religious liberty, after repeated rewriting.

According to the schema proposed by the theological commission, the state, which is based ultimately on God's creation, may favor neither indifferentism, which holds all religions to be of equal value, nor the profane neutrality or laicism of the state that closes itself to every religious reality. Both tendencies are fundamentally religious establishments on the part of the state. The negative positions were justified emphases of the papal teaching of the nineteenth century, directed against clearly liberal tendencies. But the commission's document goes further in its interpretation of both statements: thus, the state as God's creation must honor the creator, not only through its citizens, but also as such, and hence through its political representatives. It must carry out this religious cult in the manner willed by God – i.e., in the Catholic Church, the only true religion. This can hold true per se only when the State "is Catholic," i.e., when the great majority of the citizens and politicians are Catholic. In such a state, the non-Catholic religion has no *right* to religious liberty, to freedom of confession, cult and propaganda; the practice of such a religious cult can, however, in certain circumstances, and within limits, according to the interest of the good of society, be *tolerated*. If, on the other hand, the state is not Catholic in this sense, the true religion which God has revealed as such and which he has willed (and thus the *church*) has the right to full religious liberty in accordance with the natural law, and the state may not hinder this. A *personal* right to religious liberty is not explicitly considered in this present schema.

It is clear that something other than full continuity exists between this understanding, which was correctly held to be the traditional understanding, and that of the Secretariat for Unity and of the conciliar declaration; it is for the moment irrelevant to ask which historically conditioned misunderstandings led to the theses of the "traditional" understanding. The conciliar declaration on religious liberty explicitly opposes every form of indifferentism; all human persons are morally bound, and fundamentally also possess sufficient capacity, to seek religious truth and to live it as they find it. Therein lies the reason for their dignity as human persons. Human society and the state must respect this dignity, which exists as the characteristic of all human persons and includes also the fundamental right, based on this dignity, to freedom from force or hindrance by others in religious matters — even if one does not conform to the conviction of his conscience in his personal decisions (no. 2). The state is therefore not wholly profane, neutral, laicist; this, however, is not because it ought to defend and care for religious truth (the "Catholic state") and hence the good of the church, but because its competence is to care for the common good or, more precisely, for public order (*ordo publicus*); and this includes above all the protection of the personal right to religious liberty. It is not religious truth as such that establishes the rights and duties of the state in the religious sphere, but the objective right of all *persons* to religious liberty. The state as such has no competence to decide in religious matters and to exercise coercion or hindrance in religious matters as a result of such decisions; its duty is rather to protect the right of the citizens to religious liberty. Only when the right to religious liberty is misused and damages the public good or public order, e.g., by infringement of fundamental rights and fundamental ethical principles, does the state have the right to intervene as guarantor of public order (no. 7); this, however, concedes to the state a right (not further defined, and not easy to define) to decide what is and is not the misuse of religious liberty.

(2) The change outside the Council in the understanding of religious liberty can be seen in three significant texts that followed each other in the years before and during the Council. The texts are the following: (1) an article by Cardinal Alfredo Ottaviani, the prefect of what was still called the Holy Office, "Doveri dello Stato Cattolico" (Rights of the Catholic state);[6] (2) the address of Pope Pius XII on 6 December 1953 to the Italian Union of Catholic Jurists;[7] (3) the encyclical *Pacem in Terris* of Pope John XXIII, of 11 April 1963.[8]

Ottaviani's essay refers above all to article 5 of the Spanish constitution of that time (which completely conformed to Pius XI's pact with the Italian state of 30 May 1929). Ottaviani understood Spain to be a "Catholic state" and wished therefore to show, even against the opinion of some Catholics, that it is obliged to national confession and defense of the Catholic religion as the only true religion. This thesis means that other religions *as such* are not at all to be tolerated; the hypothesis is that a non-Catholic religion can be tolerated only for very serious reasons, but the propaganda of such a religion cannot be tolerated. In short, the non-Catholic churches have no right to freedom, and the person does not have a right to religious liberty; only the *truth* has a right, i.e. the truth of the one true religion, the Catholic church, and the necessary defense of this right goes so far as to exclude tolerance of a non-Catholic cult.

In his address, delivered a few months after Ottaviani's article, Pius XII clearly referred to this text. He agreed with it in its fundamental propositions, but not in its severe statements about the tolerance of non-Catholic cults. Pius XII too started from the assumption that "Catholic states" exist, but held that these cannot be considered in isolation, but must be seen in their relationships to non-Catholic states in the world as a whole. If Ottaviani's stance of non-tolerance were to be applied in individual states, this could only harm the greater good of the universal church in the world. While one cannot give a positive authorization to teach error (the error of the non-Catholic cults), it is possible for serious reasons to tolerate, and refrain from repressing, a non-Catholic cult. Pius XII, then, did not yet consider the right of the *human person* to religious liberty, but only the good of the one *true church.*

After these two texts of highly placed ecclesiastical authorities in 1953, there appeared ten years later in 1963 (during the Council, which itself was preparing a declaration on religious liberty) the encyclical *Pacem in Terris* of Pope John XXIII. He speaks in this of the outlook and needs of humanity today, which, together with the United Nations Declaration on Human Rights, cause him to speak of human rights; the Pope sees these rights in a way similar to the United Nations declaration but also, by referring repeatedly to Leo XIII, he sees them as rooted in the dignity of the human person. He also speaks in this context briefly, although at greater length than the UN Declaration on Human Rights, of the right to give private and public worship to God in accordance with the norm of a rightly formed conscience (a similar formulation occurs in the Council's declaration!).[9] It is, then, not a case of the right, freedom and tolerance of religions, churches and cults, but rather the right of each *person* to religious liberty — a right of which we are especially aware today. It is no longer a matter of rights that are based on truth or error, but of the right that is based on the dignity of the human person, to decide and to behave spontaneously in religious questions and not because of external coercion or hindrance. (As has already been pointed out, there is still no restriction in this text when the presupposition is made that such a personal decision is made in accordance with a rightly formed conscience; the final text of the conciliar declaration speaks differently.) According to the encyclical, it pertains to the possibility of making a personal religious decision, that one comes together with like-minded persons to form groups and communities. The path therefore leads, not from the freedom of the church to personal freedom, but vice versa from personal freedom to the freedom of the church, without overlooking the fact that this freedom belongs to the church from its foundation (as the later conciliar declaration also says explicitly). In Pope John's encyclical, there has been a turning away from the problematic and the concept of Ottaviani and of Pius XII to arrive at the position that was first laid before the Council in the schema of the Secretariat for Unity, and was decided, after long efforts, in the final declaration of the Council. Naturally, *Pacem in Terris* also belonged to the statements of the "more recent" popes, which the conciliar declaration wished to take up and carry further (no. 1). The texts of Ottaviani and Pius XII were not able to prevent the change introduced by the Council while the brief exposition of John XXIII's encyclical did not make superfluous a further, hard discussion at the Council.

5. Centuries-long Traditions as Background to the Council's Change-around

When the Council spoke of "carrying further," it always faced confrontation with the ideas of the past, especially with statements of the ecclesiastical magisterium in the nineteenth century, but also with those of earlier centuries (cf. the Council's remark about ecclesiastical mistakes in earlier centuries, but also the quotations in the article by the canon lawyer Cardinal Ottaviani). To understand the extent of the change brought about by the Council, therefore, it is not enough to examine the Council discussion in isolation. A short look at the official papal church teaching of the nineteenth century, is just as necessary as an albeit even briefer look at "religious liberty" in the preceding centuries of church history.

(1) The ecclesiastical teaching of the nineteenth century, taken as *terminus a quo* of the conciliar change, is largely to be understood as a reaction against the tendency of the Enlightenment to indifferentism, and against the understanding of freedom, emancipation and secular neutrality which corresponded to this tendency. Gregory XVI, Pius IX and Leo XIII attacked this tendency, although in a very one-sided manner; they were still influenced by the relationship between church and state of the preceding historical period.

Gregory XVI, in his famous encyclical *Mirari vos* (1832),[10] understood the freedoms that were demanded at that time, including freedom of conscience and of opinion (and thus also religious liberty) as the expression and emanation of a nihilistic indifferentism. It would accordingly be indifferentism to attempt to picture a ("Catholic") state without the right and duty to defend the (one and true) church; other cults could therefore at most be tolerated, under certain circumstances, but neither these cults nor their adherents could have *rights* to freedom.

Pius IX is well known not only because of his encyclical *Quanta Cura* (1864),[11] but also and above all because of the *Syllabus* (1864).[12] He opposed a naturalism and liberalism understood exclusively as hostile to the church: against this, he proposed an authoritarian church to be protected and defended by the ("Catholic") state. For him, a state understood otherwise could be seen only as the personification of indifferentism, neutralism and laicism. Pius IX too was not yet sufficiently able to see that rights to freedom can exist that have nothing to do with indifferentism, neutralism and laicism. This presupposition explains the following theses (here adduced as examples) that are condemned in the *Syllabus*:

15: Every person is free to adhere to and profess whatever religion he holds to be true in the judgment of his reason.

16: Human persons can go along the way of salvation and reach eternal salvation in every religious cult.

17: One may hope for the salvation of all who do not belong to the true church of Christ.

35: The church is to be separated from the state, and the state from the church.

77: In our times, it is no longer appropriate to declare the Catholic religion to be the only religion of the state, to the exclusion of all other cults.

78: It is therefore praiseworthy that the law provides in some "Catholic" areas the possibility for persons who emigrate there to practice their own cult publicly.

79: It is false to say that the freedom of cult of the individual and the concession to all of the right to public expression of opinion lead to the corruption of morals and minds, and spread the plague of indifferentism.

Leo XIII fundamentally carried Pius IX's fight against laicist liberalism further, and appealed to his *Syllabus;* one should note above all his encyclicals *Diuturnum Illud* (29 June 1891), *Immortale Dei* (1 November 1885), *Libertas Praestantissimum* (20 June 1888), *Sapientiae Christianae* (10 January 1890). However, he emphasized more strongly than Pius the autonomy of the state, appealing to Pope Gelasius I,[13] while demanding from the state the guarantee of the freedom of the one church and allowing it at most a certain tolerance of other cults. He understood the state in a rather authoritarian way, as lord and educator of its subjects, whom it must protect from error; there is, accordingly, no very strong emphasis on an autonomous independence of the society (and thereby also of the individual person) vis-à-vis the state. Nevertheless, Leo spoke more than Pius of legitimate freedoms belonging to the citizens, although not of a legitimate freedom of conscience. And the Pope was very fond of speaking of the dignity of the person and of his corresponding right (as a member of the church) to practice his worship of God in private and in public (against all dictatorships).

If one reflects on the teaching of these three popes of the nineteenth century, put forward with high authority, then one understands that bishops and theologians of the twentieth century faced a confrontation with a tradition that made it hard for them to think differently from these popes. This would have been easier at certain points, if they had paid more attention to the situations that determined what the popes had said, for they concentrated on a dangerous enemy and were not yet able to see the difference between certain freedoms and the indifferentism that was to be condemned. These popes themselves concentrated so strongly on their enemy partly because they too came from a particular tradition. In order to understand better the change made at the Second Vatican Council, we must reflect very briefly on the ecclesiastical "treatment" of personal religious liberty in the course of church history.

(2) Because it is necessary to be brief, it is better now not to go backward, to the eighteenth century, but to start at the beginning of church history and go forward to the nineteenth century. One fundamental thesis of religious liberty has always been upheld by the church: that coercion to accept the Christian faith is not permissible. It is another question whether on occasions in the history of the church this fundamental thesis has been contradicted in fact or in spirit; one may think of Charlemagne's efforts to convert the Saxons, or of the obligation laid on the Jews in Rome to be present at Christian sermons.

In the Roman empire, the Christian religion and the fact of being a Christian were illegal from the beginning, and were often subject to severe punishments. Christians were free only after the edict of tolerance in 311. This situation slowly changed, however, to a caesaropapism in which paganism now lost its freedom and was in general no longer tolerated. The (baptized) heretics were in the same situation as the pagans: public religious error, even of an individual, was not permitted, and it was suppressed, even with the use of violence. Augustine agreed with the severe punishment of heretics, with the exception of the death penalty (in this he differed from Thomas Aquinas in the Middle Ages). Leo I praised the vigorous actions of the emperor against heretics. Pope Gelasius I, however, finally resisted the emperor's power in religious and ecclesiastical matters, which had in the meantime become excessively great; he did so with full clarity in his famous letter about the two powers that must be sharply distinguished on this earth, the pope and the emperor (494).[14]

The medieval world of *Christianitas* (the empire and the predominant papacy) was absolutely intolerant of heretics, and did not hesitate to apply the death penalty. A broad tolerance existed vis-à-vis non-Christians who did not belong to the *Christianitas*,[15] but they were not granted any right to religious liberty.

Since the sixteenth century, there has no longer been *Christianitas,* but only nations and churches. Freedom of church and religion was in general not a dominant idea; religious confession gave the reason for killing and for fighting religious wars. Ultimately, only the prince had religious freedom, not his subjects: *cuius regio, eius religio*; the freedom to go to a region "with a different religion" was not religious liberty. It was the humanists who understood the injustice of such "solutions" and protested against them. The various attempts at solutions led later to the system of the *ancien règime*, in which the privileged church was the state religion. More liberal drives to freedom rose against this system with the French Revolution, and later the popes who came from the *ancien règime* in the nineteenth century tried to fight against these tendencies: this was the "tradition" that the Second Vatican Council had to overcome.

6. Final Considerations

It was difficult for many Council fathers to see in the declaration *Dignitatis Humanae* on religious liberty only a continuous development, without innovation and partial discontinuity, of the papal teaching of the nineteenth century, which had been carried forward in part until the time of the Council. Seeing the rich variations in the relevant teaching in the course of church history can only make such a perspective more difficult. Yet it would be false to speak only of discontinuity of ecclesiastical teaching. There was also continuity, although mixed with discontinuity.

There was continuity in the church's teaching, above all in the unbroken teaching on the impermissibility of coercion and hindrance with regard to the acceptance of the Christian faith. An aspect of continuity is likewise the awareness at every period to some extent that a just solution to the problematic of the freedom of faith and church in society must be sought. Behind this stood the constant conviction that the Christian church and Christians are owed a freedom, however this was established and described. As for the state's relationship to faith and church, it was always known fundamentally — despite the extremely varied realizations of this relationship, which were frequently historically determined — that the state may not dominate the church, nor itself be either indifferentist nor laicist-neutralist. The often changing statements about the relationship to the religiosity of those who do not belong to the "one true" church seem to show that there has always been a profound sensitivity for the sacrality of this realm — even when it was often not possible to see how to bring it into harmony with other convictions.

Within such a continuity there exists discontinuity — as the various concrete expressions of that continuity: this exists in very different forms, and also alternates from one form to another. This is shown by looking at the problematic of religious liberty during the Council, before the Council, in the last century and in the attempt over many centuries to solve the problem. Religious liberty, however, is taken here only as an example; in principle, such a possibility exists also in other ethical questions, and therefore also the possibility of tension between loyalty to tradition and the search for a possible solution to the problem today.

Were some of the teachings given in the course of the various traditions, and proclaimed by the intervention of the highest authority, false? Certainly, in the sense that they must be termed unacceptable today in the terms in which they were formulated and in the sense intended at that period. This does not exclude the possibility that the insights possible to us today were not prudent under the conditions and in the consciousness of other periods; as Karl Rahner once put it, they were neither relevant nor the only insights possible. In this sense, one could say that they were correct at that period, but cannot be transferred to the modern period. Today indeed, we can demonstrate where the insufficiency and mistakes of former insights lie; it does not contradict this to say that even then there were nonconformists who were already able to see matters in the same way, or in a similar way, to our manner of seeing them. *Dignitatis Humanae* also observes that the path of deeper insight has let us come to a more correct understanding of what people formulated differently at other periods and believed had to be formulated differently.

The Council's declaration observes explicitly that the proposed solution to the problem of religious liberty is not, in these terms, a direct statement of the gospel. Is the declaration perhaps to be understood as a declaration of the natural law — as was certainly intended at the Council, even if this was deplored by many? Would that mean that we have at last found the permanent solution of the natural law? Or must not "natural law" mean here too that we have found the correct solution, in terms of natural law, for today under the circumstances and in the consciousness of today? Similar queries may be expected in the case of other moral questions with different contents.[16]

NOTES

1 *La Civiltà Cattolica* 136 (1985, IV), 209–21.

2 M. Zalba, "Num Ecclesia Doctrinam suam mutaverit?", *Periodica MCL* 54 (1965), 461–89.

3 *Acta Synodalia Sacrosancti Concilii Vaticani II* (1962), vol. I, p. III, 65–74.

4 *Acta*, vol. III, p. II, 317–27.

5 *Acta*, vol. III, p. II, 533–35.

6 *Miscell. Comill.*, 19 (1953), XV–XXVIII; also in *L'Osservatore Romano*, 4 March 1953.

7 *AAS* 45 (1953), 794–802.

8 *AAS* 55 (1963), 257–304.

9 Cf. J. Fuchs, "'Jura hominis'. Commentarium in Joannis XXIII Litt. Enc. Pacem in terris," *Periodica MCL* 53 (1964), 8–30.

10 *Acta Gregorii XVI* (Rome 1901), 169–74; cf. DS (Denzinger-Schönmetzer, *Enchiridion*) 2730–32.

11 Cf. DS 2890–96.

12 Cf. DS 2901–80.

13 DS 347.

14 DS 347.

15 Thomas Aquinas, *S.T.* II-II 10,11c ("to avoid a greater evil"), also 10,8c and 11,3c.

16 P. Huizing gives a thorough account of the treatment of this and similar problems in post-conciliar literature: "Uber Veröffentlichungen und Themenstellungen zur Frage der Religionsfreiheit," *Concilium* 2 (1966, VII), 621–34.

XII. Married Love: Christian Pluralism in the Twelfth Century

Frequently there is a history to ethical problems and the attempts at solving them in Christianity. It is often a struggle as times change, but sometimes it is a struggle of contemporary disparate opinions. Although the contrary is often asserted, it cannot be the case historically that the church (who is understood thereby?) or those in the church always had the same solution for the many ethical problems; for this would mean that a genuine pluralism had never existed and that ethical solutions were not determined by the historicity of the human person (including the Christian), whether in the succession of periods or in a contemporaneous plurality.

In what follows, this will be demonstrated by means of an extremely interesting example, that of the way married love was understood in the twelfth century. We do not propose a full exposition of the history of this problem in the twelfth century; rather, four very different positions will be compared with one another. We are not undertaking a preliminary study of the sources; the results of such a study are presupposed here. We propose to give an insight into the variety of some (not all) understandings of married love within the Christianity of a determined period of time.

Years ago in 1949, while working on the sexual ethics of Thomas Aquinas, I observed the exceptional variety within Christian moral theology of ethical positions taken up with regard to sexuality and marriage.[1] In connection with this, I have been interested for some time in the treatise *De Amore* ("Concerning love") composed in the 1280s by the Frankish court chaplain Andreas; the Latin original, edited by E. Trojel in 1892, was issued in a new edition in 1964.[2] The royal court chaplain gives an interesting justification of the courtly thesis that love was possible only outside marriage, when he refers *inter alia* to the contemporary church teaching on marriage, terming it "apostolic." We choose as our starting-point this work by Andreas, which was significant for long periods and was translated into various languages in the course of the centuries. We shall present the following four understandings of married love which existed contemporaneously: (1) the Church's teaching on marriage at that time, which Andreas calls "apostolic"; (2) the teaching on courtly love, opposed to the church's teaching and upheld by Andreas; (3) the understanding of the critical philosopher and theologian Peter Abelard, chronologically antecedent to Andreas's work, but equally opposed to the church's teaching on marriage; and (4) the mystical effort of a contemporary of Abelard, the theologian Hugh of St. Victor.

1. The Court Chaplain (Andreas) and the Church's Teaching on Marriage

The court chaplain's writings contain three "books" (*libri*). The first two were an authority for courtly love both in Andreas' lifetime and for a long time afterward; not so the third book, which is nothing other than a cautious retraction of the contents of the first two books. On the basis of numerous observations in the work of Andreas, one could be inclined to take the true authority of the treatise on love to be less Andreas himself than the Countess Marie de Champagne. The whole work is written in such a way that it can be set beside the *Ars amatoria* of Ovid.

In the wooing dialogue D the lady points out to her wooer that she is very happily married to a very noble and excellent man and that, because of her deep love for her husband, she would never dare to admit another secret admirer into her marital fellowship. The rules of love obliged the lady who was wooed to make this response. Andreas for his part has the lady draw attention to the fact that in this wooing she is not concerned with the love of marital affection (*affectus maritalis*), but with the secret and passionately erotic love which alone deserves to be called "love" (*amor*). For various reasons, such love can exist only in a burning extramarital desire and common conduct.

In accordance with her duty, the lady objects that what her wooer desires has always been rejected throughout the world: in such extramarital conduct, she sees a sinful act. Passionate and erotic conduct may occur only within one's own marriage; it must nourish and strengthen day by day the loving unity of the spouses. Such conduct (*immoderata carnalis dilectionis ambitio*) is love (*amor*) in truth and is certainly possible between marriage partners — not only outside one's own marriage.

The wooer (or the court chaplain Andreas) now opposes his knowledge of the contemporary church teaching on marriage, as well as other reasons, to this explanation by the noble lady. To her great astonishment (and presumably that of many readers today) she hears that the conduct in marriage defended by her — erotic love (*amor*) instead of merely marital affection (*affectus maritalis*) — is condemned as a sin by the contemporary church teaching on marriage, which, it is claimed, goes back to the apostolic tradition.[3]

Unlike the lady who is being wooed, one who is to some extent familiar with the patristic and especially the Augustinan teaching on marriage, which determined the medieval teaching of the Christian church, will certainly not be surprised at the statement of the court chaplain. When Andreas has the wooer explain to the lady that every erotic enrichment that the marriage partners permit themselves, beyond their desire for children and the fulfillment of the obligation to the other partner, is not without sin, this is in accordance with the teaching on marriage of many centuries, which bore the mark of Augustine. Like the theologians of the twelfth century, Augustine understood the spiritual happiness coming from the fellowship of marriage (*affectio maritalis*) as a high human (and also supernatural) good.[4] But sexual eros and corresponding conduct have, as such, no place in this fellowship; from nature, sexual eros and becoming one in marriage serve exclusively for the procreation of children (together with their education). Augustine thereby understands children as an increase of the kingdom of God: it is therefore a matter of religious service, as Thomas Aquinas likewise teaches explicitly in the thirteenth century. Erotic desire and experience, understood in accordance with Augustine as deriving from original sin and therefore theologically evil (*malum*; not sin = *mala*), can indeed be "excused" by the devotion of married partners, understood in this sense to be religious devotion; but this does not, as such, belong to the riches of "marital fellowship."

St. Paul had some enthusiastic new Christians in Corinth who believed that, as Christians, they should renounce the erotic union of marriage (1 Cor 7). He warned them that such abstinence could also involve the danger of extramarital fornication. Nevertheless, Paul wishes this warning and exhortation to be understood only as a "concession" (*venia* or *indulgentia* in the later Latin translation), for he gives preference to renunciation, if one is able to achieve this by reason of a gift from God. In accordance with his pessimistic attitude in sexual matters, Augustine interprets the Pauline text in an un-Pauline way: the intercourse in marriage which is "conceded" in order to prevent extramarital fornication is not without at least venial sin, in Augustine's teaching, for otherwise there would be no need for *venia*, which Augustine understands not as "concession," but as "forgiveness" (of sin). This Augustinian theological interpretation remained authoritative for centuries. It is in this sense that Andreas the court chaplain has the prudish lady instructed about the sinful character of her marital conduct: it is no sin at all to "fulfill one's obligation," i.e., to grant what the partner requires — so that the danger of extramarital fornication may be avoided — but it is sinful to require this "payment" oneself.

In short, the court chaplain knows the contemporary church teaching on marriage, and employs its exposition in the wooing of the desired lady: erotic love in marriage is a sin, unless it takes place exclusively — religiously — for the procreation of children for the kingdom of God, or else — as a legal obligation — as the fulfillment of the requirement made by the partner who is in danger by reason of his original sin. The court chaplain hopes thereby to convince the lady he is wooing of the sinfulness of her marital conduct and to win her over to courtly love (*amor*).

But Andreas, who is well versed in theology, believes that he can use even more theology to woo the lady. Not only does he give her to understand that the marital conduct she defends is an "excess" of love life, i.e., a practice of erotic desire and conduct which has no justification within the religious motive of procreation or in the righteousness which carries out an obligation, and hence is the "unexcused" realization of an "evil"; he goes further and teaches that the "unexcused" realization of this evil in marriage is a worse abuse than erotic desire and conduct outside marriage, because marriage is a "holy matter" (marriage as *sacramentum*).

Finally, the court chaplain believes that he can appeal to an apostolic directive in support of his thesis. Here, however, his theological knowledge is not quite exact. For Paul did not teach this, and even the Augustinian interpretation of Paul does not say this. Rather, the text that he quotes, a text quoted for centuries before him, goes back to Jerome, who mistakenly believed it went back to Xystus, a Pythagorean; in fact, as we know today, it originated with the Stoic Seneca. In Jerome, it reads: "He (Xystus) says that a man who loves his wife too passionately is an adulterer. With another woman, every love, and with one's own wife excessively passionate love is shameful. A wise man loves his wife, not from hot desire (*impetu*), but from consideration (*iudicio*) . . . Nothing is more shameful than to love one's own wife like an adulteress."[5] In another passage, Jerome uses the formulation which is also quoted by Andreas: "One who loves his wife too passionately is an adulterer."[6]

It is clear that Andreas intends to put the lady under further pressure by means of the claimed apostolic directive. But while he is mistaken in his appeal to an apostolic directive, he does not reflect further whether the last words quoted from Jerome and from himself about the excessively passionate lover in marriage truly apply to the marital conduct defended by the lady. In fact, many theologians saw in this "excessiveness" in marriage a conduct that was "all too passionate" or "all too frequent" or "all too brutal"; others maintained the opinion of Augustine, upheld also in the late Middle Ages by Thomas and others, that erotic conduct in marriage becomes not only venially, but mortally sinful, if a man's desire for his wife is so strong that he is not even interested whether it is his own wife, and not another woman, that is his sexual object.

The theological argument that the court chaplain Andreas throws into the scales in his aim to woo a lady for courtly love belonged essentially to the genuine teaching of the church of his time, and of many centuries earlier (and later). It contains both Stoic and Manichaean influence, and also symptoms consequent upon the Augustinian teaching on original sin. These influences prevented a total and harmonious vision of the human person who is at once spiritual-personal and sexual-erotic. The ecclesiastical understanding of marriage presented by Andreas existed also in the writings of the theologians, and there is documentary evidence that it was also the subject of preaching.[7] But just as the lady says that she did not know it, so is there also documentary evidence that many Christian married people knew little about it and reflected even less upon it with regard to their way of living. Nevertheless, this teaching, or better the understanding of marriage it contained, was influential for many centuries in the church, and even in the modern period.[8] We may ask whether such an ecclesiastical understanding of marriage did not fundamentally meet with a great lack of understanding, and thus favor such traditions as that of the courtly love praised by the Frankish court chaplain.

2. The Countess (Marie de Champagne) and Courtly Love

The court chaplain attacks the church's teaching about marital love in his discourse, and his opposition itself implies the ideal of courtly love, for which, as has been remarked already, the authority of the Countess Marie de Champagne is appealed to. Naturally, we do not intend here to go into the whole problematic of courtly love, of the troubadours and poetical love; here we are interested in the understanding of "love" (*amor*) which the theologically informed chaplain opposes to the contemporary ecclesiastical understanding of marital love. According to his exposition, two broadly divergent conceptions of the personal human being and the interpersonal relationship of man and woman confront each other in the church's teaching on marriage and in the ideal of courtly love.

It is clear that the fastidious aristocracy of the twelfth century had attained a cultivated ideal of noble interpersonal relationships, full of respect for the person of the other, who was to be venerated as a whole and very deeply. The womanly element was here drawn upon in a marked manner: the wooer was to be ennobled himself through a respectful and well-mannered courtship relationship with a noble lady. (Some researchers believe that the veneration in the spiritual realm that looked to Mary as the ideal woman began at the same time. From now on, she is more and more frequently considered as "conceived immaculate" and as the *Regina caeli*.)

This tendency had a diverse effect on love and marital fellowship.

(1) On the one hand, Andreas himself attacks the narrowly sexual and even "brutal" manner in which (above all, among the common people) marriage is lived in the sexual-erotic realm often simply as physical union, *sicut equus et mulus*, as the Bible says. Against this, the relationship between man and woman should be profoundly personal, sustained by respect, reverence and devotion. He speaks here in favor of a refinement of interpersonal conduct, at least for the world of the aristocracy, and above all vis-à-vis the woman.

(2) On the other hand, Andreas condemns the tendency to exclude erotic-sexual relationships from a fellowship between man and woman. This relationship must be more than what the church's understanding of marriage holds to be a "marital fellowship," i.e. a fellowship for which, per se, the sexual-erotic reality has no value. The tendency here is toward a total relationship between man and woman, based on respect and reverence for the person of the other (the lady), and having an effect on the whole reality, including the sphere of eros. Precisely for this reason, marriage is fundamentally acknowledged, but is found to be insufficient, as the church of the period understands it: what marriage, understood in this way, cannot give must be sought and experienced outside marriage.

(3) The ideal of Andreas in his defense of courtly love attacks the reduction of the significance of sexual eros exclusively to the procreation of children in the service of the kingdom of God and as a medicine against the evil of erotic passion which derives from original sin. The court chaplain emphasizes that eros means more for the human person than this.

(4) The ideal upheld by courtly love is opposed to the church's teaching, understood in an excessively impersonal way, which sees the spouses in marriage as definitively "possessing" each other and as having a "right" to the "payment" of a marital "requirement." Love must not be the fulfillment of a legal requirement, but must always prove itself in freedom. Love cannot be demanded: it must be sought in wooing. This wooing and this response of love must occur continually; they are a continuing process, out of which nothing definitively fixed may emerge (as in the church's teaching on marriage).

(5) Courtly love has its sights set first of all on the person of the lady who is being wooed. But, according to Andreas, it always has an erotic tendency and certainly does not absolutely exclude adultery. In Andreas's three books about love there is no special insistence on the distinction that other defenders of courtly love often make between "pure love" (*amor purus*), i.e. love that excludes sexual relationships, and " mixed love" (*amor mixtus*).

Behind the ideal of courtly love, there seems to be an ideal of marriage and of marital love — unexpressed and doubtless not consciously reflected upon — which is different from the con-temporary teaching of the church on marriage. What courtly love seeks outside marriage should in some way have its place within marriage: first, personal love which does not simply appeal to "possession" and "right," but is continually sought and wooed, and given in response as a gift that is ever new; and second, a marital love that takes in the spouses in their totality and therefore also includes the erotic gift and nourishment. A marital love which is thus understood would, however, exclude the essential element of exciting tension found in courtly love, which lies in its being secretly realized without the knowledge of the marriage partner. Otherwise the temptation to go out secretly from the realm of the marriage could always remain. This is doubtless what the lady of Dialogue D in Andreas's work means, and presumably many highly placed Christian members of the aristocracy in fact lived in this way at that time.

F. Schlösser has pointed out that, although the phenomenon of courtly love was generally known in the society of that period, it was never condemned, despite its contradiction of the ecclesiastical doctrine of the church — neither in the numerous synods nor in the directives for confessors (*libri confessariorum*), even though both of these copiously drew attention to concrete abuses. Bishop Tempier of Paris condemned the work of the court chaplain Andreas — but in 1277, 100 years later.[9] But even this condemnation does not explicitly attack courtly love as such: Andreas's work is condemned in general terms in the introduction to a list of sexual-ethical teachings that are to be condemned. In any case, however, the sexual-ethical theses that are condemned may indicate corresponding theses of the court chaplain's books on love, for example, the thesis about the naturalness of extra-marital sexual conduct — for the clergy too, as Andreas explicitly em-phasizes. The definition in the decree of condemnation of how "love" (*amor*) is here to be understood is typical, and corresponds entirely to the understanding of the court chaplain: "Love is a congenital passion which emerges from looking on the form of the other sex and from un-checked thinking about this, so that one desires above all to attain the embrace of the other . . ."

It is certainly not easy to grasp why the church in fact was silent about the phenomenon of courtly love. Schlösser's suggestion that this may have been explicable on the basis of the de facto widespread mentality of that time is scarcely convincing.

3. The Opinion of the Critical Ethicist (Peter Abelard)

Several decades before Andreas had the lady instructed on the church's teaching about marriage in the course of her wooing, the brilliant but critical Peter Abelard (d. 1142) had, in his early writings [10] — i.e. before his "erotic Damascus conversion" (G. Weber) — explicitly attacked the contemporary teaching of the church and her theologians about erotic love in marriage. He fundamentally rejects the traditional negative judgment, as he understands this, on pleasurable erotic experience as such: he says simply, "pleasure" (*delectatio*).

As is well known, Abelard has his own theory about the essence of sin, and he takes this as the starting-point for his reflections about erotic love. He teaches that sin as such belongs to the interior of the human person, to the soul; it follows, according to Abelard, that it is only the inner consent (consensus) to what is not allowed and therefore may not be done "for the sake of God," that is sinful. The performance of the illicit action adds nothing from an ethical point of view to the inner consent (readiness) to the act — e.g., the pleasurable carrying out of marital or extramarital sexual intercourse. Besides, in the reflections of this critical thinker, the erotic experience of pleasure is given by nature itself, and is therefore in accordance with nature and natural; this is equally true of the act that is permitted and of the act that is unjustified.

A century later, Thomas Aquinas also insisted that pleasure as such is natural, and per se ethically indifferent; but for Thomas, far more than for Abelard, it is not only the inner consent that is connected with "sin," but also the act itself. Accordingly, the erotic pleasure which belongs to the act participates in the ethical character of the act itself; therefore it is ethically wrong in extramarital intercourse, but not so in the permitted act within marriage.

How is the difference between the two thinkers to be explained? Abelard sets his sights almost exclusively on the inner consent and thereby on the *personal* ethical character (sinfulness, goodness); Thomas, on the other hand, insists more strongly that the *act* itself has something to do with sin, although he makes the following distinction: the act as such, as Abelard correctly emphasizes, has nothing directly to do with the personal ethical character (sinfulness, goodness), but certainly what we call in modern terminology the "rightness" or "wrongness" of the act is relevant. Thomas therefore has more to say than Abelard about the ethical character of the erotic experience of pleasure.

In fact, Abelard's thesis that pleasurable erotic experience is not sin did not require an effort on the part of the critical ethicist, for already Augustine — and the contemporary teaching of the church on marriage, which accorded with his understanding (as related later by the court chaplain Andreas) — held that pleasurable passion was not, as such, a sin, but ultimately an evil traceable back to the sin of the first parents. This evil, however, was to be avoided as much as possible and could be defended only for important reasons (the procreation of children, and help to avoid fornication). Presumably, this was how it was understood by the theologians whom Abelard quotes critically, since they declared the (naturally pleasurable) consummation of marriage to be allowed, but not the pleasurable experience. Abelard too agrees with the traditional thesis that erotic desire is ultimately an evil that goes back to original sin, though only an evil in the form of a punishment, not itself a sin. But the brilliant Abelard is not interested in the subtle distinctions made by those theologians: for him, it is (correctly) the case that if the consummation of marriage is allowed, then the pleasure that belongs to this and is willed by nature, and likewise the desire for this pleasurable consummation, cannot be sinful.

It does not, of course, escape Abelard the theologian that the defenders of the teaching on marriage of his time adduce the authority of the Bible. On this, he observes, first, that it is fundamentally false to appeal simply to authorities without caring about reason; and second, that in any case, a reasonable interpretation of the authorities does not confirm the pessimistic teaching. When David prays (Ps 50:7), "In sin was I conceived," Abelard interprets this as follows: in the act of conception, the child is not in any way "sinful" (although a text quoted from Jerome would have us believe otherwise), even though it does not escape the "evil punishment" of erotic desire. This evil punishment is not due to the parents who procreate the child in their erotic experience, but rather to the sin of the first parents. When Paul wishes erotic marital love to be understood as a "concession" (*indulgentia, venia*) and not as a "commission" (1 Cor 7:5), Abelard interprets this to mean that, in this passage, the apostle does not speak of the concession of a sinful action, but views married life as the renunciation of a life of abstinence, which Paul obviously prefers.

In short, Abelard does not enter into the subtle distinctions of a well-known tradition when he opposes the theses of the contemporary ecclesiastical teaching on marriage; he departs from several propositions of that theology; he opposes to them simply his own "reasonable" interpretation. But he does not agree with the teachings of the court chaplain on courtly love. (He seems to have known about this teaching, as is shown by a remark in the present context about the many who woo the wives of the powerful for the sake of their own glory; Abelard judges that such conduct is not only fornication but also, above all, adultery.)

The later Abelard did not repeat his earlier reflections and teachings.[11] In the meantime, the cleric Abelard, who was not a priest, had entered a very deep and erotically very active love relationship with Heloise, whose uncle (a canon) had entrusted her to his special tutelage. Although Heloise, like the Countess Marie in Andreas's work, tried to refuse marriage with him, preferring a love life that grew ever anew out of her continuing freedom, Abelard's will prevailed and a secret marriage took place; the child who was born of the marriage was given away to be brought up. Heloise's uncle, enraged at this, had Abelard forcibly castrated one night, and Abelard slowly turned to introspection. Freed from his relationship with Heloise, he began to look on his castration as a grace. The converted ethicist became a monk and a priest, a famous abbot, and an important theologian and philosopher. He caused Heloise to take the veil; she did this at first more out of love for Abelard than out of conviction.

The marriage between Abelard and Heloise naturally continues to exist: Heloise points this out to her Abelard and asks him in her letters for signs of love. Abelard acknowledges the existence of the marriage, but wants it to be lived differently now on both sides: the spouse Heloise is now for him a "sister in the Spirit" (*in Spiritu soror*), no longer "spouse in the flesh" (*in carne uxor*). The converted Abelard now follows instead the mystical line of his adversary Bernard of Clairvaux. In the correspondence with Heloise he knows only one alternative, with no hint of an intermediary position: either the love of God or marriage "in the flesh." When he looks back on their earlier life together, he is indeed ready to accept what Heloise supposes and accuses him of, that love had nothing to do with it, only lust. He quotes now to his "sister in the Spirit" the arguments and authorities that we also find in the contemporary teaching of the church about marriage. For example, he replies to the "forty-second problem" of Heloise, who is putting pressure on him because of the marriage, in a manner quite different from his earlier one: "Whether one can sin when he does what the Lord permits him or indeed enjoins on him."

4. The Mystical Theologian (Hugh of St. Victor)

Like Peter Abelard, his contemporary Hugh of St. Victor (d. 1141) had reflected and written on the contemporary church teaching on marriage before Andreas's treatise on love. Hugh, however, tends to take a direction opposed to that of the earlier Abelard. Basically, he followed the pessimism of Augustine and of the centuries that followed him with regard to erotic love in marriage, although his own ideas were generally independent. In his own very positive teaching about marital fellowship, he stood rather in the mystical line of Abelard's adversary Bernard of Clairvaux.[12]

The problem that harries Hugh is clearly the erotic passion experienced in marriage, which is based on original sin. As a theologian, Hugh returns to creation doctrine, like the theologians of his time and like Augustine: according to this, it is God himself who founds marriage. He gives Eve to Adam first of all as a *help (adiutorium)*, understood one-sidedly as a help in the procreation of children (for the one active in procreation is exclusively the man, in the traditional opinion, which was held also by the biologists), and second as the *sociata* (spouse) of the man. This distinction in the creation of marriage will be decisive for Hugh's theology of marital love.

The problem arises from what was called at that period the second foundation of marriage after the fall, for out of this grows erotic passion and experience, with the result that marriage is no longer at the service only of procreation, but also serves as a medicine against the force of erotic lust. Marriage now has, therefore, a double goal in the realm of sexuality. Hugh must treat this per se as one and the same sexuality, but in practice he remains one-sidedly attentive to the erotic experience (after the fall); this is the great evil (*malum*, not *mala* = sin) that makes the marriage partners themselves "blush," and its realization, according to Augustine, needs grounds that "excuse" it (procreation, or fulfillment of the marital obligation). The theologian seeks the solution to the problem in the second element of the creation narrative that has been referred to: the woman is given to the man as spouse (*sociata*) so that man and woman in marriage are a personal fellowship. Marriage is a covenant of love (*foedus dilectionis*), while the task (*officium*), in accordance with creation, is only the procreation of children.

Hugh, like many other theologians, finds a first pointer to this solution in the marriage of Mary and Joseph, a marriage without sexual intercourse, whether aimed at procreation or used as a medicine. He finds a further pointer in the question which was discussed at his time, whether it is the marital consent or the sexual union that establishes the marriage. Naturally, Hugh stands on the side of the consent theory, although his own interpretation of this is highly idiosyncratic. Parallel to this is the question that was likewise debated at that time, whether a non-consummated marriage could be a "sacramental" sign of the relationship between Christ and the church (incarnation in the flesh!) in the terms of Ephesians 5:12. Hugh seeks a "sacramental" solution *without* marriage "in the flesh." A third pointer to the solution is found by Hugh in his understanding of the human being's quality of image of God, which for him belongs exclusively to the soul: the body and its sexuality have only the significance of an outward sign.

Hugh uses these pointers to make a distinction between marriage as *marital fellowship (coniugium)* and the *task (officium)* of this fellowship. Marriage as marital fellowship is exclusively the personal fellowship of love that is ultimately spiritual and is based on the personal love (not *amor*, but *caritas*) of the partners for each other. Its essence therefore does not derive from the sexuality, or the different sexualities, of man and woman, but from the different natures of their humanity. For Hugh, the reason why two persons of the same sex cannot enter marriage (as marital fellowship) is consequently to be found in this difference between man and woman, and not in their sexual difference.

Although the *task* of marriage, the procreation of children, belongs for Hugh to the structure of marriage, it is still only "an addition" to marriage; marriage is only "orientated" toward procreation as its "sign." The task is therefore in no sense constitutive of the essence of marriage. As has already been observed, Hugh also holds that it is the marital consent, not the sexual union, that establishes the marriage; but he interprets this position to mean that marital consent, as such, refers only to marital fellowship. With the exclusion of the task of marriage from the essence of marriage as a fellowship of love, the theologian has also eliminated from marriage as such (*coniugium*) the "problem" of erotic love "coming from original sin." This is decisive for him. Augustine had already laid down for him a path to this solution: "The good of marriage ... seems to me therefore not to lie in the procreation of children, but in the natural fellowship of the different sexes".[13] Hugh replaces the term "different sexes" with the term "in the different natures."

He refers with a certain rhetoric to the creation narrative in support of his thesis: "Therefore a man leaves father and mother and cleaves to his wife, and they become two in one flesh." We read, "therefore"; Hugh asks, "Why?" In his exegesis, the "two in one flesh" refers not to the entirety of marriage, i.e., the marital fellowship together with its task, but only to the task (*officium*). It is not for the sake of the task, therefore, that a man leaves father and mother. Love for parents, which is a love determined by one's origins, remains; but a man leaves his origins in order to make for the remaining goal. "To cleave to his wife" is the choice of love. This is the covenant. This is more than one's origins; it is the singular devotion of the heart and of love, the "unending life of that divine and deep mystery (*sacramentum* and *mysterium*) and of a fair and wonderful example of human reality." Happiness now takes the place of the existence that has been received from one's parents; the latter is given by nature (creation), the former is the choice of grace: "the definitive rest in love," in "marital" love. It is for this that God has created marriage, as a "fellowship of freely chosen and never-ending and wholly particular love for the spouse and for her alone."

Nevertheless, the Creator has also given this fellowship of love the *task* of the procreation of children. The marriage that is lived in obedient performance of this task will be "meritorious" and "fruitful" in a special manner; its value lies herein, together with a "holiness" of the marital task. The "two in one flesh" is thus something great, but the "two in one heart" or "in one spirit" is much greater: it is therein that the real holiness of marriage (as a fellowship of love) consists, even if one should not deny a certain holiness in the case of the task (as service and fruitfulness). But without any doubt, "The holiness of the sacrament (of the marital covenant of love) is more valuable in marriage than the fruitfulness of the body."

"Sacrament" in Hugh of St. Victor means here a mystery that is the sign of a holy and greater thing. In the fifth chapter of the letter to the Ephesians, the marriage of Christians is called "a great mystery in Christ and the church." While his theological contemporaries disputed whether a marriage not consummated "in the flesh" could be a mystery-sacrament of the unity of Christ with his church, Hugh sensed a danger for his understanding of marriage as a fellowship of love "in the spirit," independent of its task "in the flesh." Is it a mystery-sacrament, and therefore indissoluble? Hugh believes that he must admit that marriage as he understands it (*coniugium*) is not a sacrament in the sense of the letter to the Ephesians; but it is for him a great mystery-sacrament, indeed even greater than the one spoken about in Ephesians, i.e., the sign of a fellowship between God and the soul: the latter fellowship is "in the spirit," the former "in the flesh." Hugh believes that, in this way, he has saved his theory of marriage "in the spirit alone." After him, even before Thomas Aquinas, Peter Lombard declares Hugh's endeavor to be superfluous and supersedes it by arguing that the mystery of the letter to the Ephesians is already fundamentally also present in marriage as a fellowship of love.

In all that he writes about marriage that is "only in the spirit," Hugh's ultimate aim is to reduce the significance of the task of marriage (in the flesh) and thereby to suppress as far as possible (this is his chief goal) the "evil" of the "fleshly" sphere of marriage which has become a sphere of erotic desires and erotic experience since the fall. The ideal is the marriage of Mary and Joseph!

According to Hugh, therefore, the Christian should reflect as follows. If the union "in the flesh" is only "added on" to marriage — as a task in creation with a view to the procreation of children, since the fall as a remedy for lust — and is therefore only an accompaniment of marriage rather than constitutive of it, and is ultimately only a concession of God's compassionate mercy made to us in our fallen condition, then it is obvious that personal marital consent should be limited to the covenant "in the spirit," without linking this to the consent to union "in the flesh." It is indeed usual for marital consent to include both elements, at least implicitly; but even then, in Hugh's opinion, consent to union "in the flesh" is only the accompaniment of real consent to the marital fellowship of love "in the spirit" (*comes*, not *effector*).

It is possible, according to Hugh, to renounce explicitly at the marriage ceremony the expression "in the flesh" (as task and as medicine). In such a case, however, the marital consent establishes only a double bond: first, the renunciation of the marital fellowship of love with another, and second, the will truly to live the marital fellowship of love. The union "in the flesh" is thus excluded in this case, even though the permitted physical union always presupposes marital consent. For Hugh, marital consent with the exclusion of sexual union is more serious, true and holy than consent to a marriage that is both "in the spirit" and "in the flesh."

The spiritualizing understanding of marriage of Hugh of St. Victor had significance in the years that followed, but, as Peter Lombard was able to supersede Hugh's reflections on a double mystery-sacrament of marriage, so, after him, Thomas Aquinas declared the impossibility of consent to a marriage that would not also include the right to union "in the flesh."[14] It was thus not possible to uphold Hugh's spiritualizing tendency, born of a pessimism with regard to erotic desire and experience. This pessimism, however, even though it did not take refuge in the marital mysticism of Hugh of St. Victor, persisted in the thirteenth century and later.

5. Pluralism and the Understanding of Marital Love

It is undoubtedly materially correct to speak of a pluralism in the understanding of marital love in the church of the twelfth century. The chief question posed was how sexuality, understood as deriving from original sin and experienced erotically, could be built into the personal fellowship of marriage.

In fundamental points, there existed a common ecclesiastical understanding about this question; the court chaplain Andreas could hold this up before a lady who was being wooed. This teaching on marriage is aware of the high natural (and supernatural) value of marriage as a personal fellowship; it is the sexual-erotic sphere in marriage that is problematical for this understanding. This is already true when it is considered as a reality of creation, for it is seen here exclusively as a means of continuing the human race; but it is especially true when the experience of erotic passion is understood and evaluated as an evil that is a consequence of original sin. As an evil, it is believed that one must exclude it from marriage as far as possible; it is even less possible to integrate it positively into marriage.

Hugh of St. Victor deepens and spiritualizes in a mystical manner the personal marital fellowship of love and life, but he seeks precisely in this to divide marriage, thus understood, from sexual reality, both as regards the commission given in creation to continue the race and above all as regards the "evil" of the lust that is experienced erotically and is understood as a consequence of original sin. His deepening of the personal understanding of marriage finds a certain parallel in courtly love, albeit in the extramarital sphere. This latter introduces erotic love into the sphere of the extramarital personal encounter, and stands thereby in complete contradiction to Hugh.

Hugh's contemporary Abelard, on the other hand, attempted in his earlier writings to integrate erotic love into marital fellowship. In this, he takes a position against the contemporary teaching on marriage, and above all against the ideas of Hugh. He distinguishes himself from the advocates of courtly love by integrating erotic love into the relationship between man and woman, but allowing this integration only (at least in theory) in marriage. Courtly love aims at a personal relationship between man and woman, and also integrates erotic love into this, but only outside of marriage; in this, it takes a position against Abelard, Hugh and the entire contemporary ecclesiastical teaching on marriage. There may have been many reasons for doing this; the question remains whether a motive may also have been the general banishment of erotic love, evaluated negatively, from marriage in the contemporary teaching on marriage.

In the twelfth century, a genuine pluralism existed in the church in the understanding of marital love, as can be documented both in the theories of the theologians and in the different lives of different Christians. All wanted to be Christians. Christianity is not only an objective "given," but also life that is lived, and hence also a continuous "search" – a human search and consequently often also an "interested" search.

NOTES

1 J. Fuchs, *Die Sexualethik des hl. Thomas von Aquin* (Cologne, 1949).

2 *Andreae Capellani Regii Francorum de Amore Libri Tres*, ed. E. Trojel (Copenhagen, 1892, 2nd edition, Munich, 1964).

3 F. Schlösser has subjected this statement of the court chaplain to a historically based analysis: "Die Minneauffassung des Andreas Capellanus und die zeitgenössische Ehelehre," in : *Zschr. f. dt. Philologie* 79 (1960), 266–84. On the history of the theological discussion about marital love, cf. the still valuable study by D. Lindner, *Der usus matrimonii. Seine sittliche Bewertung in der katholischen Moraltheologie alter und neuer Zeit* (Munich, 1929).

4 *De bono conjugali* III, 3: PL 40, 373–96; here 375 (cf. note 13 below).

5 *Adv. Jovinianum* I, 49: PL 23, 293.

6 *Commentary on Ezechiel* VI, 18: PL 25, 173.

7 D. Lindner cites, for Germany, Berthold of Regensburg (op. cit. 142).

8 The centuries-old pessimistic teaching on marital love is today superseded in principle. The encyclical *Casti Connubii* of 31 December 1930 explicitly acknowledges motives for marital intercourse that a centuries-old tradition had tried to exclude (DS 3718). In his celebrated discourse of 29 October 1951, Pope Pius XII explicitly approved of the search for the erotic experience of marital intercourse, in words which could have been taken from Abelard (AAS 43, 1951, 835–54, 851).

9 Cf., on this, the arguments of M. Grabmann in *Speculum* 7 (1932), 75–9, and A.J. Denomy in *Mediaeval Studies* 8 (1946), 197–249.

10 Thus Abelard in *Ethica, seu Scito teipsum*: PL 178, 633–678; here 178, 639–642 could be especially interesting.

11 On this, cf. the *Problemata Heloissae*: PL 178, 677–730, especially *Problema Heloissae* XLII: ibid., 723–30. Cf. also the fictional collection of letters *Historia calamitatum*: PL 178, 113–82.

12 Hugh's teaching on marriage is found above all in the treatise *De sacramento coniugii* (PL 176, 479–520) of his chief work *De sacramentis christianae fidei*: PL 176, 173–618. It is based on his earlier work *De Beatae Mariae Virginitate*, with the fourth chapter added later (PL 176, 857–876). On the whole topic, cf. H.A.J. Allard, 'Die eheliche Lebens- und Liebesgemeinschaft nach Hugo von St. Viktor' (excerpt from dissertation, Pont, Gregorian University, Sittard 1963).

13 *De bono conjugali* III, 3: PL 40, 373–96, here 375.

14 *Suppl.* 49, 2 ad 3.

XIII. Disposing of Human Life: Recent Problems in Bioethics

There can be no doubt about the great relevance today of the theme of this essay. Magazines and newspapers report the new discoveries by research and technology in past decades, and even within the last few years, that make it possible to dispose of human life in its various forms. New possibilities confront the biologist, the biotechnician and the bioethicist with ethical questions: what experiments and applications of the new possibilities in the realm of human life can be justified morally? In what follows, an attempt will be made to answer three questions: What do "bioethics" and "disposing of human life" mean? What are the problems of today's bioethics? Who decides?

1. What do "Bioethics" and "Disposing of human life" mean?

(a) *Bioethics*. The word "bioethics" is a recent coining,[1] and is used above all in the United States. In German, the older terms, still used today, are *medizinische Ethik* ("medical ethics") and *ärztliche Deontologie* ("deontology of the physician"); the latter expression especially shows that the chief concerns here are the ethical questions that arise in the relationship between doctor and patient. In the meantime the intermediary form *biomedizinische Ethik* ("biomedical ethics") has come into existence; whereas the older form indicated that the primary concern was the ethics of the relationship between doctor and patient, the word "bioethics" points rather to *human life as such* and to the researcher, technician or practitioner who is interested in "life." The object of biology and biotechnology is "human life"; the subject, the human person, is understood to a high degree as the object of scientific activity. However, inasmuch as human life is the life of human persons (actual, potential or future), the question arises of how far it is ethically possible to grant the experimental researcher and technician, and the practitioner who treats human persons, the right to dispose of human life — and this is precisely a bioethical question. Bioethics is not a fundamentally new ethics, but the application of ethics and its basic principles to the new possibilities opened up to us by modern biology and biotechnology with regard to human life.

The manifold problematic of modern bioethics is, of course, known not only in America, but also in Germany and other European countries but it tends to be treated in a systematic and organized manner above all in the United States, as can be seen both in specialized periodicals and in a four-volume *Encyclopedia of Bioethics* (1978),[2] and also in the establishment of several specialized academic bioethical centers, especially those of the Hastings Center in New York State and the Center for Bioethics of the Kennedy Institute of Ethics at Georgetown University in Washington, D.C. The members of these centers are philosophers, theologians, jurists, biologists and doctors. As far as I know, such research centers do not exist in Europe, with the exception of a newly established center in Brussels and the seat of a bioethical research group of the international Union of Catholic Universities in Brussels, Barcelona and Washington, D.C. Apart from this, one should note that the European studies in bioethics tend to be purely theoretical ethical studies, whereas the American ethical studies generally also look to the "public policy" of representatives of the professions, of the hospitals, the legislature and the political administration.

Since biology, medicine and genetics — both as research and as technology — are competent only in their own respective limited fields, it is necessary to pose the bioethical question. Questions of the significance of research and technology in the biological life of the human person, of what goals they should aim at, and of what paths they may or may not take, are questions that bear on the person as a whole, and are thus ethical questions. Naturally, these questions occur also to the researcher and technologist as human beings, and can therefore per se be answered by them as human beings, though not exclusively by them. Bioethics, or the bioethicist, explicitly confronts the ethical question; but this is possible only on the basis of sufficient information from the researcher and technologist. The ideal, in consequence, is collaboration between the researcher and technician on the one side and the ethicist (philosopher or theologian) on the other.

It will thus be possible for bioethics to accompany the work of research and technology, and for bioethics to reflect on the possibilities which are not yet realized but are indicated for a near or more distant future. This is important, for otherwise ethics appears too late on the scene, while research and technology have gone ahead freely in their limited sphere of human existence and have prevailed. At present, bioethics has this preventive function to a large degree in the realm of genetics.

(b) *"Disposing of human life."* The basic problem of bioethics is the disposing of human life — in any manner. How is the ethical problem to be resolved, either fundamentally or in exceedingly complex cases that have become possible only because of ultramodern research and technology? It would be too easy for the Judaeo-Christian tradition to appeal simply to the relevant prohibition of the Decalogue, for that speaks only of murder, and indeed of the murder of a member of one's own people, not of killing in general, and even less of the various other ways of disposing of human life that are possible today. Nor is the frequent reference to God as the only lord of human life valid, for theologically speaking, God is the only lord, not only of human life, but in the same way of all that is created: it follows that such a discourse excludes an arbitrary disposing of human life. The discovery, therefore, of what disposing of human life — as a high and fundamental value for the individual and for society — is defensible remains a task reserved to human insight and reason. This is a reflection that involves the whole human person.

We must also note that the term "human life" is capable of being used, and is used, in an analogous sense, not only in a univocal sense (life/death), and hence does not always mean the same thing. One may, for example, think of the still lively discussion about whether embryos in the first days after fertilization are only potentially "human" life or are already individual and personal life, i.e., human life in the full sense. It is obvious that the answer to this question could have consequences for the disposing of human life, here above all for the problems of abortion and of experimentation with embryos, if these last mentioned are supposed to be human life but perhaps not human individuals or persons.

We also see the analogy in the use of the term "human life" in the problematic cases at the end of life. We have one who is still a "human person," but is irreversibly in the process of dying; and we have one who is "no longer" (or simply "not") a human person, e.g., one who has suffered brain death or one who has no brain (from birth onward, or because of an accident). In both cases, we have a "human" reality, and in some sense "human life," but only in the first case is there an individual-personal human existence. Once again, the distinction will have consequences for the "disposing of human life."

The use of the term "human life" is to be understood in another sense and in another way when it is a case, not of human life that already exists, but of the *beginning* of such life. It is not a case here of disposing of human life in the traditional sense, but of disposing of the manner of the *coming into being* of human life — and with various consequences for the one who will perhaps one day exist. Such disposing is possible today through artificial fertilization and now also through fertilization in a test-tube. There is also the possibility, either today or in the near future, of disposing in various ways of human life that already exists but is not yet born, on the basis of prenatal diagnosis.

"Disposing of human life" is, therefore, not a univocal concept, but an analogous term. Bioethics has to work with many analogous ways of disposing of human life that have been made possible above all by modern research and technology.

2. Problems of Today's Bioethics

We shall now indicate more concretely what problems are faced by bioethics today in view of the manifold possibilities of disposing of human life. Obviously, it is not possible to aim at completeness here; thus only a few areas of bioethical concern will be presented. We shall look at the following areas: (1) killing and allowing to die; (2) disposing of life that is coming into being: embryo and fetus; (3) the problem of extracorporal fertilization; and (4) problems of today's genetic technology.

(a) *Killing and allowing to die.* In disposing of human life, there is a general disposition not to kill, but to do nothing against dying, i.e., to allow to die. Life remains the fundamental, if not the highest value of human existence, and the living human person has the dignity of realizing his own life meaningfully and freely in history. The bioethicist knows this; but he also knows that the value of human life is not absolute, for otherwise it would be impossible to understand the traditional teaching about the possible justification of self-defense and capital punishment, and also the concession of the possibility of sacrificing one's own life under certain circumstances, or indeed of even taking one's own life (e.g., as the only way to preserve an important state secret). Consistently with this, the bioethicist asks whether there may not be a justified possibility of killing in his area too: whether the price to be paid for maintaining life may not be too high, as for example in the case of a mentally defective person or a dying person who is lying in an irreversible coma and needs care that is found to be meaningless and often "inhuman."

But instead of killing, one often prefers to allow the person to die, either by posing no further obstacles to the hopeless process of dying, or by refusing to consider a maintenance of life (e.g., by means of artificial respiration or artificial feeding, or by treating a new additional illness) that is judged to be meaningless.

One can, of course, ask whether allowing a person to die is not also a way of killing: for one who abandons a possible fight against death, or a possible struggle to maintain life for a longer period, although he has the possibility of helping further, cannot deny that his conduct too is one of the *causes* of the death that now ensues.

Some bioethicists, including theologians,[3] theoretically uphold the position that there is no ethical difference between allowing one who lies hopelessly in the process of dying simply to die (perhaps painfully), and freeing him from his situation by means of a fatal intervention. Against this, it has been correctly pointed out that the refusal to kill — including the refusal to take one's own life, and the practice of only allowing a person to die rather than ending life — expresses reverence for human life more strongly than does killing and such an attitude has a high value in human society. Certain persons could be especially bound to this because of their particular position in society; I am thinking of the priest, the father of a family, the doctor. Indeed, in a society doctors must be forbidden to kill, so that the sick can retain their confidence in the medical profession.

We have already observed that there is an important distinction in the case of allowing to die: it is one thing to refuse to prolong dying, and another to refuse to prolong life. In the case of a refusal to prolong dying, there is no difference between refusing to begin a treatment (e.g. in an intensive care unit) and finally breaking off a treatment; but if one allows death by refusing to undertake treatment to prolong life, then one must ask whether one should be ready to pay any price for a certain prolongation of life. The moral theology and medical ethics of the past have not asserted this, and there is no obligation to do so on the part of the patient who is capable of deciding about his own life, or of the relatives, or of the doctor. In such cases, a reasonable and prudent reflection is necessary. We cannot expect such a reflection to lead to the same conclusion in all cases, with unanimity among all those involved.

Must one artificially feed the brain-damaged, even though they are presumably not (or no longer) to be regarded as personal human individuals? Must one provide artificial feeding for someone who lies hopelessly in a coma? Opinions differ here. Older moral theology would have said that artificial nourishment was an "exceptional" means (today one would perhaps say, "not proportionate"), and therefore not obligatory.

The gynecologist will find himself confronted with similar difficult situations. We see from the world-famous case of Baby Doe in Bloomington, Indiana (1982) how little unanimity (and therefore perhaps how little certainty) there can be in the judgment of such situations. In this case, the parents of a newborn mongoloid baby (Down's syndrome) knew about the sad future of their child, who needed an immediate operation in the esophagus if she was to remain alive. Because of the mongolism, the parents refused consent to the operation, and received explicit permission for this from the competent court. The mongoloid child died of hunger after a few days in the hospital. The Reagan administration judged the case differently: all those born and living in the United States have the same right to full care, without discrimination, and so the child had the right to the operation which would have prolonged its life. The *Washington Post* entitled an editorial: "They are still killing in our hospitals." (Killing includes what we call the "abandonment" (*Liegenlassen*) of physically or mentally damaged newborn babies when they are allowed to die.)

(b) *The beginning of life: Disposing of embryo and fetus.* The biology of the beginning of human life likewise poses new bioethical questions. It is generally held that it is with the fertilization of the ovum that individual and personal human existence begins. The destruction of the embryo must therefore be seen ethically as killing — even in the first period after fertilization — in analogy to the prohibition of killing in the Decalogue (although often in the legal sphere one speaks of abortion only after implantation in the womb). The thesis that individual and personal human existence begins from the moment of fertilization rests above all on the fact that the particularity of the human person who is to come into being is established *genetically* at fertilization.

The contrary thesis rests on a biological observation and a philosophical-theological reflection. The biological observation is that the fertilized ovum can still divide itself, for example into 2-4-8-16 totipotent cells, which can be brought back together into a unit again. The philosophical-theological reflection is that as long as cells can divide in order to separate from one another, they cannot be a human individual and a human person; but according to biology, this possibility exists until about the fourteenth day. It is further held that the existence of the person is given with the development of the brain, which can be established by an electroencephalogram (EEG), parallel to the widely accepted loss of human existence when the EEG establishes that brain activity has ceased (brain death).

These theories, above all the first, can be considered well founded. If the second thesis is correct, the elimination of the embryo in the early period or the prevention of implantation would be abortion but not an act of killing, although it could be allowed only for important reasons.[4] Such a theory could also be significant in the evaluation both of the methods of preventing implantation and of experimenting with embryos. If one does not reckon this view of things to be certain, and takes into account accordingly the possibility that the embryo is already a human person, one must still reflect whether this slender probability always deserves to be respected, rather than other factors which certainly exist.[5]

Another biological observation adds significance to these considerations, viz., that a large number of naturally fertilized ova are lost spontaneously in the first weeks, mostly without this being noticed; the percentage is generally placed between 50 and 80 per cent. The question then is whether we are dealing with as many human persons, for whom nature (and thus the Creator) no longer cares, or with pre-individual and pre-personal "human life." One could formulate a bioethical question: what care are *we* obliged to provide for what is in the first phase of the development of human life?

The situation of the fetus in the womb is that of a human subject living in another human subject; it is already a separate entity and yet depends on the other in its development. Particular legal relationships result from this: first, one speaks, within a broad tradition, of the fundamentally equal right to life of both human existences; then one tries also to specify the rights of the mother, both because of already existing duties in family and society and also because of her specific function in helping the development of the fetus. From an ethical point of view, such specifications can be significant in a situation of conflict, to help evaluate rights.

Biology too has known for decades the significance of the mother's existence for the fetus; but recent biology now seeks to have direct access to the fetus as a human existence in its own right, within the maternal organism. (I am aware that many biologists and philosophers would criticize my formulation, "human existence.") This attempt by biologists presupposes that one can attain sufficient information about the biological conditions of the fetus, and also that one is able to direct treatment of the fetus through the covering of the womb.

It is possible today to get information about the fetus and also to treat it. The information is possible first through amniocentesis — i.e., through cultivation and analysis of cells of the embryo that are taken from the amniotic fluid of the womb; and second, one can establish quite precisely the situation of the fetus through ultrasonic testing. Both methods, especially the first, are not without risks for mother and child, and the ethical requirement is therefore that they not be carried out as a matter of routine, but only for correspondingly important reasons — e.g., where there is a reasonable suspicion of the presence of a significant genetic defect and at the same time the probability that it can be healed. Blood transfusion is a possibility that has already been tested and found to work; the same is not true of the genetic treatment of hereditary defects. It is nevertheless hoped that it will be possible in the future genetically to treat certain illnesses by means of prenatal alteration or transplantation of genes; at present, these techniques are so risky that they could be attempted only as the last possibility in a hopeless case. It follows that today prenatal diagnosis with a view to genetic treatment could have only the following outcome: either an attempt at a risky treatment, or a refusal to treat, or abortion; in many cases, the motivation of a prenatal diagnosis will have been this last possibility.

(c) *The problem of extracorporal fertilization.* Apart from the possibility of reaching the fetus directly, an attempt is also being made to produce the embryo itself in a test-tube (a "test-tube baby"). Apart from the interest of the researcher, there is a general and justified interest in helping particular married couples, who will never have their own child in the natural way because of biological reasons (e.g., because both Fallopian tubes are closed), to have their own child through *in vitro* fertilization. The usual procedure today is to take some mature cells artificially from the woman and fertilize them in a test-tube with the sperm of the husband; an optimal number of embryos are brought to the point of division and are then transferred into the womb. The chances of success are however, as yet, small (about 10%). This process has been judged ethically impermissible, especially among Catholics, mainly because the embryo is not the fruit of an *act* that is simultaneously one of personal love and of procreation. I believe, however, that one can correctly argue against this[6] that such an "artificial" procreation of a child can be an extremely concrete sign of the personal love of the marriage partners. Is not such a procreation a work of love, in that procreation and personal love coincide?

It is not, however, only the ethical permissibility of *in vitro* fertilization as such that is questioned; other difficulties in detail are often raised too.[7] It is asked: are not many fertilized ova lost in *in vitro* fertilization? Many biologists reply: scarcely more than in natural procreation! It is asked: are not many embryos, which are in one particular case or another not transferred into the womb, abandoned to a speedy death or to the researcher's experiments? Biologists reply: It is a fact that most of the embryos perish in a speedy death in the case of natural procreation; it depends on the attitude of the researcher whether the remaining embryos in *in vitro* fertilization are used for research purposes. The researchers in Erlangen, Germany, emphasize that all the embryos there have been transferred into the womb; but this is not the general praxis today. If one holds the embryos to be already human individuals or persons, one will perhaps feel happier with the praxis of Erlangen. Independently of this question, a group composed mainly of

Catholic researchers in Belgium recently expressed the opinion that there is no reason why superfluous fertilized embryos, if they exist by chance, should be left to a speedy death rather than be used for experiments that benefit mankind; the case would be different if one wanted to employ *in vitro* fertilization systematically to produce embryos for experimentation. It is reported that the possibility now exists of avoiding superfluous embryos.

Individual cases (usually abuses) must be judged in the light of the particular circumstances, e.g., the possibility of fertilization with the sperm of a man other than the husband, or that an unmarried woman can have the child of an unknown man through procreation in a test-tube, or that the transfer can take place in a substitute mother; the same is true of the possibilities of freezing and storing ova, sperm and embryos. The decisive question is how far such actions display a lack of respect for human life, for the ties of marriage and family, and for the possible child that is to be born. What would one say about the possibility of *in vitro* fertilization along with the development of the procreated human person without the transfer into the shelter of the womb? An attempt to achieve this would be considered inhuman and therefore not morally acceptable.

(d) *Gene research and gene technology*. The most revolutionary of all biological discoveries – only a few decades old – is in full swing today in genetic research and technology. It is well known that genes are the smallest units of DNA, the acid that gives structure to the chromosomes and thus to the nucleus of the cells. The genes contain a particular heredity; is it therefore possible to manipulate the hereditary characteristics of the human person? It is important to note that the cells of *all* living creatures (man, animal, plant) consist ultimately of genes that are structured in a determined way; it follows that it is possible in principle to unite human, animal and plant genes in order to alter them or substitute one for the other. In principle, then, man has the entire life of our planet in his hands. We are, however, only at the beginning of gene research and technology.

The transplantation of genes in bacteria has already been used to produce medicinal insulin through the multiplication of genes; the pharmaceutical industry already knows about the possibilities that lie in store for it. A few years ago it was thought that the creation of new types of genes (recombinations of DNA) was dangerous, but this opinion is no longer held today.

It is possible to analyze the genes of a human person, and thus to establish the hereditary substance of the human person without having recourse to family trees. In the United States the "genetic passport" has already begun to be demanded when an applicant seeks a post in a firm; whether this is morally permissible, or can be seen as legally permissible in a society, is a new question for social ethics.

It is also possible to analyze the hereditary substance of the fetus through prenatal diagnosis and to establish the existence of hereditary illnesses. It is possible in principle (though not yet in practice) to replace defective genes with normal genes, thereby eliminating a hereditary illness from the organism. It is said that the majority of the beds in hospitals are occupied by people with hereditary illnesses; this shows how significant gene therapy could be. It is in principle also possible to alter genetically, or replace with other genes, the genes in the sexual cells, i.e. the cells that determine the procreation and thus the condition of future generations.

Bioethically speaking, a gene therapy carried out with all due precautions is not to be judged differently from other therapies. The same is to be said even when it is not simply a case of healing therapies, but of a direct intervention to improve the health of a person; it is, however, true that the boundaries between therapy and improvement are fluid. What has been said is true also of the genetic treatment of sexual cells. This could not be said of the attempt at the eugenic alteration of future generations through gene technology; this judgment is based both on the principle of the equality of all human persons and on the difficulty of establishing criteria for a eugenic improvement.[8] The same would have to be said for the breeding of "subhuman" human beings, which is perhaps genetically possible.

3. Who Decides?

After having exposed today's bioethical problems, we must now turn briefly to another question: who decides? We are thinking here not so much of the question of who decides the bioethical problems — they are not to be decided, but solved — but rather of the question of who decides when confronted with the difficult question of what should be done in an individual case, whether with regard to a human person who is to be treated, or with regard to experimentation (research and technology) in our society.

(a) *The decision with regard to the patient.* We shall call the human being concerned the "patient" for short, although the action of the practitioner aims not only at therapy, but also in certain circumstances at improvement, taking into account besides this the coming into being of the human person and the good of future generations.

It is obvious that one must do whatever is possible to inform a conscious patient about the nature, expectation of success, and risk of a treatment or of an experiment that is to be carried out on him, and it is then the patient who himself decides about the action of the doctor. To this type of decision belongs also, at least within certain limits, the decision of parents about the good of their unborn child or living child, as well as the decision about the attempt to prolong living or dying. In many situations, however, the patient will not be capable of understanding the problem sufficiently well, so that the doctor, or sometimes the relatives, must act in his place, although it is an open question here whether they are able to discover the true intention of the patient, or simply decide for what they consider to serve the true good of the patient.

If the patient himself cannot decide — for example, because he lies in a coma or because he is not yet born or is only a child incapable of deciding — the decision of the relatives will in general be decisive; but it is often the doctor alone who must decide, mostly in accordance with what he holds to be the true intention of the patient, or else what he holds to serve the true good of the patient. It is possible that circumstances could arise in which he would have to act against the wishes, e.g. of parents, for the sake of the true good of the patient; in the United States a court decision would often be required in such a case.

In general, however, the freedom of decision on the part of those directly concerned is upheld; a certain "paternalism" on the part of doctors, which exists in secret, is not accepted. Difficulties arise for the doctor when there are insufficient supplies of the existing means for a therapy (e.g., technical appliances); in such cases, it is not always easy for the doctor to make the right choice, guided by prudence and fairness.

(b) *Consultations and guidelines.* The conclusion to what has been said is that it is often not the individual doctor, technician or researcher who should make the decision as to which treatment or which experiment is to be carried out. There has been an insistence in the last couple of years in the United States that a philosopher too should be present in large hospitals, for ethical consultation. But as is clear from the examples adduced above, the judiciary and the government are also interested in bioethical questions that touch on the public good, and commissions have been set up to work out guidelines on these. It is said that there is the danger, at least in Europe, where such commissions also exist, that they may be composed for the most part of researchers themselves, or indeed of researchers and technicians who are active in pharmaceutical industries that have an interest in these questions, although society is interested precisely also in the point of view of the non-specialists on such commissions. Guidelines that are produced in this way can be very significant. There is some discussion about whether they should not be made obligatory by the organs of the state. It is also important that the reality of modern biology and the corresponding bioethical problems be made known to the public and treated as subjects for discussion.

Our intention in this chapter has been to show what bioethics is and how it copes with the ethical questions that arise from today's possibilities of disposing of human life. It has certainly become clear that there is no secret ethical "deposit" for this. Bioethicists, reflecting in the light of the most general ethical principles, seek to discover means of disposing of human life that correspond not only to the sphere of biology or to the immediate interests of the human being directly concerned, but affect the human being as such in all his reality, looking both to his present givenness and to his human future. In this way the ethical norms of right behavior are found.

NOTES

1 *The Challenge of Life. Biomedical Progress and Human Values,* eds. R.M. Kunz and H. Fehr (Roche Anniversary Symposium: Basel, Stuttgart, 1972); D. Callahan, "Bioethics as a Discipline," in *The Hastings Center Studies* I, no. 1 (1973), 66–73; K.D. Clouser, "Bioethics: Some Reflections and Exhortations," in *Monist* 60, no. 1 (1977), 47–61; T. Beauchamp, L. Walters, *Contemporary Issues in Bioethics* (Belmont, 1978); T. Beauchamp, J. Childress, *Principles of Biomedical Ethics* (New York, 1979); *The Hastings Center Studies* (from 1973); *Bibliography of Bioethics,* ed. L. Walters (from 1975); O. Höffe, *Sittlich-politische Diskurse* (Frankfurt, 1981), 173–218; J. Mahoney, S.J., *Bioethics and Belief. Religion and Medicine in Dialogue* (London, 1984).

2 *Encyclopedia of Bioethics,* ed. W. Reich, 4 vols. (New York, 1978).

3 On this, cf. J. Keenan, S.J., "Töten oder Sterbenlassen," *Stimmen der Zeit* 201 (1983); 825–37, and the authors cited there: G. Hughes, S.J. (1975), J. Rachels (1978), R. Ginters (1982).

4 On the preceding reflections, cf. also F. Böckle, in *Hdb. d. christl. Ethik,* vol. 2 (Freiburg, 2nd edn., 1979), 43 ff.; J. Splett, "Wann beginnt der Mensch?", in *Theol. Phil.* 56 (1981), 407–19; *Manipulating Life. Ethical Issues in Genetic Engineering* (Geneva: World Council of Churches, 1982), 31f.; J. Mahoney, op. cit., 52–86; while Mahoney is rather cautious about the second consideration, he is all the more sure in the case of the first consideration: humanity is "rather unlikely" in the first period (82), "quite unlikely" (83), corresponding behavior "cannot be homicide" (85) and is accordingly justified "for ... most serious reasons" (85) and "not, even objectively, morally blameworthy" (83). The often quoted positions of the Göttingen embryologist E. Blechschmidt seem not to take the philosophical-theological reflections with sufficient seriousness.

5 The Congregation for the Doctrine of the Faith, in note 19 of the 1974 document about abortion, explicitly left open the question of the beginning of life, but required, because of the existing discussion and uncertainty, the choice of the safer way. On this, cf. the commentary by Mahoney, op. cit.; also C.A. Tauer, "The Tradition of Probabilism and the Moral Status of Early Embryo," in *Theol. Studies* 45 (1984), 3–33.

6 So also F. Böckle, "Biotechnik und Menschenwürde," in *Die neue Ordnung* 33 (1979), 356–62; similarly J.G. Ziegler, "Extrakorporale Befruchtung," in *Theol. d. Gegenwart* 25 (1982), 254–60; cf. H. Hepp, "Die In-vitro-Befruchtung," in *Stimmen der Zeit* 201 (1983), 291–303.

7 On this problem, cf. e.g. U. Eibach, "Menschliches Leben ist unantastbar," in *Luth. Monatsheft* 23 (1984), 462f.; also Mahoney, op. cit., 11–35. On the English Warnock Report (Report of the Committee of Inquiry into Human Fertilisation and Embryology,

London 1984, HM Stationery Office), see the very critical account by H.-B. Wuermeling in the *Frankfurter Allgemeine Zeitung*, 1 November 1984, 9f.

8 Pope John Paul II expressed himself in a similar way in a discourse on 29 October 1983: *L'Oss. Rom.*, 30 October 1983.

Author's postscript: The manuscript of this chapter went to the publishers several months before the Vatican Congregation for the Doctrine of Faith published an Instruction on bioethical questions (22 February 1987), declaring that some procedures, and especially any fertilization *in vitro*, were, for ethical reasons, not allowed.

XIV. "Catholic" Medical Moral Theology?

At the end of his 1975 Père Marquette lecture on "The Contributions of Theology to Medical Ethics,"[1] James M. Gustafson comes to the conclusion that these contributions are not particularly great. The volume *Theology and Bioethics. Exploring the Foundations and Frontiers,*[2] edited by E. E. Shelp, confirms this conclusion. It follows that we can hardly expect greater things when we deal here specifically with the contribution of *Catholic* theology to medical ethics. Nevertheless, reference is made frequently to Catholic medical ethics, presumably because Catholic moral theology and the Catholic church have dealt more frequently in the past with questions of medical ethics than have other religious institutions.

1. Medical Ethics

Catholic medical ethics has generally presented itself as a philosophical ethics: its reflections, its principles and its reasonings differ hardly at all, in a formal sense, from those of a philosopher. But if it is to be specifically Catholic, it cannot simply be philosophical, but must proceed from the Christian and Catholic faith. It is obviously possible for Catholic faith to give support to such an ethics without displaying it; it is indeed perhaps possible that the moral theologian in his endeavors is not consciously aware of his faith as the basis of his endeavors.

This presupposes that, although the Catholic faith and Catholic theology wish to be significant for a Catholic medical ethics, this latter is in principle possible — at least as normative ethics — without explicit reflection on the faith. This in turn means that it is taken in principle to be possible to arrive at this ethics on the basis of a common dialogue between the believing Catholic and the nonbeliever.

Faith itself, which must serve as the basis and starting-point of a Catholic medical ethics, requires a moral justification that is (logically) antecedent to itself and hence, as such, cannot derive from faith alone. It follows that medical ethics cannot appeal to a faith as its ultimate basis. In medical morality the self-understanding of the human person as a moral being (logically) precedes every faith and every believing reflection. This means that every medical-ethical reflection that derives from faith occurs within a human self-understanding that (logically) precedes faith; the immediate application of this is merely that the human person understands himself as a moral being, and therefore necessarily understands medical conduct and action also to be moral conduct and action. In other words, because medical problems are human problems, they are always moral problems too; their moral quality does not derive in the first place from a faith.

This is true also of the content of medical problems. It is not the case that they have a moral solution because a God in whom we believe has ordained things in a particular fashion. The familiar saying that everything is allowed if there is no God as starting-point, is false. Nor is it true that medical conduct or action is right only because a God has willed it thus. Rather, the question of what medical conduct and action correspond to humanity must be solved on the basis of the self-understanding of the human person.

Accordingly, a medical ethics deriving from Catholic faith or Catholic theology can have no value if it is unable to accord with human self-understanding. Without such a correspondence, an ethics based on faith or on theology could not be understood humanly, and could therefore not be understood as morally obligatory. It would be humanly meaningless.

Medical ethics is thus an autonomous ethics – in the sense that it is not merely imposed on the human person from outside himself. Catholic Christianity per se is therefore not an original source for replies to questions concerning right medical conduct and action. If one is not afraid of the concept of natural law or moral natural law (understood not statically, but dynamically), this is the right category for medical ethics. Understood theologically, this means the created being of the human person in its orientation toward the future; both something given, to which one must correspond, and a future which must be discovered. It is the human person's task to seek and to find. It is his tragedy that he can go astray in this and arrive at false solutions, just as it is humanity's tragedy that different people can arrive at different solutions to the problems that present themselves in this search.

Plato and Hippocrates did not understand humanity with its value and dignity in the same way. Unlike Hippocrates, Plato saw humanity in its usefulness for the state as a whole, and believed he knew which human life should be procreated, born, and kept alive. Today too, the question of "Who may live?" is posed, though rather from an individualistic or indeed egotistical point of view. A similar question arises from the point of view of the quality of life, in the case of very young or very old human life, or utterly weak human life; what should one risk and undertake for such life? Besides this, when is human life in fact the life of a human person, and what is the consequence of the doubt that is indicated here? And finally, who is to decide how a human life is to disposed of?

This does not mean that the God of faith, and thus faith and theology itself, are irrelevant to human attempts at solutions. The God of creation and redemption wills the search to be a search for true solutions, i.e., solutions that truly correspond to humanity. An utterance of God — for example, through his prophets such as Moses, or through the Bible — insofar as it genuinely intends to address medical ethics, can only be an utterance that is in accord with the human person; it follows that it is fundamentally comprehensible to the human person and that the human person himself is capable of thinking it. This does not mean that such a word of God is superfluous; it has a maeutic function for the human person in his reflection and his search, and gives him additional certainty vis-à-vis what he himself discovers; it can indicate an orientation or a direction in which a good solution to the problem must be sought and found.

2. Theological Medical Ethics

Medical ethics is theological, and hence Catholic-theological, ethics if it proceeds from faith, i.e., from the Catholic faith. This faith is ultimately not the assertion of the truth of certain faith propositions, but an act, in the depth of the person, of giving and entrusting oneself to the God who reveals and imparts himself to us. Naturally, no concrete ethics — and therefore no medical ethics — can be developed out of faith understood in this way.

God's self-revelation and self-gift to man seek man's salvation, i.e. his life in God instead of his death. The self-giving of the Son is a self-giving "for us" — for the others. Jesus' self-giving in his earthly life is a pouring out of himself "for us" — for the others. His life is a life for the "salvation" of the world, i.e. a life and activity and self-giving for our life with and in God, instead of death. His concern for the conduct of our lives is that we, like him, should be "just" instead of sinners who are egotistically closed in on ourselves, and hence that we should be open to all that is right and good, to the others and to God. Jesus' way in the world of human persons was one of doing good, helping, and healing — all an image of the God who reveals and imparts himself for our salvation. Here medical research and the endeavors of doctors for the good of men are called upon: where or how do moral norms exist for them?

Our act of giving and entrusting ourselves to the God who reveals and imparts himself to us is, at the same time, an acceptance of our own self. For its part, this self-acceptance which takes place in the depth of the person is the acceptance of the task of understanding this self and developing it in the direction of self-realization. Thus, the human and philosophical attempt to understand and develop oneself vis-à-vis medical problems is ultimately an attempt that derives from faith and is propelled by faith. This is so even when the believer does not reflect explicitly on the deepest basis of his search. What seems to be human philosophy is, therefore, the attempt in faith to think out and translate this faith into the concrete medical realm of human reality. It is in this sense that the medical ethics of the Catholic who holds on to his faith in his moral reflection is a Catholic ethics, even though it works with the intellectual tools of the philosopher. This, however, is only a partial truth, because living faith signifies also an interior disposition to seek the truth, the whole truth, and nothing but the truth, and such a disposition, present in the basis of faith, has primary significance for the seeking and discovering of medical moral norms.

Medical ethics of this kind serves also to make explicit Catholic theology. For the faith is also made categorial in faith propositions, in which it is affirmed how God is in Jesus Christ vis-à-vis man, man who has become a sinner, and every man. At the same time, much is also affirmed about man in such propositions. Here, for example, it is made clear what the ultimate dignity of the human being, and every human being, consists in; it becomes manifest that this dignity belongs to every human being and that ultimately, therefore, all human persons have the same dignity. Should such affirmations create difficulties in the human-philosophical endeavor, the believer can derive their truth from his faith and a corresponding theology. Should such anthropological affirmations not exist, or fail to convince, in the search for norms of a medical ethics, then the faith can become the "light of the gospel," to use the words of the Second Vatican Council. In this way, faith can also be significant both in terms of the contents of medical ethics, and for the doctor. It remains true, however, that the faith and a theological anthropology only offer help and support for the establishing of a medical ethics, and that they cannot replace human and philosophical reflection, seeking and discovery. But the danger of mistakes remains, as does the possibility that the many who seek the elements of a Catholic medical ethics on the basis of their faith may not all arrive at the same result. This is unavoidable, since the various elements of a medical ethics are not revealed, and hence are not the object of faith: they must be discovered "in the light of the gospel" in a human search — but the search remains human.

One should note that what has been said holds true for a normative ethics (moral rightness), but not only for this: it is true also of the morality of virtues (moral goodness). If one understands and accepts the human person, including the patient, in the ultimate reason for his dignity, one will arrive at an attitude and a conduct that would perhaps otherwise have been absent. One who understands human life (and this means, in fact, human existence) in this way will more easily discover right conduct and a correspondingly right action, than one who must discover his path without a correspondingly solidly based ethics. Here we may think of the example posed by the complicated problematic of euthanasia.

3. Catholic Tradition

It is well known that the Catholic Church and its theology attach great weight to the Christian tradition, and orientate themselves accordingly. This is understandable, since revelation and faith are given in advance: it is on the basis of revelation and faith that theology is possible as a reflection on the faith. Tradition, however, has a different meaning for theology than for faith; for theology, as human reflection, is conditioned by human elements of the reflection and can therefore in certain circumstances arrive at diverse theologies. The significance of tradition for ethics, including medical ethics, is even more problematic.

There are fundamental revealed and believed truths that are relevant to ethics. On this basis, it is established that God has taken up all human persons into his love, that all have become sharers in this love, that the dignity of human beings lies most deeply therein, that all persons have become sharers in this dignity in the same manner, that all must acknowledge this dignity in all persons, that therefore no one may close himself egotistically in himself, that he must be fundamentally open to all persons: such truths are established as the foundation of all Catholic ethics.

It is a different matter when such truths are to be made concrete. Here revelation and faith no longer have the last word, for here human reflection begins. The reference to the fundamental dignity of the human person no longer suffices; the more concrete question is how a particular act, observing human values, does or does not preserve the dignity of the human being; and this question is not answered by revelation and faith. Nevertheless, great value is attached to tradition in Catholic moral theology. Once it was thought that the Christian past always developed its concrete ethics "in the light of the gospel" and believed that it certainly found itself, in the ethics developed at each period, on a path in harmony with the gospel and thus with the faith; in addition it was thought that the Holy Spirit is always with the church of Christ in her seeking and discovery, and that he guarantees for her teaching at least the presumption of truth.

Today, people of various outlooks on the world, including Catholics, make a somewhat different judgment with regard to such moral solutions of a Christian tradition. Indeed, Catholics have given different answers to individual questions at different periods in the history of Christianity. We ask; where then is the tradition that is to help us? Do we today perhaps know human reality in a somewhat different way from that of earlier periods? Do we perhaps make human judgments differently? Do we perhaps make a different interpretation of human situations from a moral point of view? If so, then a different human evaluation, and a different moral norm-setting must occur. This holds true also for questions of medical ethics.

We are confronted here with a decisive problem. If neither faith nor dogmatic theology can offer us concrete solutions to concrete moral problems, and can do no more than preserve the light of the most general principles, then the concretization of such principles in the concrete circumstances of life must take place in another way, i.e., by means of the human evaluation and moral interpretation of the given human realities by the Christian as a human being — hence in a way that is fundamentally available even to the non-Christian person, even if the Christian acts always "in the light of the gospel." This is the way that we are accustomed to call the "moral natural law." Given the lack of corresponding biblical affirmations, the Christians of the first centuries often adhered to evaluations and norms given by pagan philosophers (e.g., Stoics or Gnostics) in their search for moral norms, provided that they believed they could find no incompatibility between the concrete moral norms given by the pagan philosophers and the fundamental attitudes of Christians. For example, Christians generally took over the doctrine of *apatheia*, which had as its aim a conduct that was not at all guided by passions; this was held to be a very high moral ideal. One of the consequences of this was that in Catholic moral theology in general, for many centuries — even if not today — sexual intercourse within marriage that was not concretely motivated by the will to procreate new life was held to be (at least venially) sinful — clearly, a doctrine that could acquire importance within medical praxis also.

But this is only one single example of a one-sided and rather mistaken moral interpretation of a human situation. More significant is the way in which the Stoics taught that the given nature of the human being should be understood as the norm of moral conduct. The Stoics held the human givenness, called nature, to be divine in a pantheistic sense. It follows that what nature indicates is understood as the divine will: if nature shows the growth of a beard as God's will for man, then man must not shave. If nature gives us to understand that the only goal of sexual activity is the procreation of new life (as was mistakenly thought) then all sexual conduct that does not correspond to this objective is to be judged immoral. Christianity, which understood human nature, not pantheistically, but as the work of the Creator, took over this teaching, thus "Christianized," from the Stoics. This was true not only of the teaching about marriage, but in other spheres of life as well. In the middle of this century, the permissibility of transplantation of an organ from a living organism was still a much discussed question; for it was argued that nature (the Creator) had, for example, willed this particular kidney for this particular organism and not for another. One can readily suppose that such an understanding also plays a role in problems of the most modern bioethics. The traditional teaching about the natural law is a treasure of Christian moral theology, but it is not to be adopted blindly. As a norm of moral conduct, it must be brought into relationship with "right reason," which has to achieve a balance among various human goods and values.

We may draw attention to other problems of Christian tradition. One of the jewels of the entire Christian tradition is its insistence on the value and dignity of human life. But, even on this fundamental point, tradition had a different understanding during the first centuries than in later periods, e.g., regarding the question of killing in war, which was excluded in the earlier period. In order to preserve the unity of Christians in the one Christian family, tradition did not always guarantee the protection of life — that is, unlike today, it allowed killing. At all times Christian tradition has been the protector of newly born life, i.e., in rejecting both abortion and infanticide. When both problems are discussed afresh today in wholly other circumstances and possibilities, can one simply appeal, without further question, to a tradition that, in different circumstances, came to a judgment about the protection of human life? This question must at least be posed.

In short, the tradition of Christian moral theology developed generally in "the light of the gospel," but as a Christian-human attempt at concretizing the principles of the gospel. This tradition is so valuable for us because Christians could consider it for long periods as corresponding to their fundamental Christian outlook. But since it was always also a human attempt, and as such could stray from the truth, Catholic moral theology must not take it over blindly in all points. Only in this way can it serve today as Catholic tradition.

4. The Church's Magisterium

It is well known that the Catholic church attaches great importance to its tradition, even in questions of ethics; it is even better known that it officially prescribes a Catholic moral doctrine, and so likewise a Catholic medical ethics, as its obligatory doctrine. This is connected to its understanding of the church's tradition: within the church's fellowship with its tradition, there is an official and thus valid exposition and interpretation of this tradition. Moreover, inasmuch as tradition is always understood in an ultimate relationship to the doctrine of the faith of the church, the official teaching in questions of ethics, which is upheld in each period and today as valid (e.g., in questions of medical ethics), is seen as standing in an ultimate relationship to the doctrine of the faith of the church. It is precisely for this reason that the church, as the guardian of the faith, intervenes in an official way in questions of moral theology, including those of medical ethics.

This is of interest, inasmuch as the church's doctrine of the faith does not as such contain the many concrete moral questions, and therefore generate them out of itself: they do not belong to the treasury of the church's faith. There is no special knowledge about the essence of sexuality, and correspondingly about right sexual conduct, in the treasury of the church's faith, nor is there special knowledge about the beginning of human life, about the reality of embryos, or about the nature of genes. Nevertheless, corresponding knowledge about these matters is presupposed in moral affirmations about human behavior with regard to these realities; for general moral principles do not suffice. The church, however, insists on its magisterium in questions of medical ethics. The many interventions of Pope Pius XII are still well remembered, and the interventions of the present Pope are well known.

In this way, the magisterium of the church shows itself as the competent authority not only in questions that count as revealed, but also in nonrevealed questions of natural moral doctrine (natural law).[6] This claim is explicitly asserted, as was done several times during the Second Vatican Council. There are, however, formulations both in the Second and in the First Vatican Councils which indicate that questions of natural law are not bound to the magisterium in the same way as questions that obviously have to do with Christian revelation. Here, it is clear that not all questions have yet been resolved.[3]

Nonetheless, if one is questioned about doctrine in matters of medical ethics, one refers to papal and episcopal statements. Many Catholics feel bound for their instruction and their praxis by such statements; this is also true of biologists and theologians. But this does not apply to all moral questions. It belongs to Catholic tradition and also to the teaching of both Vatican Councils that only a few ecclesiastical pronouncements have to count as "infallible." The "noninfallible" statements include teachings which are not found in the treasury of the church's faith, but, for example, like concrete moral norms, derive only from human reflection (from moral ethical law). The church's magisterium does indeed emphasize very explicitly that one must adhere religiously to such teachings too; if questioned, it would insist upon this. But dissent would not be absolutely excluded; this is clear from the totality of the proceedings at the First and Second Vatican Councils.[4] The faithful of the non-Catholic Christian churches of the West do not feel bound in the same way as Catholics by an ecclesiastical magisterium or by a Christian tradition in questions of ethics, including those of medical ethics. In part, this is because these churches do not understand themselves to be hierarchically structured in the same way; consequently, the church's leadership is not so important and so conspicuous in them. They do, however, make statements, both for their own believers and for all men of this world. These leaders believe that they have a mission to do this, believing that they should give light from the resources of the Christian faith; but they issue fewer requirements and commands in dealing with their faithful. Like the church leadership, the pastors and the theologians of these churches do the same, though on a different level.

This is so although the theology of the other churches makes less use in its work of the concept of natural law than does the Catholic church. They believe rather that one can and should speak more directly of God's will. This, however, is often not a revealed will of God, e.g. in the Bible, but rather insight gained in the Holy Spirit which the believer possesses — together with a willingness to take into account, in great freedom, the directives of the pastors, the theologians, and the church leadership. To take an example of some theologians: many hold the commandment "Thou shalt not kill" to be an absolute divine requirement, but see that in particular cases the requirement is too much for the weak and sinful person. They deduce from this in the Holy Spirit that God too does not insist: the act remains a sin, but the sinner is certain of pardon. In other words, God justifies, not the act, but the sinner. Catholic theology thinks otherwise: when one reflects precisely in terms of natural law, in the Holy Spirit, it is seen that God's requirement is not so extensive as it could at first sight seem to be. The requirement of God, thus acknowledged, is, however, absolute; there is no need either of a justification of the deed or of a justification of the sinner.

NOTES

1 Milwaukee: Marquette University Press, 1975.

2 Dordrecht, Holland: D. Reidel Publishing Co., 1985.

3 Cf. J. Fuchs, *Christian Ethics in a Secular Arena*, (Washington, D.C.: Georgetown University Press; Dublin: Gill and Macmillan 1984), 57–67.

4 Cf. loc. cit.

Acknowledgments

Chapter I, "Christian Morality: Biblical Orientation and Human Evaluation." Public lecture, College of St. Thomas, St. Paul, Minnesota, 1986. First published in: *Gregorianum* 67 (1986), 745–63.

Chapter II, "Vatican II: Salvation, Personal Morality, Right Behavior." German original, F. Heil: 'Sittlichkeit, richtiges Handeln. Die christliche Morallehre des Zweiten Vatikanischen Konzils': *Stimmen der Zeit* 205 (1987/1). Italian: "Vaticano II: Salvezza, Moralità, Corretto agire," *Rassegna di teologia* 28 (1987) 1–12.

Chapter III, "Our Image of God and the Mortality of Innerworldly Behavior." German original, 'Das Gottesbild und die Moral immerweltlichen Handelns': *Stimmen der Zeit* 202 (1984), 363–82. Italian: "Immagine di Dio e morale dell'agire intramondano," *Rassegna di teologia* 25 (1984), 289–313.

Chapter IV, "God's Incarnation in a Human Morality." Public lecture, Catholic Academy in Bavaria, Munich, 1985. First published in *Stimmen der Zeit* 204 (1986), 241–52.

Chapter V, "Christian Faith and the Disposing of Human Life." Lecture delivered to the Society of German-speaking Catholic moral theologians, Brixen, 1985. First published in: *Theological Studies* 46 (1985), 664–84. German text in *Christlicher Glaube und Moral*, ed. K. Golser, Innsbrück, 1986, 14–42; shorter version in: *Stimmen der Zeit* 204 (1986) 663–75.

Chapter VI, "Early Christianity in Search of a Christian Morality: 1 Cor 7," slightly altered version of a section of the text of Italian lectures "Essere del Signore", Rome 1981.

Chapter VII, "Morality: Person and Acts." Lecture in Italian at the Pontifical Gregorian University, Rome, 1985. First published in: *Stimmen der Zeit* 204 (1986), 473–84.

Chapter VIII, "The Phenomenon of Conscience: Subject-Orientation and Object-Orientation." Lecture at an international and interdisciplinary Colloquium in Salzburg, 1984. Published in: *Conscience: An interdisciplinary View*, Reidel, Dordrecht, 1986.

Chapter IX, "Conscience in a Pluralistic Society." German original, *Gewissen und pluralistiche Gesellschaft: Lebendige Katechese (Beihefte zu Lebendige Seelsorge)* 7 (1985), 107–12.

Chapter X, "Self-realization and Self-alienation." German original, '*Selbstverwirklichung und Selbstenfremdund*', *Stimmen der Zeit* 202 (1984), 651–61.

Chapter XI, "Continuity in the Church's Moral Teaching? Religious Liberty as an Example." German original in *Stimmen der Zeit* 205 (1987), 242–56.

Chapter XII, "Married Love: Christian Pluralism in the Twelfth Century." German original, 'Eheliche Liebe: Christliche Pluralismus in 12 Jahrhundret', *Stimmen der Zeit* 203 (1985), 803–17.

Chapter XIII, "Disposing of Human Life: Recent Problems in Bioethics," slightly altered version of a lecture given at the annual meeting organized by the Landes Kuratorium of Baden-Württemberg for the Union of Societies of the German Sciences, Stuttgart, 1984. First published 'Verfügen uber menschliches Lebens? Fragen heutiger Bioethik' in: *Stimmen der Zeit* 203 (1985), 75–86.

Chapter XIV, " 'Catholic' Medical Moral Theology." Lecture at a Symposium on the philosophical and theological foundations of Catholic medical ethics, Washington D.C., 1986.